Beyond Babel

New directions in communications

Brenda Maddox

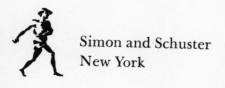

Simon and Schuster
New York

First U.S. printing
SBN 671-21436-5
Library of Congress Catalog Card Number: 72-83632
Manufactured in the United States of America
Printed by Mahony & Roese, Inc., New York, New York
Bound by H. Wolff Book Mfg. Co., Inc., New York, New York

1723938

TO JOHN

Acknowledgements

I would like to thank the many people who took time to tell a technically unsophisticated journalist how their machines and organizations worked. I am particularly grateful to those who talked with me at the British Broadcasting Corporation, Bell Telephone Laboratories, the British Post Office, the Communications Satellite Corporation and Comsat Labs, the Foreign and Commonwealth Office, the Independent Television Authority, the International Telecommunication Union, the Marconi Company Ltd., the Ministry of Posts and Telecommunications, N. V. Philips Gloeilampfabrieken A.G., Plessey Ltd., the Rand Corporation, Rediffusion Ltd., the Relay Services Association of Great Britain, the Reliance Telephone Company Ltd., the National Aeronautics and Space Administration, the National Cable Television Association, the New York Telephone Company, the U.S. State Department, the Sloan Commission on Cable Communications, Standard Telephones and Cables Ltd., Siemens A.G., the Telephone Manufacturing Company Ltd., the Telephone Users' Assocation, and UNESCO.

I would also like to thank Nancy Balfour of *The Economist* for encouraging my interest in communications and giving me time to write this book; Richard Natkiel of *The Economist*, who did the charts and maps; Delia Doherty, Marianne Isch and Janine Triboulin, who looked after my house and children while I wrote it; and Joanna, Bronwen and Bruno Maddox, who coexisted with it for what seemed a very long time. I would also like to thank my husband, John Maddox, for his many explanations of the difference between frequency and wavelength. I still do not understand it but I am grateful.

Contents

List of figures

Foreword

This book is about change and resistance to change in communications. By communications I mean the techniques and systems of carrying voices and print and pictures over distance. It is not a technical book. Communications is a political subject, for it concerns who may say what to whom at what price and in what place. Moreover, the means through which human communication can take place if people are not in the same room – the medium – affects the nature of what they can say to each other – the message.

Among the great array of new techniques and devices I have chosen to concentrate on three: satellites, cable television and telephones. These are the ingredients of the revolution in communications which is going to occur, making available cheap, portable, instantaneous two-way communication among people all over the face of the globe. I have chosen not to join the general clamor about video cassettes or electronic video recording. They are exciting new products but in essence they are also old-fashioned, the television set's phonograph records. They do not offer communication in two directions, which is what the impending revolution is all about, and they are physical objects. They gather dust, and their need to be transported by hand or by truck from place to place is, in terms of communications technology, a regressive characteristic. Although cassettes may have a bright future, much of it will be achieved through cable television, a development which may turn out to be more revolutionary than the much more spectacular communications satellite.

Because communications is a new technology peculiarly in the grip of the past (unlike atomic energy or aeronautics, for example), I have included a fair amount of historical material on the difficulties encountered by some of the earlier innovations in the field. The story of the advance of communications technology is, in a way, one of fear. Each new arrival has been seen as a threat to the survival of the old. The fact that these fears have generally proved groundless – radio did not mean the death of newspapers, television did not kill off radio – has not meant that they have disappeared. The new technology, for all its promise, will have a difficult time in taking hold.

I have devoted an amount of attention which I do not believe to be excessive to the tribulations of a little-known organization called Intelsat. The world's press, by and large, has ignored Intelsat, driven off by the bad breath of technology. Yet Intelsat, the international communications satellite organization, shows the politics of communications in microcosm, or perhaps macrocosm; no other organization has tried to involve so many governments in an international commercial enterprise. The brief experience of Intelsat also shows that the older institutions which run communications have no monopoly on conservatism and on failure to come to grips with the social implications of the new technology.

This book has grown out of work I have done over several years for *The Economist*, in London and in Washington, and reflects my own transatlantic imbalance, that of an American journalist living in London and writing largely about the United States. Perhaps it is an American prejudice that leads me to prefer the more comprehensive word, communications (as in Federal Communications Commission) to telecommunications (as in Ministry of Posts and Telecommunications) which refers more specifically to the technical processes of long-distance communications. As for other prejudices, I must confess to a preference for American telephones, British television, and government officials and corporate executives who will talk to a journalist without a chaperone from the public relations department in the room.

I have used as few technical terms as possible. There is a glossary in the back of the book but I hope that it will not be needed.

BRENDA MADDOX

Part One
Introduction

Chapter 1
A Liberating Technology

To admire technology is all out of fashion, yet there is a great deal to hope for in the burst of new ways to communicate over distance. Communications satellites and refinements in electronics have made it possible to think of ending isolation, illiteracy and the tyranny of the mass medium. It is conceivable that because of improved communications techniques a good deal of drudgery – letter carrying, newspaper delivery and commuting to work – could also disappear. It is even reasonable to hope that cheaper and more flexible communications equipment will give people more influence over the world around them, as they become able to talk across national boundaries, to pay close attention to a number of levels of the political process and even to vote without leaving their homes.

If some of the hopes placed in the new technology are extravagant – can a solar-panelled drum 22,300 miles above the earth really teach anyone to read, let alone create world brotherhood? – the fears aroused by it are probably exaggerated too. Little harm can come from more communication among more people. The experience of the International Telecommunication Union, the agency of the United Nations which looks after communications arrangements between nations, has been that there is little room for malevolence in something as reciprocal as communications. The worst that can happen has probably been seen already: whole populations sitting listening to a single voice, international telephony a private sport for the rich and most parts of the world so ignored by commercial communications that only a calamity of biblical proportions can get them mentioned in newspapers in Western Europe or the United States. In 1970 when one million or more people died in a tidal wave in East Pakistan, several days passed before the fact became news.

What is cheering about the technical developments in store is that they will make much more versatile two instruments which are not reserved for an elite and which are already in the hands of millions of people – the telephone and the television set. (See chart 1.) The functions of both will change drastically in the next few decades. Both will become more flexible and more responsive to individual needs, eventually carrying several different kinds of information. Telephones, all with push-button dials and some with picture screens, will deliver and receive streams of electronic information. They will also become portable; telephone numbers will eventually be assigned to people, not to places. Television will have dozens of channels, some for private communication with other television sets, some for communication with computers, a great many for public television programmes which will come from diverse sources – local and international and educational as well as national. The television set will also print out newspapers and deliver facsimiles of letters.

Yet there are many sophisticated people who have come to despise technology in all its forms and who fear the future as their ancestors used to fear the afterlife. To them, the new technology of communications is as repellent as supersonic aircraft or artificial food. There is nothing to look forward to in the year 2000 but future shock. 'I am not interested in communications,' announced a pretty young London mother, proud of her capacity to breast-feed and make her own bread. 'I am interested only in communication.' She stressed the last syllable. 'Relations between people interest me, but not between machines. All this about newspapers tumbling out of the television set and telephones with buttons instead of dials spoils what is essentially human in communication. The world is moving too fast. We must do what we can to slow it down.'

It is possible to retard technological change, but in communications it would be wrong. A crowded planet needs nothing so much as the sense of community and the pooled intelligence that cheap, easy and instantaneous communications can give. There is no excuse for letting the dull mechanics of the process obscure the fact that there are people (or at very least computers which are occasionally consulted by people) at each end of all communication links. The whole direction of communications technology means that more people can convey

World telephones, television, & population

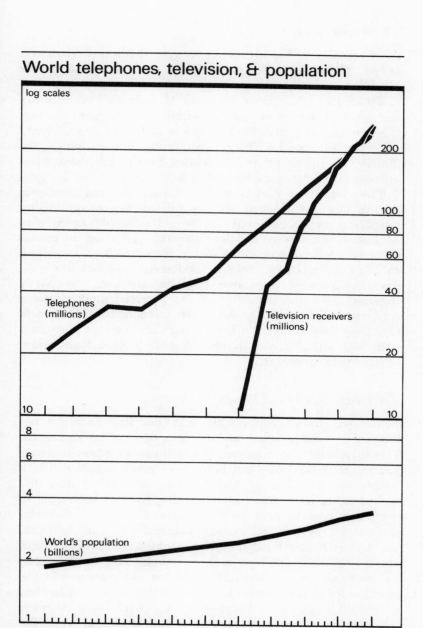

log scales

Telephones
(millions)

Television receivers
(millions)

World's population
(billions)

200

100
80

60

40

20

10

10
8

6

4

2

1

1921   25   30   35   40   45   50   55   60   65   70

more complex and subtle ideas over greater distances than ever before. There will be less centralized control over what people say and hear.

To lift two of Professor Marshall McLuhan's axioms out of the mud of his prose (as he surely intends them to be), 'Electric circuitry profoundly involves men with one another,' and 'Instant communication transports not so much the message but the viewer and the sender. Even by telephone, "you are there" and "they are here".' (*The Listener*, October 8, 1970.)

The poor in New York City who suddenly acquired telephones in the late 1960s when welfare officers began subsidizing telephones as necessities of life would probably agree with McLuhan. They were not dehumanized by having an instrument of telecommunications within their reach. They began calling their relatives, and the sudden surge of talk along an unexpected path, from one slum to another, was partly responsible for the humbling of the biggest communications company in the world. The American Telephone and Telegraph Company may not recover from being caught out of touch, not with electronics, but with the changing needs of communications in the world around it.

The Present is Not Good Enough

Bewildered by change people may be. But they are not shocked enough by what has not changed in communications. The British telephone service is a national disgrace, not only because it works badly but because so many people still lack telephones. The United States, trying to awaken from the nightmare of its commercial television, has not been able to work out how to provide a permanent source of financial support for its national non-commercial television network. The United States, for that matter, paid for the development of communications satellites and put them into international service in the mid-1960s, but it still has not managed to use satellites for its own domestic needs. In Britain a company has developed a system for bringing dozens of television channels into the home, but it has had to peddle it abroad while the Ministry of Posts and Telecommunications ponders whether or not British viewers may have a fourth channel to watch.

All over the world families are being sent to live twenty or thirty floors off the ground without a telephone. The pricing of telephone services, for those who have access to them, has been unimaginative, to say the least. Television news is too often a colored-slide show; there is not enough motion-picture film, let alone live coverage, of news in action. Everywhere there is a callous tolerance of the primal pain of separation. Too often people waiting at airports look as if they were waiting at the entrance of a coal mine. Why shouldn't they have spoken on the telephone to passengers in the air? It is not because air-to-ground telephoning has not been invented yet. Neither is there any technical reason why so much of the world's business should depend on men who get up at dawn and trudge around pushing packets of paper through doors and into mailboxes and who, quite understandably, go out on strike.

The Threat of the New

Technical change is swift; social change is slow. Everything that is necessary for the electronic delivery of letters or for telephones in motorcars or for television in the jungle is invented already. The basic discoveries were made just after the war. What has inhibited the use of these inventions is not only the enormous cost of putting new equipment in the hands of millions of people but also sheer inertia. There is an inherent conservatism in communications because the existing systems represent an enormous investment and because their smooth working cannot be interrupted. Everything new must be compatible with equipment twenty and thirty years old.

Within the next two decades the whole structure of the world's communications as it now exists will be shaken. Until now, communications have been under the control of national governments. There has been little international standardization of equipment beyond what was necessary for the flow of messages. Telephone instruments, for example, have differed considerably and it is often harder to master the use of the telephone in a foreign city than to learn the bus routes.

Yet satellites have made nonsense of what was at best a pretense that communications can stop at national boundaries. Cable television, which transmits television over a wire and not through the air, may make the same nonsense of what are now quite serious, strict and necessary governmental limitations on broadcasting within a single country. Computers and the communication between them are showing up the inadequacy of telephone lines and forcing the consideration of alternative kinds of network. The telephone and television networks may some day fight each other for the same business.

The institutions now in charge of telephones and television do not relish the prospect of surrendering their old jurisdictions. They are conservative, old and powerful. In the United States and Britain, the telephone networks are in the same institutional hands as they were before the turn of the century. And television, while it has been flourishing for just over twenty years, is largely run by the organizations that went into radio just over fifty years ago. The convulsion that was required in Britain in 1954 to break the British Broadcasting Corporation's monopoly on all broadcasting and to allow commercial television gives some idea of the kinds of upheaval that must come. For the challenges will not be from new groups wanting to provide familiar services but from new organizations wanting to offer something quite new altogether. For example, one question that will have to be answered in the not too distant future concerns the newspaper printed by the television set. Who is to be the publisher – a broadcasting organization or a newspaper? Who is to pay how much to whom? If the newspapers pay the broadcasting organization to transmit their daily editions, in which order shall various newspapers be transmitted? Who shall decide?

The worrying thing is that these decisions, which are political, not technical, may very well be made by men who are preoccupied with the enormous cost of their existing telephone network or with the size of their audiences and the costs of producing programs. It is not easy to dream up new uses for the telephone when they would make 255 million instruments obsolete, or new opportunities for television, if the result were to bring hundreds of competitors into the business. Conceivably only new institutions can cope with the new possibilities of telephones and television, but it will not be easy to establish them.

Yet the opportunities must be taken. The world's appetite for communications seems to be insatiable. The floors of the planners are littered with discarded growth charts. 'We are always surprised,' says Professor James Merriman, head of engineering for the British Post Office, with disarming candor, 'at how much greater the demand for a new service is than we expected.'

All that is really certain is that there is an enormous pent-up demand for all kinds of communication; the better the connection and the cheaper the service, the more people who will find a need to use it. What is more, the easier it is to get a line, the longer people talk, and when an inferior service is supplemented by a superior one, people tend to desert the cheaper for the more direct. Telephoning, for example, is more satisfactory than telegraph because there is no waiting for an answer. The communication is two-way and instantaneous and, if an answer is wanted swiftly, worth far more than an exchange of two one-way messages.

Predicting growth is difficult because the planners can only guess at the amount of demand that has been suppressed by a shortage of circuits and high prices. The rise of the transistor radio shows what can happen when the price is attractive. From a beginning around 1953, the numbers in the world grew to 600 million by 1971 and are rising by 100 million a year. The first telephone cable across the Tasman Sea between Australia and New Zealand in 1964 raised New Zealand's international telephone traffic by 85 percent. The fifth transatlantic cable, TAT-V, which opened in 1970 and gave southern Europe better telephone lines to the United States, more than doubled Portugal's international traffic. What seems to be happening is that the suppressed demand is at last being met by an explosion in supply. The number of telephone circuits across the Atlantic has grown from a few dozen in the late 1950s to roughly 10,000 by 1971. At the same time, rates have been dropping and, were it not for the financial conservatism of telephone authorities, might have dropped faster in the late 1950s and early 1960s.

For the developed world, international traffic seems likely to keep on growing by 20 and 30 percent a year. AT&T now handles about twenty million international telephone calls a year and expects about 140 million by 1980. The British Post Office expects to go from a yearly 37 million to 200 million international telephone calls in the same period.

TABLE I

Cost of a Three-Minute Telephone Call from London to New York
History of New York–London Telephone Charges
Cheapest Rates for a Three-Minute Call

	USA	UK
1927		
(£1 = $5)	$75	£15
1928	$45	£9
1930	$30	£6
1935	$21	£4.4.0
1936	$15	£3
(service suspended 1939–45)		
(£1 = $4)	$9.60	£2.18.0
1967	$5.70	£1.17.6
(£1 = $2.80)		
1970*		
(£1 = $2.40)	$4.05	£1.10.0
* international direct dialing introduced – minimum call, one second		

Source: AT&T, British Post Office

Yet these are conservative estimates, based on solid evidence of past practice. The extent of the demand for services which have been held back, such as mobile radios and telephones for cars and trucks, can only be imagined. As far as developing countries are concerned, the only certain thing is that the suppressed demand for domestic communication within their national boundaries is even greater than that for communicating abroad.

Liberating the Technology

But the future is not preprogrammed. The growth estimates do not have to be fulfilled. The new uses for the telephone and television do not have to be developed in the foreseeable future. Whether they are or not will depend on decisions made in the next few years. In Britain in 1976 there will be a review of broadcasting when it will be decided whether or not television will be allowed to become less strictly controlled and to become like publishing, open to anyone, or whether it will continue to be restricted to a few national services. In the United States, the next few years will show whether the telephone network will be superseded by more sophisticated national information networks which could, quite incidentally, provide a national educational television channel. Internationally, the 140 or so countries which are members of the International Telecommunication Union will have to decide whether they will allow it to become, as it is not at present, a strong international organization with power to assign various satellite systems to various places in orbit around the earth or whether it will let the present anarchy in space continue. The developing world will have the toughest decisions of all, whether, for example, to put their hopes for educating their population into satellites or into less glamorous resources such as radios, films and teachers.

The danger is that opportunities, once missed, are lost for a long time. Both the United States and Britain have spent nearly twenty years trying to make up for the mistake of the early 1950s when they allowed television to develop in the crowded VHF (Very High Frequency) bands. In Britain, much of the telephone equipment now being installed will blight the telephone service until well beyond 1990.

Communications is a field waiting for action by consumers and civil libertarians. If the new technology is to be used to solve the problems of the cities, to reduce traffic on the roads, to give the poor more contact with a larger world, then the demand for change must come from outside the organizations which now provide communications services. They are less responsive to change than are the manufacturers of goods and they do not vary their wares nor lower their rates unless they are forced. Communications is a liberating technology in need of liberation.

Chapter 2
Why Now?

I

With communications at such a stage that television viewers switch off if pictures from the moon are fuzzy, it is hard to reconstruct the primitive state of affairs at the end of the Second World War. The radio was then the center of the home, a bulky altar which often as not supported photographs and pots of flowers. Telephoning overseas was for heads of government and was accomplished by means of short-wave radio, the signals traveling from Rocky Point, Long Island, to Rugby, England. There were three times as many public telegrams as there are now, and they were treated with respect; the arrival of a telegram was dramatic enough to provide the turning point in the action of a play. One out of three telephone calls in the United States and in Britain were completed manually by a telephone operator, and most people had never laid eyes on a television set.

The war was a fertile mother of invention but the inventions took time to develop. The first telephone cable (as distinct from telegraph cable) was not placed across the Atlantic until 1956. The first communications satellite, the size of a grapefruit, was not launched until 1958. A picture telephone was a curiosity at the New York World's Fair in 1963–64. In the short stretch of time since then, satellites the size of a London taxi have been launched, and 45-channel television systems are being built. In a few years pipes called waveguides carrying a quarter of a million telephone circuits between cities will be put into operation in both Britain and the United States, and the gradual mastery of techniques for putting signals on beams of light suggests that the shortage of telephone lines and television channels will disappear forever. (How this sequence of technological events has come about is not excessively complicated for those who are curious about it. Those who are not should turn to the next chapter.)

Radar and All That

Wireless communication – radio – is possible because waves of electromagnetic radiation can be sent out into space and made to travel through the air. The waves flow outward when bursts of electric current pass through an aerial. The current is fed into the aerial in the form of electrical oscillations. The oscillations can be thought of in terms of how many up-and-down movements they make a second. The faster they go, the higher their frequency and the shorter the waves that travel out from the aerial.

The range of waves that are useful for purposes of communication is called the radio spectrum. (See chart 2.) Before the Second World War, the usable portion of the spectrum lay between 10,000 cycles a second and 300 million cycles a second. The lower limit, called Very Low Frequency or VLF, or long-wave, was used for radio broadcasting and the upper limit, the Very High Frequency or VHF, was used for television, such as it then was.

Radar, the use of radio waves to detect a solid metallic object (by sending out signals from an aerial and then picking up the signal reflected from the object) was invented in Britain in 1924. The techniques were refined and kept highly secret with the approach of the war, but there was one drawback. The waves were long – about thirty feet, as long as an aircraft. To define these objects accurately, shorter waves were needed. The solution came (just in time, from Britain's point of view) in 1939, with the invention of an oscillator that could produce very powerful and very short (half an inch) waves. This meant that an entirely new portion of the radio spectrum was opened up for use. It was the band of microwaves that lies above the waves of Ultra High Frequency, or UHF. What is particularly valuable about microwaves is that they can easily be made into beams which can be pointed with great accuracy in particular directions. When a wave is long, it bends around corners or buildings or mountains. When it is short, it travels only in straight lines. It was not until after the war, when Rudi

Kompfner, an Austrian scientist working at Bell Telephone Laboratories in New Jersey, invented a traveling wave tube that can strengthen and process microwaves so that they became particularly suitable for use in communications.

Microwaves have enormous advantages over the slower, long waves farther down on the radio spectrum. They can carry much more information and they do not interfere with the radio communication lower down. For this reason, microwaves are used for communication with space satellites and the mastery of microwave techniques in the 1940s was an essential step in the invention of the communications satellite in the 1950s. To be sure, there are some snags – microwaves with wavelengths in millimeters are affected by clouds and even rain.

Microwave technology liberated telephone networks from the ground. In order to carry thousands of telephone conversations from city to city, microwaves require only a chain of relay towers in line of sight from each other. On the towers, antennae shaped like horns or dishes catch the incoming waves and shunt them, strengthened, on to the next tower. Microwaves have made it possible to extend telephone networks without digging up the ground and have brought telephone and radio communications to jungles and mountaintops where cables could never go.

The higher portions of the microwave frequencies are at present useful only for communication to or from objects in the sky – astronauts, stars, aircraft or satellites. Above that in the spectrum, the waves are so short that they cannot be sent through the air without being lost in clouds and rain, although there is some hope that scientists may solve this problem, however, just as they have now perfected methods for transmitting extremely short waves through tubes in the ground (see below).

But the constant progress in exploiting the capacity of the electromagnetic spectrum has not been confined only to extending its outer limits. There has also been rapid technical progress in squeezing more channels of communication into the middle of the spectrum which is, like the middle registers of the piano keyboard, the easiest to use. The bands of Very High Frequency (vhf) and the lower uhf are desirable because the waves are long enough to be able to be received with fairly cheap equipment within a radius of thirty miles or so – just right

The radio frequency spectrum

Megacycles	X-RAYS ↑	Wavelength
300,000 million		0·000001 millimetres
30,000 mn	ULTRA-VIOLET RAYS	0·00001 millimetres
3,000mn		0·0001 millimetres
300mn	VISIBLE LIGHT	0·001 millimetres
30,000,000	INFRA-RED LASER FREQUENCIES	0·01 millimetres
3,000,000		0·1 millimetres
300,000		1 millimetre
30,000	MILLIMETRE WAVES	1 centimetre
3,000	MICRO-WAVES	10 centimetres
300	UHF	1 metre
30	VHF	10 metres
3	SHORT WAVE RADIO	100 metres
0·3	MEDIUM WAVE RADIO	1,000 metres
0·03	LONG WAVE RADIO	10,000 metres

for commercial communications within a city area. A two-way radio connection, the staticky kind that taxis have, can now be fitted into one-tenth the band width (or spread of frequencies) that once was needed. As a very large chunk of the VHF and UHF is now occupied by television broadcasting, one of the most contentious issues in what is called spectrum management is whether or not some of these frequencies can be taken away from television and given over to small companies and private citizens for use in mobile radio communications.

A Common Code

Codes have always been important in communications, and the challenge has always been to design the most efficient code for the type of message to be carried over a particular channel. The code that Morse produced for the electric telegraph was excellent. It could not be made more than 15 percent more efficient, according to some estimates, if it were redesigned by computer today. To make his code, Morse assigned dots and dashes to the letters of the alphabet according to the frequency of their use in English language. (He judged their comparative amount of use by looking at the assortment of letters in a printer's tray.) Accordingly, *e*, the most commonly used letter, has the simplest code, a single dot, and so requires the smallest amount of electricity and time for transmission.

In 1947 the code which was to revolutionize modern communications appeared at Bell Labs. Dr Claude Shannon brought it about with his classic paper, 'A Mathematical Theory of Communication'. His theory made it possible to break down all communication into its smallest components, units of information. The basic unit, according to Shannon, is the smallest amount of information which resolves doubt or uncertainty. It answers the question yes or no. Shannon called this unit a 'bit', for binary digit. In binary arithmetic, only two numbers are used, zero and one. Any number can be expressed in binary terms (one, two, three, four and five are 1, 10, 11, 100 and 101).

To be able to break down any kind of message into a code of just two symbols meant that anything could be expressed electrically as on or off, or as the presence or the absence of an electrical pulse.

Shannon's information theory made it possible to consider separate forms of communication – pictures, voices, telegraph signals – as using the same language. It made it possible to calculate the most efficient way of expressing a given message into the fewest possible bits. His theory also made it possible to work out how many bits a particular channel of communication could carry – a telephone circuit cannot carry a television signal, for example. This is very important to communications engineers, for economy demands that circuits be as full as possible – that they carry as many signals as possible without producing the kind of distortion or noise that destroys the message.

The digital code made it possible to wring the maximum advantage from another discovery of the 1930s, pulse code modulation. A. W. Reeves, working at the laboratories of Standard Telephones and Cables Ltd in Harlow, outside London, worked out a method of interleaving telephone conversations so that twenty-four calls could be carried on a line designed for one. In PCM (pulse code modulation), instead of sending the full signal made by the voices in the conversation, only portions are sent. Samples are taken of the amplitude of the waves made by the voices. If they are taken often enough – 8,000 times a second – enough information about the sound is obtained to enable the listener at the other end to hear what sounds like a full voice. The technique is something like the screening which produces photographs in newspapers. All that is printed is black and gray spots but the human imagination can fill in the rest. The advantage of PCM is that samples of other conversations can be inserted in the gaps, so that the carrying capacity of the circuit is increased.

The code, called digital, has as much as any one thing destroyed the old barriers, which once made technical sense, between various kinds of communication. Combined with a number of packaging techniques, such as PCM, it has made possible the jumbling together of different types of communication for quicker, cheaper, more accurate transmission. Eventually, all the world's communication will wash back and forth in waves of digital codes once obstacles in the form of the existing telephone networks are overcome.

Smaller and Smaller

Another basic problem in communications is keeping a signal, or an electrical pulse, or a telephone call, strong during transmission. The farther it gets from its source, the weaker it becomes. Communications depends on amplifiers, devices to restore the signal to strength as it travels along.

Bell Labs again produced the major discovery which divides communications, present and future, from the past. In 1948, the year that Shannon published his mathematical theory of communication, Bell Labs announced the invention of the transistor. The transistor was the small, cheap amplifier the world was waiting for. It allowed communications devices of all kinds to become small, light and cheap. The transistor led to the transistor radio, the space satellite and the eavesdropping martini olive.

Before the transistor, amplifying had been done by vacuum tubes or valves (the Englishman's valve is the American's vacuum tube). Made of glass, valves were bulky, fragile and, after they warmed up, hot. The first computers, put together after the war, held enough rows of valves to look like a bottle vending machine. The transistor eliminated all these disadvantages. Transistor radios and television sets need no warming up time; they are either off or they are on. Transistors did away with most of the heat generated by valves, but not all.

It was war work once again which had paved the way. Bell Labs had been engaged in wartime research on the behavior of electrons in solid materials. Some solids, metals particularly, conduct electricity very well. Others, like rubber, do not. A Bell research group led by William Shockley, Walter Brattain and R. B. Gibney was concerned with materials, such as germanium and silicon, which were called semiconductors because they will conduct electricity only if certain conditions are created. The team found a way to control the movement of electrons in semiconductors by adding very small amounts of impurities. The electrons could be made to flow or to stop flowing simply by applying an external source of current. Nothing appeared to move; little heat was generated. What they had invented, in short, was an on-and-off switch which works in what the world now knows as the solid state.

For their discovery, Shockley, Brattain and Gibney received

the Nobel Prize in 1956. For his, Dr Shannon did not, thereby joining a long list of distinguished scientists whom the Nobel Prize committee forgot.

Radar, then the traveling wave tube, then information theory and the transistor, laid the foundation for the whole explosion in communications technology which is now developed to the point where it is ready for use in public telephone and television networks. It is worth noting that AT&T, the company which symbolizes the American belief in private ownership, has been prevented by the federal government's anti-monopoly restrictions from receiving money from the patent rights on the inventions which came out of its Bell Labs.

II

The next major development was miniaturization, which brought an increase in the carrying capacity of communications links, along with a lowering of their price and an improvement in their reliability.

By 1958 it was possible to make transistors so tiny that enough of them could be combined on a small chip of silicon to make a complete electrical circuit. That compact package is called an integrated circuit. To have, as is now possible, hundreds of such complete circuits pressed together in a chip of material as insignificant in size as a shirt button (and not much more expensive) is called large scale integration. To achieve such compactness, the problem that had to be solved once again was that of heat. Electric current had to reach all the tiny amplifying points without causing the microcircuit to grow warm to the point where the signals were blurred. The answer was to find ways to make the microcircuit run with even smaller amounts of power and, when it was accomplished, there was a gain in the reliability of the circuit as well as a reduction in size. The smaller the circuit, in other words, the greater the reliability. Two results of miniaturization are the computer, which can perform millions of operations in a second and yet fill no more space than a filing cabinet, and the communications satellite, which can keep on working for years on the amount of power consumed by a feeble light bulb.

A Common Axis

Another reward of miniaturization is the increased number of conversations that can be squeezed into an ordinary sized telephone cable. Until microwaves came along, coaxial cables were the most common way of carrying telephone calls from city to city, and they still bear about one-third of the burden of long-distance telephone and television traffic in the United States, and about a quarter in Britain. Although coaxial cables have been doing telephone duty since 1941, transistors have swelled their capacity so much that if it were not for the vast expansion in demand that public telephone authorities expect in the next ten or fifteen years, coaxial cables might seem to be all that any communications engineer would hope for.

A coaxial cable is a tube for carrying waves – VHF and UHF waves – from specific points to other specific points. Television broadcasting uses VHF and UHF waves, but it throws them out onto the air and they must be caught by aerials. Coaxial cables are a way of confining these waves, making them run around corners and into telephone exchanges. They can carry communications signals into homes (which is the basis of cable television). They can carry them under oceans. And they can carry enormous quantities. The cable consists of a fine copper wire packed round with insulating plastic in such a way that the wire rests exactly in the center of a copper sheath; the tube and the wire share the same axis – hence 'coaxial'.

When coaxial cables came into service for long-distance telephones, during the war in the United States, after the war in Britain, they represented a big leap forward. Until then, telephone conversations over long distances had to travel over small paired wires, a pair for each conversation, that are still the kind of connection between telephones in a house and the trunk cable in the road. A coaxial cable can carry a great many conversations at once because it packs them all together. Each two-way connection is put on a separate frequency and all of these are carried along together on an all-enveloping carrier wave. Because the total range of frequencies is broad, several million cycles wide, coaxial cable communication is called broadband communication. When the carrier wave arrives at its destination, it is broken down into its individual parts, which travel to their destination on the narrower telephone wires. These are narrow not so much in diameter but in bandwidth.

The distinction between broadband and narrow band is important. Television, which is a bandwidth eater – one channel requiring as much band width as 600 to 1,200 telephone circuits – requires a broad band of frequencies for its transmission. When it goes from city to city, it travels by microwave or coaxial cable. Computers, spewing out data to be carried to another computer, also require broadband channels. They take bandwidth equivalent to a dozen telephone circuits. In contrast, ordinary telephone calls need only narrow band transmission. (One telephone call requires a bandwidth of only 4,000 cycles a second. The world's telephone networks are designed for narrow band transmission. And while computers and eventually picture telephones (which will take as much bandwidth as 300 telephone calls) do use the telephone network, they consume so much bandwidth that congestion easily results. They are, one might say, road hogs. Or one might say that the road is too small. The possibility of widening the road – providing broadband networks which lead not only between cities but within them and straight into homes and offices – is no less contentious than that of putting superhighways through cities. Whether it will be taken or not is a question involving many entrenched interests and many challengers and a very great deal of money. It is a bitter battle about the future which has begun already.

The first coaxial telephone cable, laid by AT&T, between Minneapolis and St Paul, in 1941 carried 480 telephone calls. In 1953 a New York to Philadelphia coaxial cable was opened, carrying 1,860 telephone calls. By 1965, thanks to transistors, coaxial cables were carrying 17,000 circuits. And the transition from the 30,000-call cable to a 90,000-circuit cable is in progress.

Transistors also did wonders for submarine telephone cables because they allowed the repeaters – the bulky amplifiers that had to be placed at intervals along the line – to be made smaller and lighter. Many more calls could be squeezed through existing cables. The first transatlantic cable, TAT-1 (TAT stands for transatlantic telephone), originally had forty-eight circuits.

Its repeaters were based on old-fashioned valves. It required a separate line for each voice in a two-way conversation. In contrast, the fifth transatlantic cable opened in 1970 held 720 circuits in a single cable, and there are plans for more capacious versions, nearly 2,000 circuits, to be put in place in the near future, and current research is directed toward 3,500-circuit undersea cables. Cable engineers hope to fit 10,000 conversations in these cables by the end of the decade.

The Next Step

The next dramatic improvement in transmission technology will open up the vast reaches of the spectrum above the micro-waves for commercial communications use. There lie the milli-meter waves – waves so short that they cannot go through the air without being soaked up by clouds and cannot be confined in coaxial cables without dispersing. For a long time it was recognized that if millimeter waves could be sent underground through hollow tubes, they would offer fantastic communica-tions capacity – one-quarter of a million telephone calls or 150,000 television channels. But the problem of going around corners seemed insoluble. When the tube was bent, as it had to be if it were going to be used outside the laboratory, the waves struck the side of the tube and were lost.

Once again Bell Labs found the solution, although the British Post Office and British universities have not been lagging in their research into waveguides (as the tubes are called). One way out seems to be a carefully wound helix of wire, where the coils seem to be able to help the waves to bend. Another seems to be an extremely smooth tube with carefully designed inner surfaces. The result is that not only can waveguides be bent but, in the cheerful words of an engineer at Bell Labs, 'now they can be tied in knots. They can be laid anywhere.' Waveguides are now being tested in the New Jersey country-side and will soon be tested in Essex, at Martlesham, where the Post Office has its new experimental station.

What is holding back waveguides and their quarter of a million telephone calls right now is not theoretical but practical. A waveguide delivered to a building site represents only one-third to one-tenth the actual cost of the waveguide installation.

The tube cannot go into existing cable ducts. It must be buried separately and as straight as possible. Buying rights of way and clearing the land is expensive. Lakes and roads in the way add to the cost. The initial investment to put a waveguide system into operation will be enormous, but as it will make available a quarter of a million or more telephone lines the cost per circuit mile will look cheap. There is not yet sufficient demand to fill such capacity, and the stepping up of coaxial cables to 90,000 circuits has provided telephone engineers with some severe qualms about plunging ahead with an exotic new form of transmission. But both AT&T and the Post Office have now committed themselves to waveguides for the 1980s. They are confident, perhaps overconfident, that there will be a commercial demand for picture telephones, which occupy an enormous chunk of bandwidth – as much as 300 telephone conversations. Yet even without picture telephones the heavy rise in demand for long-distance telephony and intercomputer communication makes it likely that the waveguides, when installed, will not have much capacity going to waste. They offer a chance to install new trunk lines, designed solely for digital transmission.

Then Come Lasers

The higher you go in the radio spectrum, the smaller the waves, the more difficult they are to handle, and the more bandwidth – room for communications circuits – there is. Beyond the millimeter waves lie the waves of light. They have always been the prize at the end of the road. If light waves could be made usable for communications, if they could be made to carry signals and prevented from diffusing into the air, then the shortage of circuits would be over forever. Now, with the development of lasers, the prize is within reach. It is possible to think of the day when there could be 900,000 television channels – in color. There could be telephone lines by the billions – each person could have his own television telephone.

Lasers are intense, concentrated beams of light. They are now becoming practical possibilities for communications because ways are being found to make the beams of light which they produce carry signals just like radio waves. They travel through thin glass tubes as fine as a human hair. The systems that use lasers will be called optical systems. They will not come quickly, but when they do, perhaps by 1990, perhaps by the turn of the century, the search for higher frequencies, greater bandwidth, more space to carry all kinds of communication, will be ended. Alec Reeves, the inventor of pulse code modulation, predicted in 1968 that by the year 2020 the world will be shot through with laser-carrying glass tubes. With thousands of fibers, each carrying the equivalent of several television channels, that would seem sufficient message-carrying capacity for however many billions of people will be living then. Anything beyond that would seem to come out of science fiction – the electrical transference of thoughts from one person to another. But research is certainly under way at Yale University and elsewhere into the stimulation of the brains of chimpanzees by remote electrical current, and science fiction in the past has often proved to be merely a cheap method of technological forecasting.

III

So much for the technique. What are the practical manifestations of the new technology?

The ability to send printed or written materials over telephone lines will be greatly expanded in the future by the greater carrying capacity of cables. Even now it is commonplace, or nearly so, to have documents copied by a facsimile machine which sends a copy over the telephone lines. News agencies use this technique to distribute photographs. With the introduction of digital sampling methods, it becomes possible to deliver such printed materials at enormous speeds. As long ago as 1949 the Radio Corporation of America demonstrated the transmission of letters and documents over a television circuit at fifteen to thirty pages a second. What this means is that it would take only two minutes or so to transmit all of *Gone with the Wind*. The reason why such services have not been developed on a wide scale by now has been the shortage of bandwidth. When it becomes available, then it is possible to think in terms of the electronic delivery of mail and even of books – a library service – to the home by wire. The device that is needed is a facsimile recorder, which is activated by a code. When the code rattles along the line, the machine knows that a message intended for its reception is coming and switches on.

By 1980, in parts of the United States, the development of broadband networks should mean that letters, at least business letters, can be delivered electronically. Almost all the country's financial transactions are expected by then to be taking place by such means, or by push-button telephones that feed electronic information into computers. (See Chapter 11.) It will be possible for letters to be taken to a post office, or photo-copying office, to have them scanned automatically, transmitted to their destination, retranscribed on paper and put into an envelope, sealed and addressed, and unread by human eye. The letter that reaches the recipient may not have the charm of one written in thick black ink on expensive stiff writing paper, but it will look like a letter, not like a telegram – resembling, in fact, wartime V-mail. Eventually these facsimile receivers will make their way from offices to the lobbies of blocks of apartments to homes. When they are combined with the ordinary television set, then the apparatus for the home printing of newspapers will be at hand.

Wired Cities

In time, as coaxial cables extend not only between cities but within them, right into homes, what futurologists call the Wired City will come to pass and the cable will be the pipe along which the print and pictures and data will flow into the home. Such a new kind of broadband cable network would mean, odd as it may seem, that there could be a surge of radio communication which does not use cables or wires at all. What inhibits the use of mobile radios now is the congestion of the airwaves. Yet if cities were strung through with broadband cables, radio signals could feed into the cable network by being picked up by small antennae that could be located at every street corner. Then the radio power emitted by moving vehicles or people carrying two-way radios could be very weak, perhaps one-hundredth the strength needed for a taxi radio today. It is this possibility, of cables and radio working together, that makes it reasonable to think that every car will some day have a telephone and that perhaps every person will as well, each having his own individual telephone number. A person-to-person telephone call then will be literally possible.

The increasing use of weak radio signals on a more modest scale has already begun the introduction of pocket pages, devices that bleep or buzz when the wearer is wanted on the telephone. Sometimes this device is used simply to tell the wearer that he is wanted by his hospital, commanding general or news editor. Sometimes it can deliver crude messages, by buzzing in simple codes.

Picture Telephones

Work is being done in the United States, Britain, Sweden, West Germany and Japan to provide the telephone with a picture screen. Commercial picture telephone service on a very limited scale and high cost ($100 a month originally) began in the United States in 1970. The British Post Office has its own version, designed for it by Plessey Ltd., and will introduce it at some unspecified date in the future, but not before 1980.

The drawback to their introduction is the enormous amount of bandwidth the picture telephones consume, 100 to 300 times as much as an ordinary telephone call. This would not be such a handicap if they traveled to their destinations on broadband coaxial cables, but they do not – they use ordinary telephone lines. Before picture telephones become cheap enough so that the business community in any rich country becomes interested enough in the service to subscribe to it, the millimeter waveguides, promised for the mid-1970s, will have to be in place. They will provide the intercity capacity for picture telephones. But as long as the internal wiring of cities is still narrow band, any telephone authority that encourages a boom in picture telephones is inviting massive congestion of the telephone lines.

Who will own the broadband communications networks of the future, and who will supply the increasingly varied services that can travel over them, is the single most contentious issue in communications today. Moreover, the legal complications presented by the distribution of printed materials by electronic means are staggering. The technology is ready but the road to its introduction is not.

Chapter 3
The Caretakers

'A master butcher does not divide up his activity under the headings of Veal, Beef, Pork, Mutton and Liver.'

GERALD GROSS, Secretary General of the International Telecommunication Union, 1960 to 1965

I

More and more, communications is turning into a single commodity – a medium for carrying messages. Television, telephone calls, telex, facsimiles of photographs and data from computers all travel along together. As they go from one place to another, they probably pass through several different means of transmission – microwaves, cables, high-frequency radio. It doesn't make much difference as long as they reach their destination quickly in the desired form.

But the organization of communications is still handled as if various kinds of messages and different types of transmission were quite distinct from one another. What Gerald Gross saw to be wrong with the ITU was the archaic structure of compartments which it used to preserve order in the world's communications. Yet the same inefficient division of responsibility within the ITU reflects a similar disorganization and confusion on the national level. Within most countries there is no coherent national policy on the use and development of communications. Instead, the various special interests – the military, the broadcasters, the space researchers, the airlines and the telephone and telegraph authorities – concern themselves with their own particular requirements, often unaware that their actions are in direct conflict with those of another agency of government or public life. The result is that the structure of communications is a hodge-podge, nationally as well as internationally.

Of course, communications would not be possible at all without fairly strict rules. The radio spectrum could not carry the amount of traffic that it does unless there were agreement on assigning different varieties to different lanes. Telephones and telegraph also must of necessity conform to standards. A country could not conduct its business, let alone its private life or its national defense, were there rival telephone systems, with some people plugged into one and others into another.

The various organizations that have grown up to do the job of rule-making tend to bear the marks of the evolution of communications technology, like rings on a tree. The telegraph service is often separate from the telephone service. What goes through the air may be dealt with by men who work in quite a different part of town than do the men responsible for communications through wires. Satellites, in the United States at least, are treated as if they were a strange kind of technical beast to be kept isolated from other forms of transmission.

A National Grip

The most glaring anachronism in the organization of communications is its division into national compartments. All countries treat their communications systems as a matter primarily of national concern. While they do conform, for the sake of convenience, to the international recommendations of the ITU, they do so only if it pleases them. They are under no compulsion to do so. Who would compel them? The ITU, like other agencies of the UN, has no powers to enforce its decisions.

From the first days of the international exchange of telegrams in the 1840s, it was clear that the nations that were rich and powerful enough to want the service considered that their sovereignty came first, ease of communication second. At first the problem was solved by having telegraph lines stop at national boundaries. Telegraph operators copied the messages down by hand and messengers carried the pieces of paper across the border, where another operator took it and translated it back into Morse code. This absurdity was ended in 1849, when Austria and Prussia signed a treaty linking their telegraph lines. Even then, the priorities were clear, and put into the treaty: government messages came first, those concerned with railway operations second, public messages last. By 1865 the obvious desirability of making such treaties centrally rather than bilaterally brought about the creation of the International Telegraph Union. Within it, the twenty richest countries of the time were able to work out uniform agreements on rates, equipment and operating technique. When telephones came along in the 1880s, the ITU worked out similar arrangements so that telephone calls could cross borders. Today's basic unit of time for charging for telephone calls – three minutes – was laid down in an ITU conference in Budapest in 1896.

When radio became a practical form of communication around the turn of the century, it seemed so unique (telegraph signals that went through the air without the use of wires) that an entirely separate international organization was established to cope with it. The International Radio Telegraph Union was created in 1906 to end the chaos at sea, where ships often could not communicate because of incompatible radio equipment. The first international radio conference, forerunner to the many that have taken place since, was held in Berlin that year. It drew up the first international regulations for the use of radio which obliged radio stations along coastlines to be connected to the international telegraph service, to give absolute priority to distress signals and to avoid radio interference as much as possible. It also made the first allocations of frequencies and distinguished between services for the public and those 'not open to public correspondence' – that is, military and naval radio.

Not until 1932 was the radio union taken under the wing of the ITU which, without having to change its initials, adjusted its name to the more catholic International Telecommunication Union.

Soldiers First

Radio might have led to the creation of a strong international communications organization, one which operated a service itself and told countries fairly flatly what frequencies they might use in international communications. Radio, unlike telegraph and telephone, was inherently international; its waves wafted across national borders whether there was permission or not.

But radio had just the opposite effect. It intensified the determination of governments to retain the freedom to make their own rules, for they recognized the great political power that lay in a means of reaching into homes and speaking to citizens unseen. Moreover, radio was essential to national defense; military needs always took precedence over civilian interests – in the First World War both the British and American governments took over all radio and banned international agreement on the use of wavelengths. So strong was the determination of governments to keep their grip on radio that not until 1948, when chaos threatened, was there any international agreement on the use of wavelengths. To this day there are governments in some parts of the world that do not allow mobile radios for commercial use because each transmitter is a potential revolutionary broadcasting station. The separation of military from civilian communications is standard practice and likely to remain so.

The rise of broadcasting – sending radio signals to the public at large – arose in the 1920s and created another niche in the communications hierarchy. Broadcasting presented two opportunities for regulation: permission had to be given to organizations to engage in it, and some form of watch had to be kept on programs to see if the broadcasters were using the airwaves in the public interest.

Today the methods of operating and regulating communications vary around the world. In some countries the government's control extends so far as to have a Ministry of Broadcasting with sole authority to make radio and television programs. Other countries put communications into the hands of private companies over which the government exercises some control. Others have mixtures of public and private operation or quasi-public authorities to which certain responsibilities are entrusted. Assorted as the arrangements are, it is possible to generalize. The operation of communications the world over is regulated, but its future course is not planned and its regulation is done through compartments which now make technological nonsense.

Obviously these compartments are a handicap in planning for the introduction of new devices that changing technology has made available. Yet the organizations in charge are slow and inflexible and often are concerned above all to ensure their own survival. They are caretakers of the past. A tremendous amount of discontent and frustration is rising up against them, for planning needs to be done and innovation cannot be held back forever. Satellites are creating the same kind of pressure for international control as the telegraph did in the nineteenth century. Simplifying and strengthening the rule-making framework for communications is a major task for the 1970s, yet one that may be impossible, for the weight of tradition and investment lies behind the existing sprawl. A rough description of the basic organizations of communications in the United States, Britain and the ITU may help to show just how formidable the reorganization task is.

II

The Federal Communications Commission

Communications in the United States is regulated by the Federal Communications Commission. Perhaps the most significant thing about the FCC is that it was not founded until 1934 and that the weak Federal Radio Commission which it had superseded had existed only from 1928. By 1934 it was too late; the American communications industry was fully grown. There were more than thirteen million radio sets, three powerful radio networks supported by commercial advertising and more than twenty million telephones, the majority of them the property of AT&T. The FCC was supposed to provide unified regulation for both broadcasting and common carrier communications companies (those, like the telephone and telegraph industries, which are message carriers for hire by the public), but it was not supposed to provide very much. While it was to control the award and revocation of broadcast licenses, it was not supposed to exert any form of censorship over the content of programs. In the years since then it has not been given a big enough budget or staff to do really thorough investigations of the financial or technical arrangements of the giant communications companies. The FCC embodies the primary concern of Congress to leave American communications in the hands of strong and private corporations, subject only to the minimum discipline necessary to keep service good and rates low.

The FCC is called an independent agency, which means that it is not part of any department of government. It is accountable only to Congress for what it has done, and it can be thought of as holding an assignment from Congress to keep an eye on industries which affect the public interest, yet which Congress has neither the time nor the expertise to watch itself.

But Congress does manage to find time to watch the FCC. There are two subcommittees of Congress which make communications their business. The Senate's subcommittee is headed by the tiny and formidable Senator John Pastore of Rhode Island, who may be the single most powerful influence on America's communications policy. If the FCC shows signs of too much independence, Senator Pastore tends to hold hearings of his subcommittee, over which he presides, intoning such pronouncements as: 'There is only one electro-magnetic spectrum' or 'I agree with your standpoint of view'. There is a kind of tug-of-war between him and the FCC, and while each side waits for the other to tackle a really controversial issue, such as domestic satellites for the United States and payment of copyright for cable television programs, years can roll by with nothing being decided at all. The House of Representatives' subcommittee on communications is run by another New Englander, the florid Torbert Macdonald of Massachusetts. Recently he has worked hard enough on behalf of the new non-commercial public television network to have become known in Congress for some other achievement than having been John Kennedy's Harvard roommate.

The FCC's decisions are made by seven commissioners. They are appointed by the President (although the Senate and in particular Senator Pastore's subcommittee must give its approval) and they serve for seven years. The President chooses one of the commissioners to be chairman. To some extent the chairman stamps his personality on the commission; he presents its case to Congress and makes a great many speeches which are taken as interpretations of the FCC's policy, before gatherings of various branches of the communications industries. Yet the primary job of the commissioners is to vote – on the award of licenses to broadcast, on proposals to raise telephone rates or to allow or refuse a merger between companies – and the chairman's vote counts as no more than one out of seven.

In the interests of keeping the FCC non-partisan, the law forbids more than four of the commissioners to belong to the same political party. In practice, this means that it is nearly always partisan – the Democrats voting in general for tighter federal control of the industries, the Republicans for less. In 1969 President Nixon appointed an archetypal Republican as chairman, Dean Burch, who had been head of the Republican National Committee during Senator Barry Goldwater's presidential campaign in 1964. The appointment was seen as a maneuver to counterbalance the most flamboyant Democrat on the FCC, the liberal Nicholas Johnson, who had gone as far as anyone could to make the FCC a household word. Nixon's maneuver worked, surprisingly enough. Not only was Burch less concerned to protect the traditional big broadcasting interests than had been expected but Johnson seemed almost deliberately to squander the reputation he had built up as a crusader against the greed of the commercial broadcasters by lashing out at an indiscriminate number of targets. Liberals came to be embarrassed by Johnson and to have a grudging respect for Burch. In 1971 the political balance on the FCC shifted in favor of the Republicans.

The FCC regulates American communications through five bureaus. They cover broadcasting, common carrier services (which include satellites as well as telephones and telegraph), safety and special radio services (industrial communications and mobile radio), field engineering (which monitors radio stations around the country for technical performance) and cable television. The commission is not quite as compartmentalized as it looks, for the commissioners have an integrating function. They make decisions on cases which come up through the bureaus. Many of the matters that come before the FCC are contentious – notably those concerning the award of licenses for television stations. There is a whole branch of the American legal profession specializing in communications law and a whole breed of Washington lawyers which feeds off the FCC. Many cases never come before the commissioners but are argued before and decided upon by a hearings examiner.

Traditionally, the FCC had been feeble, a joke. Fred Friendly, television adviser to the Ford Foundation, has called it a tower of Jello. Its most conspicuous failure has been its inability to raise the quality of programs on commercial television. It was a former chairman of the FCC, Mr Newton Minow, who described American television as 'a vast wasteland'. Recently, the FCC has begun to show some signs of courage. It urged Congress to ban cigarette advertising from television and begun to ask that radio and television stations pay some faint attention to their responsibilities for providing something other than music, quiz shows and advertisements. It has also begun to take an enlightened approach to the management of the radio frequency spectrum. (It will have regional centers through which the use of the airwaves can be planned to suit local conditions. To allocate frequencies on a national basis has been wasteful. Bands that are congested in New York City might be available for mobile radio in the Southwest.) It is also trying to deal with the war between cables and satellites by taking a long-range view, examining national requirements for overseas communications links ten years ahead. The old FCC would have dealt with each request for a new satellite or undersea cable as it came up.

For all its straining to become a policy-making agency, however, the FCC cannot change very much. Congress does not want it to be strong and will probably keep it underfinanced and understaffed. It simply is not possible to bring intelligence, speed and flexibility to bear on the economic and technical problems of complex and changing industries on a budget of $30 million a year. With a staff of only 1,500, the FCC must supervise the affairs of eighty common carriers, including AT&T, more than 7,500 radio and television stations and eleven international communications carriers.

It must also decide, as the technical means of communication change, what is within its jurisdiction and what is not. (To the great relief of the computer industry, the FCC has decided that it would not in general regulate the data-processing business.) The truth is that the FCC does not have the information it needs to formulate national policies for communications. It could not, for example, suggest a direction for the use of satellites for education because it does not know enough about current educational problems nor the policies of other parts of the federal government. Because the FCC is a creature of Congress it can exercise no broader vision than Congress permits.

The Other Half

The FCC regulates only American civil communications. It has little power over the communications systems used by the federal government, including the Department of Defense, and these are both vast and generally undisturbed by congressional curiosity. The Defense Department has not only its own communications satellite network but its own telephone and data transmission network. The non-military departments of the federal government have their own private telephone systems, and all together, military and governmental, they use and control well over half of the radio frequency spectrum. The responsibility for coordinating government communications with that used by the rest of the country lies not with the FCC but with the President, and the task of coordinating American communications policies with those of foreign governments belongs to the State Department.

Well before the FCC existed, the United States President had an Interdepartment Radio Advisory Committee to coordinate the assignment of frequencies among various government claimants. Depending on whether the United States was at war or not, successive Presidents held different ideas about whether IRAC should be under military or civilian non-military control. Between 1951 and President Nixon's administration, IRAC served six different masters. But none of them was the FCC. Although sixteen government departments and agencies which are major users of communications are on the committee, the FCC is not. It must rely on a liaison officer to find out what the government is doing with its share of the spectrum.

The federal side of communications has been such a tangle that President Kennedy was both disgusted and alarmed by it during the Cuban missile crisis of 1962. He put together what he called the National Communications System, with the Secretary of Defense in charge, to make sure that there was some plan for uninterrupted communications for the government under all conditions from normal through nuclear attack.

President Nixon went even further. He took the control of the government system away from the military and placed it securely under his own Executive branch. He did this by creating a new Office of Telecommunications Policy, whose objective was not only to eliminate inefficiency and tighten communications links but to provide an office through which the President could speak his views on general issues of policy. For communications, this development was a distinct step up in the world. Many Presidents had thought the subject worthy of coordination before, but not of grand, bold policy bearing the presidential stamp.

The new OTP has not settled down to the extent where the FCC, Congress or the Defense Department – three potential rivals – know whether it is weak or strong. On paper, the OTP is formidable; it now holds the power to coordinate the government's use of communications, to allocate frequencies among federal users and to identify inefficient or overlapping programs, administer the national communications system in case of emergency, and to conduct studies, do research, give advice, testify before Congress and be general factotum for the President on all communications matters. To do this it has a budget of about $2.6 million a year, about 50 percent more than its predecessor, the Office of Telecommunications Management. There haŝ been some concern that the first man to be given the important job of director of the OTP was Dr Clay T. Whitehead, the ambitious young technocrat who suggested its creation to President Nixon in the first place. The stronger the OTP becomes in the years ahead, the less likelihood there is that the United States will create what it may need – a new Department of Communications which could do what the Department of Transportation is doing – sponsoring research, suggesting the reorganization of the existing facilities and in general trying actively to make tomorrow's technology solve yesterday's problems.

III

The British Post Office

The British Post Office is one of the most powerful organizations in Britain. It is a nationalized industry created by Parliament out of an old department of state to run all posts and telecommunications. It runs a banking service and a data processing service as well. The Post Office, with its 400,000 workers, is one of the largest employers of manpower in the country. Its employees are about equally divided between the posts and telecommunications. The profits are not. In its first six months as a public corporation, the Post Office lost £15 million on the postal services and made £22 million on telecommunications. Unlike some other post, telephone and telegraph authorities on the Continent, the Post Office does not pool these revenues. The posts and telephones are kept financially separate. The postal side, as elsewhere in the world, is moribund; it is the telecommunications side of the Post Office that is looking confidently ahead to the years 1990, 2000 and beyond. (Whether this confidence is justified will be discussed in Chapter 12.)

The Post Office is powerful first because it holds a total monopoly on all forms of communications, domestic and international, except for radio and broadcasting. It supplies virtually all the public communication service in the country, including the interconnection of computers and transmission of data. Yet its monopoly extends much deeper than the mere supply of service. The Post Office has an absolute veto on all communications equipment that is designed to work with its telephone network. No new devices may be attached to the network without its permission. Moreover, it holds (largely because its unions demand it) a monopoly on the maintenance of all equipment connected to the network. Suffice it to say that the Post Office *is* the British telecommunications system. What it does not choose to adopt in the way of technology is banned in Britain. No rejected inventor takes the Post Office to court. No one outside Parliament can make it change its mind.

The Post Office has the kind of total executive power over its own assets that the private American communications companies envy. They have to ask the FCC's permission for virtually everything they do. The Post Office does not have to ask anybody's permission before it invests in a new transatlantic cable. It is the owner of the British end of its overseas cables. It owns the Goonhilly Down cluster of satellite earth stations and it is the Post Office's money which is invested in the international satellite consortium called Intelsat. Britain's position at international conferences is presented by the Ministry of Posts after consultation with the Post Office, the Foreign Office and relevant ministries.

Before October 1969, the Post Office was a department of of state, and its day to day affairs were controlled by a Postmaster General, a Member of Parliament appointed by the Prime Minister. Parliament could ask detailed questions at any time about any aspect of the Post Office's operation and the Minister could try to wheel the whole institution around to follow the prevailing philosophy. The result was that the Post Office permanent staff was overly cautious, jittery, afraid of making decisions.

In 1969 the Labor government under Prime Minister Harold Wilson put a bill through Parliament to change the Post Office into a public corporation so that it could take a longer view of its development and make decisions on a more businesslike basis. The bill created an enormous amount of political controversy. The Conservative opposition believed that the new Post Office Corporation would have an even more extensive monopoly on communications than it did in its old form; some of them argued in Parliament and in letters to *The Times* that the development of inventions that would make telecommunications more efficient and more economical to the consumer would be held back by the veto powers of the corporation. Moreover, the Conservatives opposed the bill's provision for the Post Office to engage in the manufacture of equipment for use in connection with its services. Their fears were brushed aside by John Stonehouse, the Postmaster General under the Wilson government, who said:

'The monopoly is the monopoly is the monopoly. If it were less than total, it would not be a monopoly. For that reason, we must ensure that possible technical developments are caught within the monopoly ... before they are invented and before they become competitive with the monopoly, for that would be a very embarrassing position.'

The bill passed, the Corporation was created, Prime Minister Wilson appointed Viscount Hall of Cynon Valley, a retired naval surgeon and investment director, to be its first chairman. Not many months later, the Labor government had lost a general election and the Conservatives were in power.

The abrupt change of political climate took away much of the new confidence and security that the Post Office was intended to have. It also took away its chairman. Not that all of those who had direct dealings with Lord Hall minded. He sat in a canary yellow velvet chair, embossed with his lordly crest, and was not embarrassed to reveal an unfamiliarity with tele-communications. (During an interview with the author he turned to his personal assistant to ask: 'What's the name of that new pipe, David? Oh yes, waveguide.') Yet his abrupt de-parture reminded the Post Office board of directors, an inbred group largely drawn from the top of the old Post Office hierarchy, that they were still under parliamentary control, even if more obliquely than before. They began to fear that bits of the monopoly would be taken away and that the profit-able parts of the telecommunications operation would be turned over to private industry; what Parliament gives it can also take away. In short, reorganization does not seem so far to have given the Post Office the desired sense of security.

Parliamentary control is exerted by the new Ministry of Posts and Telecommunications, created at the same time as the Post Office Corporation. The Ministry retains all the powers over the licensing of broadcasting that the Post Office has as a department of government (an example of the importance that governments attach to radio as distinct from other forms of communications). The Minister of Posts, moreover, has the authority to guide the Post Office in international agreements and to supervise the general direction of its policies so that they pursue the national interest. He receives its financial reports and, as Christopher Chataway showed in 1970, he may dismiss the chairman of the Post Office.

The Ministry of Posts has, subject to Parliament, supreme power to regulate broadcasting. It awards licenses for the use of the airwaves, for everything from radio-guided toy boats to the BBC. It coordinates the Government's use of the radio spectrum – although so furtively that no one will say how it is done, except to say that the Ministry of Posts is the coordinating authority in an interdepartmental committee which is not only secret but nameless. The enormous power of the Minister over the organization of broadcasting was shown by the issue of local radio. When he came to the job in 1970, for example, Chataway had the power to decide whether local commercial radio should be introduced into Britain and, if so, whether or not the BBC's newly created local stations should be allowed to operate as well. He was finally persuaded by the BBC's engineers that there were enough wavelengths – sufficient room in the medium wave band radio spectrum – for all if certain procedures under the ITU's Copenhagen agreement of 1948 were invoked, in which Britain could use frequencies allocated by the ITU to other countries, so long as they did not cause interference. But the power to make the political decision based on technical choices was the Minister's alone (although he was guided by his party's pledge to allow commercial radio on a local basis). The Minister of Posts will become increasingly important as 1976 draws nearer – the year in which the BBC Charter expires, the Act empowering the Independent Television Authority runs out and the licenses of all the private relay companies which provide radio and television transmission by wire for a fee from subscribers. The future of British broadcasting will be reshaped in this Ministry's shabby building at the wrong end of Waterloo Bridge. As the stakes rise, it becomes all the more curious that the post, like that of its predecessor, the Postmaster General, is considered a junior one, not of Cabinet rank.

Britain organizes its entire institutional apparatus for broadcasting around a belief that broadcasting to the public is an activity that must be tightly controlled. This control is not exerted directly by the Government; it does not mean official censorship or political meddling in the preparation of programs. But the few organizations which are allowed to broadcast to the public through the air are expected by Parliament to keep a careful eye on what they send out. They have an obligation to serve the public interest, to inform and to teach, as well as to entertain (and to do so largely at their own expense). In Britain the concept of broadcasting implies authority.

In 1922, when the Post Office first decided to allow regular public broadcasting, it did so under very strict conditions. It allowed broadcasting on one wavelength only – a limitation deliberately imposed to avoid repeating what was seen as the horrible example of the United States, where independent, unlicensed radio stations were having such a free-for-all on the airwaves that almost none could be heard clearly. The one organization that was allowed – the British Broadcasting

Company – at first was not even permitted to transmit music. Not long after, Parliament turned the company into a public corporation, but it was a very long time before Parliament allowed any competitive source of broadcasting within Britain.

Today the BBC, like the Post Office, is immense, powerful and vulnerable. The new technology of communications will, in the years ahead, force some radical changes on broadcasting, and these will inevitably affect the structure of the BBC. As an institution, it is less secure than the Post Office. It could theoretically be abolished by Act of Parliament in 1976. It exists because it has received temporary leases of life in the form of charters from Parliament in 1927, 1937, 1947, 1952, and 1964. The 1964 charter was revised in 1969. The BBC is in some ways under the thumb of the Minister of Posts. It must provide all services required by the Minister and it may not (nor can its rival, the commercial Independent Television Authority) broadcast more than the limited number of hours a week set by the Minister. It is the Minister who has decided that Britain may at last have television in the morning.

Yet the BBC has remained remarkably insulated from political control, not as much as it might be, perhaps, but enough to make it the envy of a great many other countries which cannot design a comparable institution – public yet independent.

While Parliament has ultimate control over the BBC, the day-to-day responsibility for its policies and programs rests with its nine governors. The governors are appointed by the Queen (which means the Prime Minister) and they are powerful. Many people would rather be a governor of the BBC than a lord. (Some manage both.) They bring the pressure of their views to bear on the Director General of the BBC and the upper hierarchy of administrative officers. Until 1954 the BBC had a monopoly on all television broadcasting in the United Kingdom, and it is only now that its monopoly on radio broadcasts is being broken. But British audiences have not entirely lacked an alternative source of programs. They have long been avid listeners to Radio Luxembourg, the French-owned station located in Luxembourg which beams programs (and advertisements) in English at English audiences. They also eagerly tuned into the pirate stations in the early 1960s until these were forced to stop broadcasting from ships off the English coast. It is because Parliament has recognized the national hunger for programs outside the BBC that it has gradually broken into the BBC's monopoly.

Yet the search for more freedom of choice has always been accompanied by an awareness of the risk involved – that of impairing the quality of the BBC. There are few of its critics who do not accept it as one of the most civilizing institutions in the world, perhaps Britain's greatest contribution to the twentieth century, and certainly the most admired broadcasting organization in the world. Such an asset is not to be battered about casually. One of the greatest challenges that Britain faces in the years ahead is to design a less rigid structure for broadcasting without destroying the BBC. The BBC will fight hard to keep broadcasting as limited as it now is. Its leaders claim that to have a diversity of television sources and a strong national television service is impossible.

The haughty, powerful BBC is in a far stronger position to make its views prevail than is its rival, the weak, defensive ITA. The BBC has the weight of more than fifty years of tradition behind it, plus the awesome reputation acquired by its broadcasts during the war. It has a monopoly on two of the three television channels and it operates, as a special service in the national interest, subsidized by public funds, a world broadcasting service in which it broadcasts, from Britain, in forty languages, programs of news and comment for twenty-four hours a day. And it is justifiably proud that this much-admired world service is not considered by the forty million listeners, ill-informed as they are about the BBC's political independence, to be in any way the mouthpiece of the British government.

The BBC's most vulnerable spot is its method of financial support. It derives the bulk of its income from license fees, an annual charge that is supposed to be paid by each person who rents or owns a television set. This is an increasingly unsatisfying source of income. In the first place, there are about one million defaulters. In the second place, the money is not collected by the BBC directly but by the Ministry of Posts, which in 1970 kept nearly £5 million out of nearly £100 million – to cover the costs of collection. As the BBC begins to face the possibility of a deficit, this charge looks more and more like a needless loss of rightful revenues. Moreover, permission to raise the license fee can only be awarded by the Minister, who is reluctant to do so as it is a politically unpopular act. Then too the fee is an unprogressive tax – it does not rise in step with the rise in the BBC's expenses. Moreover, it is unfair. Some people watch only commercial television – which gets none of the license income – and yet must pay a yearly tax to subsidize the BBC. It seems clear that as the costs of producing television programs rise (and as the demand for international programs brought in live by satellite increases) the BBC is going to have to find an alternative source of funds. One possibility (requested by the BBC, rejected by the Wilson government) was that the Ministry of Education should pay directly for the educational television programs for schools which the BBC makes and on which it now spends about £2 million a year.

The Independent Television Authority, as its name implies, is a supervisory agency. It oversees the fifteen regional companies whose programs and advertisements fill the third television channel. The ITA is supposed to ensure that their programs are in the public interest, well balanced in content, and that the advertising is in good taste, coming only at natural breaks in a program. The Authority also has the responsibility for transmitting the programs of the member companies to the viewers. Its transmitters reach a fractionally smaller proportion of the national audience than do those of the BBC because its assigned frequencies are higher and more difficult to receive. The companies pay a rental to the ITA and they also support jointly an independent news service, called Independent Television News.

For all its virtues, the ITA suffers from an aura of being slightly *déclassé*. The Pilkington Committee, which inquired into the future of broadcasting in 1960, did not try to disguise its dislike for what many people still refer to as 'the other side'. The sense that there was something not quite nice about advertisements was not helped by the reference of Lord Thomson of Fleet to a commercial television company license as 'a license to print money'. That phrase hung over the ITA even when it became untrue. In the late 1960s heavy extra taxation of about 25 percent was imposed on the companies, calculated on their total revenues rather than on their profits, and it hurt the quality of their programs, for the burden fell at a time when advertising revenue was falling and color television was being introduced. Yet the ITA incurred rather more censure than pity, because it failed to improve the quality of programs in spite of a monumental reshuffling of contracts in 1967. In the national debate about the future of broadcasting in Britain, the troubles of the ITA will inevitably be a major subject.

IV

The International Telecommunication Union has its headquarters in Geneva across the road from the Palais des Nations. It is the oldest of the UN's specialized agencies. It is also the most complex. The two characteristics are related, for its complexity is a sign of its age. Unlike more recently formed organizations such as the World Meteorological Organization and the World Health Organization (also based in Geneva), the ITU was not designed; it just grew. As has been mentioned, it acquired its responsibilities gradually, beginning with international telegraphy more than a century ago. And because the countries which are its members have never wished to surrender their sovereignty over telecommunications, the ITU has been kept weak and deprived of a strong central executive body.

It is an organization much despised by many who deal with it, yet its accomplishments are considerable. International communications could not exist without it. The ITU makes it possible for various national systems to work together without interfering with each other. Its most important work is perhaps the preparation and publication of a volume called *Radio Regulations*, covering the allocation of the radio frequency spectrum for the entire globe. They do so by dividing it into three regions, specifying for each the basic division of radio frequencies which allows radio communication to be conducted in an orderly way, without harmful interference. Certain bands, for example, are by international agreement assigned for television broadcasting, others for satellites and research by radio astronomers. Some bands are reserved for aircraft and others for amateur radio broadcasters. Imperfect as the organization is, there is no question of doing without it. The alternative would be chaos.

The ITU keeps the same kind of order in telephony and telegraphy. It works out traffic patterns for international telephone calls to follow. It makes recommendations on standards for acceptable telephone quality, on the size and shape of telephone instruments, on dialing codes for international dialing, and on a new international telegraph alphabet, and it tries to make as uniform as possible the kinds of busy signals used in various countries. It works out development plans for the growth of communications in Africa, Asia and Latin America.

The ITU, like other of the specialized agencies, has 140 member nations, a wider membership than that of the UN itself. Switzerland and West Germany, for example, belong to the ITU but not the parent organization. One undoubted achievement of the ITU has been to provide a place where men with similar interests and with conflicting political philosophies can work together, amicably solving practical problems. Those closely connected with the ITU are both conscious and proud of its political neutrality and fear that were it stronger the organization might not be able to retain its neutrality.

The weakness of the ITU lies in its cumbersome procedures and the fragmentation of its responsibilities. The organization is governed by a general meeting of all its members, called the Plenipotentiary Conference, which meets roughly every five years. Large delegations of diplomats and engineers gather from the four corners of the earth and spend weeks reworking the entire convention (a kind of constitution) of the organization, down to tiny administrative and budgetary details. Then they submit it to their governments for approval. They elect a Secretary General, his deputy and twenty-nine men to go to Geneva once a year to serve as an Administrative Council. Then they go away again and as far as major policies or reforms are concerned, nothing can be altered until the whole ponderous exercise can be repeated in five years' time.

The ITU's regulations concerning international telephone, telegraph and radio are drawn up at large conferences rather than by the administrative staff at Geneva. The important radio regulations, for example, are revised periodically at World Radio Administrative Conferences, of which the most recent was held in Geneva in the summer of 1971 to decide on permanent allocations for space communications. The method is far from ideal. The conferences – also held to revise the telephone and telegraph regulations – are too large, their agendas oppressively long. The really important people either do not come or do not stay for the duration. Decisions about complex technical matters are made by majority vote, but all participants are not equally qualified to comprehend them. Yet the rules they agree upon must remain in force until another conference gathers again.

The ITU does have a permanent staff in Geneva but it is divided into four distinct sections. These are practically autonomous and not overly disposed towards cooperating with each other. The four are:

1) *General Secretariat.* Headed by the Secretary General, this branch of the ITU has responsibility for preparing ITU conferences, publishing the various ITU recommendations and carrying out the directives of the administrative conferences. It has no real responsibility for the workings of the other branches.

2) *International Consultative Committee for Radio* (known as the CCIR). Its job is to study technical and operating questions about radio communications and to make recommendations.

3) *International Consultative Committee for Telephone and Telegraph* (CCITT). It has similar responsibilities for telegraphy and telephony.

4) *The International Frequency Registration Board.* Founded at an ITU conference in Atlantic City in 1948, the IFRB maintains a register of all radio frequencies used for all purposes (except military) throughout the world. Even though it is concerned with radio, it does not work closely with the CCIR.

The chairmen of the two consultative committees are elected by the members of the committees. The five members of the IFRB are elected by World Administrative Radio Conferences. In other words, they work for separate constituencies of particular specialists. The Secretary General and his deputy are the only officials who owe their jobs to the full membership of the ITU, the Plenipotentiary Conference. What this confusing arrangement of elections means is that the leaders of the ITU have no incentive to pull together. If they want to ensure their continued tenure in the comfortable life of the international service, they must not give offense to their constituents. The Secretary General and his deputy are the only officials of the ITU who owe their jobs to the majority vote of the full membership. That means that they must not give offense to anyone. The current Secretary General, a bland, grandfatherly Tunisian named Mohamed Mili, fills this requirement very well.

The two consultative committees work through study committees which take practical problems, work on them and make recommendations. Some of the subjects studied in recent years have been the international accounting for collect telephone calls (CCIR) and standards for television recordings to facilitate the international exchange of programs. These committees contain not only representatives of 140 governments, but of forty-nine private communications agencies, forty-three scientific or industrial organizations and twenty-seven international organizations. Although their recommendations must be accepted by Plenary Assemblies which meet every three years, before they constitute formal international regulations, they practically always are accepted. Rebelliousness is not a characteristic of communications engineers. Yet what this method of drawing up regulations means is that quite often it is the manufacturers and broadcasters of the richest countries who suggest the technical standards upon which world practise and investment depend. The standards for the world's telephones, therefore, are likely to be suggested by men from AT&T and for radio transmission by engineers from the BBC. Needless to say, the countries of the underdeveloped world feel that their needs are not well represented by such an arrangement and that the richer countries tend to suggest, as the world standard, equipment which is compatible with what they have already. Sometimes, for newer countries, more sophisticated equipment would be a better buy, for they do not have to protect their existing investment. The Eastern Europeans too are wary of the dominance of the big industrial nations. So they insist fiercely that the ITU's branches continue to be run by elected officials rather than administrators appointed by a central executive. In that way they can ensure that their interests will not be submerged.

Radio has been the most troublesome of the ITU's charges, and it is the radio committee, the CCIR, that has produced the ITU's two conspicuous failures. It was unable to produce an agreement on standards for color television around the world (the French and Russians use a system that is incompatible with the British and German, which is a modification of the American system), and it has been unable to produce any agreement at all on the use of short-wave radio for broadcasting. (Short-wave radio, useful over long distances, has been too valuable for propaganda.)

The most beleaguered branch of the ITU is the frequency registration board. It might be thought of as the only branch of the ITU truly concerned with making rules for international communications, but its function is purely passive. It simply keeps a list of frequencies that members of the ITU declare their intention of using. The IFRB can inform them that such a use would cause interference, yet it can do nothing to prevent it. In fact, unless someone writes in and complains about radio interference, the IFRB has no way even of knowing that its recommendation has been disobeyed; it has no monitoring service. If the frequency is registered and not used, that too is unnoticed. The IFRB cannot even demand technical assistance from the CCIR; the radio committee may request some advice but if it does not get it, or receives it too late, there is nothing it can do.

In 1965, at the ITU's plenipotentiary conference at Montreux, the United States, the Soviet Union, Canada and the Western European countries all together proposed abolishing the IFRB and transferring its powers to a more modest, efficient department under the Secretary General. But their combined influence was not enough to produce the desired reform. The developing countries in their greater numbers insisted that an independent body, headed by elected officials and representing the various regions of the world, were more immune from political pressure and would better safeguard their interests.

It is easy to find people who believe that the ITU is in need of radical reform. It is almost impossible to find anyone who can suggest how this might be accomplished. Mr Gerald Gross, the American who had worked for the ITU for eighteen years before he stepped down as Secretary General in 1965, put an excellent scheme before the Montreux conference that year. He suggested that the ITU needed a simpler and shorter convention and that the traditional division of its work into radio, on one side, and telephone and telegraph on the other, was obsolete. The work of the organization, he suggested, should be divided into its three functions: administration, regulation and research. But the plenipotentiary conference did not take his advice. It did agree, however, to work on the preparation of a charter which would eliminate the need to keep rewriting the convention.

Since then an advisory committee of the United Nations has recommended that the next plenipotentiary not give undue attention to the traditions of the past and pay more attention instead to the fact that the old dividing lines between telegraphy, telephony and radio, as well as between transmission by cables and by wireless, were disappearing. An American foundation, the Twentieth Century Fund, has also put a lot of thought and money into the problems of reorganizing the ITU. It has suggested that the Secretary General be the only elected official among the permanent officers and that he have some authority to preside over the rest of the organization. It also suggested simplifying and unifying the work of the IFRB and the two committees.

But no reform can succeed unless it passes the necessary test – acceptance by a majority of the ITU's members. And a majority of them would prefer to have the ITU inefficient and with too many elected officials than to have it streamlined and in the control of administrators over whom they had no power. Yet there is no place in a weak, slow-moving, timid organization for the kind of regulation that communications satellites will demand. As the number of different systems goes into orbit and as anxieties over the possibility of a scarcity of space in orbit grow, there will be increasing need for an international organization to exert some regulatory and coordinating authority over them all. It is a need that will tax the present creaky structure of the ITU to its limits.

Part Two
Satellites

Chapter 4
Middle Age Ahead

'*The communications satellite knows no geographic boundary, is dependent on no cable, owes allegiance to no single language or political philosophy.*'

LYNDON B. JOHNSON, 1967

It is easy to idealize and even to anthropomorphize the communications satellite. The usual kind of satellite rides 22,300 miles above the equator, virtually equidistant from every country and every person within its enormous range. Only three are necessary to make a single television audience out of almost the entire globe. So small and so high, it seems to vault over the past, over mountains and oceans, and invites the whole world, jungle and suburb, to speak through it. The symbolic power of the satellite is so great that it is believed to have almost magical powers to educate, almost diabolical powers to persuade. The deep feelings that the device has aroused have bedeviled its short life. Planning for its orderly and effective use has been difficult and may become more so.

In theory, satellites are little different from the microwave relay towers that dot the landscape. Microwaves that are used for television and other broad-band communication because of their great information-carrying capacity are brought to a stop when they meet a physical barrier. Usually they are shunted from towers placed in line of sight with each other. There could have been intercontinental television exchange before satellites were developed if there had been chains of microwave towers across the ocean. But as there are not, long-distance over-water television had to wait until Telstar was launched in 1962, providing a relay tower in the sky.

Satellites, although using microwaves just as terrestrial communications do, have unique capacities. They do not link two points but many. They can receive from many places at the same time and transmit to many more, sending the whole range of message forms simultaneously – television, telephone, telex, photo facsimile and computer data. Satellites have also revolutionized the economics of communications. In every other form of transmission, undersea, underground or through air, the cost of sending a message depends on the distance covered. Farther costs more. Yet for satellites, at the altitudes which have turned out to be best, the distance between the senders and receivers on the ground is practically irrelevant. Communications between San Francisco and Tokyo, a distance of over 5,000 miles, and communications between San Francisco and Los Angeles, less than 500 miles, would both require the same facilities: two earth stations and a satellite.

Irrelevant too are the historic patterns of the world's communications which used to be funneled through the capital cities of what were once the colonial powers, all in the Northern Hemisphere. A telephone call from one African country to another had to go through London, or through both Paris and London. In Latin America, a call from one country to another often had to go through New York or even London.

The latest generation of satellite, the Intelsat IVs, can link any one of many earth stations within its range to any other. Even better, it can connect them on demand without prior booking. It can do this by keeping a pool of circuits in reserve for random requests and infrequent combinations – Morocco to Brazil, for instance.

How They Grew

Satellites went from dream to reality very quickly. The British science writer Arthur Clarke put forth what turned out to be a brilliantly accurate hypothesis in 1945. In the British magazine *Wireless World*, he pointed out that if a satellite could be flung into an orbit 22,300 miles above the earth (a fanciful suggestion in those early days of rocketry), it would travel at the same speed as the earth. It would thus appear to be stationary and would be in line of sight of sending and receiving stations with about 40 percent of the globe. So, Clarke concluded, only three satellites would be needed for global communications.

There are two ways in which an artificial satellite in orbit around the earth can be used for communications. It can be an inert bouncing board to deflect signals sent from earth back to earth again, without amplifying them. Or it can be an active working relay tower, taking the received signal and sending it back strengthened and on a different frequency to avoid interference. Both possibilities were remote in 1955. No artificial bodies at all had been made to travel around the earth. The United States showed some bravado that year when, announcing its plans for the forthcoming International Geophysical Year to begin in 1957, it set itself the task of placing a small satellite in orbit around the earth.

What happened, of course, was that the Soviet Union did it first. Its first Sputnik, a 184-pound ball, was put into orbit in October 1957, sending the whole of the United States, from President Eisenhower down to children in primary school, into shock. American space ambitions had been slowed down by the rivalry between the Army, the Air Force and the Navy, each of which had their own rocket candidate for the job. The Navy won the assignment, but its first attempt failed humiliatingly when the Vanguard rocket exploded on the launch pad. Into the breach stepped the Army; its Redstone rocket made by Wernher von Braun and his German team at Huntsville, Alabama, put the United States into space at last in January 1958 with Explorer I, which discovered that the earth is surrounded by belts of radioactivity. Von Braun and his team were soon absorbed into the new civilian, non-military space agency, NASA, set up that year.

Things progressed more smoothly after that. A primitive communications satellite called Score, carrying a tape-recording of President Eisenhower's voice, was in orbit by the end of 1958, broadcasting presidential Christmas greetings from space. In 1960 the first passive communications satellite was put to use; a huge silver balloon called Echo received signals from the United States and reflected them over to England and France. The first active communications satellite was Courier 1B, launched for the US Army in October 1960. It was active in that it could receive information from one ground station and transmit to another. But it could not do the two simultaneously, as it was not high enough in the sky to be within line of sight of two stations at once. The information from the first had to be stored in a tape recorder until the satellite had traveled in orbit over the second.

By 1962 the United States government was urging that satellites be used for commercial communications. But what kind? Of a number of proposals for active communications satellites the satellite made by AT&T, a private company, looked to be the leading contender. It was called Telstar and had been designed by Bell Labs' ageless *wunderkind*, Dr John Pierce, whose earlier work had helped to make microwaves useful for communications and was built with AT&T's own money. After its launching in July 1962, Telstar gave the world its first live transatlantic television pictures, such as they were. British viewers missed them on the first pass of the satellite because of the misalignment of a small part at the Goonhilly earth station.

Telstar traveled in a fairly low orbit over the earth. The earth stations which worked with it at Goonhilly and at Ploumeur-Boudou in Brittany and at Andover, Maine, were highly sophisticated radio telescopes, capable of being focused on any part of the sky. When Telstar came over the horizon, they started tracking rapidly, moving to follow the path of the signals beamed toward earth as it crossed the sky. When the satellite disappeared below the horizon, the signals were gone, the show was over.

A commercial system of low-level random-orbiting satellites like Telstar would have required a whole series of satellites following, one after the other, in orbit. In that way there would always be at least one within receiving range of the antenna. This idea seemed sensible. AT&T placed its hopes on the random orbit and so did the Radio Corporation of America, which built two low-level satellites called Relay, one in 1962 and the second in 1964, financed in part by NASA in order that AT&T would have a competitor. Both companies were hoping to win or to share the job of providing the American end of a commercial international satellite system.

Their hopes were shaken by the Hughes Aircraft Company. Hughes went straight for the synchronous orbit of 22,300 miles above the earth, suggested by Arthur Clarke. Its Syncom 2 got there in July 1963 and stayed – not exactly stationary as planned – but fixed enough so that ground stations could keep it in view all around the clock.

Obviously a system that needed only three satellites and comparatively little tracking was more desirable than one that needed a great many satellites and a lot of tracking. Yet synchronous satellites had one drawback which prevented them from being recognized instantly as the answer for commercial communications. When a satellite is at such a great height, one quarter of a second elapses while the message travels up to the satellite and down to the ground again. This lag was no deterrent to the Defense Department, which had sponsored Hughes's research into synchronous satellites, nor to NASA, which had commissioned Hughes to build Syncom. But it was a monumental obstacle to AT&T. Many people then believed that the time lag would make synchronous satellites useless for telephone service, the main job for which commercial satellites were intended. If speakers interrupted each other in mid-sentence and heard echoes of their own voice coming back at them, the result would be a telephone connection of inferior quality, hardly something that the world's largest telephone company wanted to pursue.

The time delay turned out not to be offensive to the public. Telephone men, however, who have more sensitive ears, still maintain that it bothers them; they hate the time lag as Christians hate sin. One executive in Brussels orders a cable circuit when he telephones New York. Some at AT&T feel that the time lag would not be acceptable in American domestic telephone service, that the public does not mind a few crackles on an international call but will object when it gets the same distortion on a call from New York to California. Meanwhile the ITU, which makes the international rules, has declared that a telephone call relayed through more than one satellite should be avoided whenever possible. The American Communications Satellite Corporation – Comsat – wants to see a change of ITU policy.

The Intelsat System

In 1962 the United States decided to press ahead with the development of a commercial communications satellite system to serve the world. And Comsat, the corporation that Congress created, decided early in 1964 that synchronous satellites would offer the most elegant, swift and economic way of bringing that system into existence. The technical progress of the international system created by an international consortium called Intelsat, under Comsat's auspices, has been spectacular. Intelsat's contributions to international harmony have been less so. (See Chapter 5.)

Early Bird, the first commercial satellite, made by Hughes for Comsat and the international partners it had recruited, was launched in 1965. For a few months after its launching there was a great burst of transatlantic television exchanges, but the enthusiasm ended when the experimental free-of-charge weeks were over and the use of Early Bird for television cost broadcasting organizations $8,500 for ten minutes in the week-day peak period. Television charges have dropped substantially since then but are still heavy enough to be a deterrent to the use of satellites for television. Little of the total satellite time is being used for television. That satellites are so little used for the intercontinental service which they, unique among other methods of transmissions, can provide has been disappointing, one of the first signs that the new technology might not fulfill its potential and would be ruled by the telephone business.

Early Bird was put to work on the North Atlantic route, which carries more international traffic than the rest of the world combined. There were only five earth stations in existence which could work with the satellite. It provided 240 telephone circuits or one television channel, on an either-or basis. When the satellite was wanted for television, all the telephone lines had to be cleared.

The satellite that followed Early Bird, the Intelsat II, first launched successfully in January 1967, was under the same restriction, but could be used by more than two earth stations at the same time. The development of the Intelsat II was largely paid for by NASA, which reserved much of the capacity of the series of satellites for its Project Apollo moon landing program. The Intelsat II arrangement was a great help to Intelsat, permitting it to take a step toward a global system of satellite communication earlier than had been expected.

In 1967, when an Intelsat II became the first satellite to be stationed over the Pacific, it effectively doubled the number of communications links between the United States and the Far East and made transpacific television possible. It also brought Latin America within range of satellites for the first time. One by-product was the first global television program, 'Our World'. It was made possible by linking satellites and land lines to form a network around the globe. But the technical achievement of the program was overshadowed by its banality. The scenes of people swatting mosquitoes simultaneously near the Arctic Circle and along the Mediterranean, suggested that global television programing was going to present more subtle problems than global television transmission.

The next series of satellites, the Intelsat III, brought a few political problems (see Chapter 5) but it was a great leap forward in capacity – 1,200 telephone circuits instead of 240. The Intelsat III was the first of the Intelsat series to have an antenna that remained pointed to the earth. Earlier satellites had antennae which spun round with the satellite, wasting most of their power on empty space. But on the Intelsat III, the antenna spun clockwise. This kept the antenna pointed toward the earth. It had a number of much publicized technical troubles, chief among which was the paralysis of the new Atlantic Intelsat III just as the only program of truly global interest was about to begin – man's first steps on the moon. (Nonetheless, temporary arrangements, including the recall to service of Early Bird, enabled the moon landing to be seen on six continents.) In spite of various difficulties, the Intelsat III became the backbone of the commercial satellite system, providing coverage over the Indian Ocean and a truly round-the-world service for the first time. It also allowed television rates to be lowered substantially.

By the end of 1969 the Intelsat system had grown to include thirty-six earth stations in twenty-four countries. It contributed several thousand circuits to the world's international communications capacity, only seven years since the uncertain days when no one knew what the best height for a communications satellite should be. And it had done so at half the estimated cost. The investment in satellites by the end of 1969 was only $100 million instead of the $200 million that had been anticipated. Yet even this economy was to provide a source of political embarrassment, as will be shown later.

The latest generation of commercial satellite is the Intelsat IV. First launched in January 1971, it is so sophisticated as to make all three earlier generations together look primitive.

INTELSAT's SATELLITES

Satellite	Capacity	Positions	First successful launch	Design Lifetime	Weight in Orbit
Intelsat I (Early Bird)	240	Atlantic Ocean	1965	18 months (but operable long after)	38·5 kg.
Intelsat II	240	Atlantic and Pacific Oceans	1967	3 years	87 kg.
Intelsat III	1,200	Atlantic, Pacific and Indian Oceans	1968	5 years	126·8 kg.
Intelsat IV	3,000—9,000	Atlantic, Pacific and Indian Oceans	1971	7 years	557 kg.

The Intelsat IV is roughly five times heavier than the Intelsat III and can offer three or four times as many telephone circuits. Alternatively, it can carry as many as twelve color television channels. Its most dramatic advance, however, is found in its two saucer-shaped antennae. These can concentrate its power on the areas of heaviest traffic, while two smaller antennae can radiate their power, like the earlier satellites, on an entire third of the globe beneath. As many as 9,000 telephone circuits are available when the Intelsat IV is switched to make maximum possible use of its large antennae. In this way, less of the satellite's power need be wasted on sending signals to the oceans. And because the satellite radiates eight times as much power as Early Bird, it can work with a great many earth stations at once. (Earth stations are, in a sense, a drain on the satellite. Early Bird could work with no more than two without its faint signal being lost.)

All its press releases boast about how big Intelsat IV is, but, like all spacecraft, the astonishing thing is its smallness. Intelsat IV is only eighteen feet high, only ninety-four inches across, and when it is in orbit, having shed some fuel and the cladding that protected it during the fierce shaking of the launch, it weighs only 1,225 pounds. Several of these objects, with an expected lifetime of seven years, are being relied upon to provide the backbone of a 30,000-circuit Intelsat network by 1972. The Intelsat IIIs should last through 1973 and the Intelsat IV, if they last the seven years intended, should suffice the Intelsat satellite system until the end of the 1970s.

Competition from Cables

The dramatic rise of communications satellites came at a time when submarine telephone cables were also improving rapidly. The capacity of these cables increased after their introduction in 1956 so steadily that by 1965, when 240 commercial satellite circuits became available over the North Atlantic, the number of transatlantic cable circuits had risen from the original thirty-six of 1956 to 548. The expansion of cable capacity has continued and is there to be matched against each new generation of satellite. Cables and satellites are – although some try to deny it – rival technologies.

The economics of cables and satellites remains a controversial subject. It is difficult to find an unbiased view, as the FCC found when it set about to plan for the communications facilities for the Atlantic basin in the years leading to 1980. In terms of flat purchase price, a satellite would seem to be cheaper. All eight Intelsat IVs together cost about $104 million, while TAT-V, the fifth transatlantic cable with 825 circuits compared with the thousands offered by each Intelsat IV, cost $86 million. Yet the operating expenses and risk that accompany satellites are high. The satellite must be launched at a cost that has gone from $6.5 million for the Intelsat IIs to $15 million for the heavier Intelsat IVs. It has to be guided into the synchronous orbit by radio signals from the ground and steered into its assigned position over the equator (and steered back when it wobbles off its path). Its signals must be received by earth stations which cost about $3 to 5 million, which require highly trained operators and which must then transmit them to central exchanges before they can pass into the national communications network – a process which adds to the costs. All of this investment is necessary to get the required performance out of a device that is a total loss if a very small part malfunctions – something that could be repaired with a screwdriver were it on the ground – and which, in any event, has a comparatively short life. The Intelsat IVs, most durable of the satellites so far, have been designed to last seven years.

Cables last about twenty years. They plug straight into national telephone lines; their reliability has been proven and they are reparable if damaged. The most common cause of loss of service on undersea cables – lines dredged up by fishing trawlers – has now been fairly well eliminated by sea plows which bury the cable in sand. Moreover, their costs have been going down. TAT-1 cost $305 a circuit mile to build. TAT-5 cost $30 a circuit mile, and the TAT-6, which AT&T will build by or before 1976, is expected to cost $8 a circuit mile.

For a while in the late 1960s it seemed as if the fierce rows over which was cheaper – cables or satellites – would fade away. An excellent study of the comparative economics of the two, prepared in 1970 by B. M. Davidziuk and H. F. Preston of Britain's large cable manufacturer, Standard Telephones and Cables Ltd., concluded that there is a considerable gray area where neither has a clear economic advantage. 'The final choice of the medium is influenced by issues other than economics,' they said.

One of those issues is reliability. Telecommunications men the world over will swear that reliability is all to them and that to ensure it they must have what they call a mix. On this basis, the British and Canadians have decided to build a second cable (of 1,840 circuits) between their two countries by 1974, and the FCC, after hearing bitter debate, authorized the building of a TAT-6. The FCC announced as its formal conclusion that the public interest required the promotion of both cable and satellite technologies if the 20,000 circuits expected to be needed in the Atlantic basin by 1980, to keep up with the expected demand for automatic international dialing, were to be available.

Yet there is more at stake than a common-sense wish not to rely on only one kind of transmission. What obscures the economic choice between cables and satellites is the question of ownership. The Intelsat satellites are owned by Intelsat, the international consortium. The various companies and national authorities that invest in Intelsat do not *own* satellites in the true sense. They rent circuits from Intelsat, on the one hand, and they receive a return on their investment on the other. When they decide to put money into a transoceanic cable, in contrast, they get virtual ownership rights for their money. For as long as the cable lasts, their share of circuits is theirs. They can plan for its use and the allocation of its revenues without consulting anyone else. Telephone authorities in Europe, like AT&T in the United States, prefer facilities which they own and can control. For AT&T, cables have an added attraction: they count toward the company's rate base – the assets on which the FCC calculates how much profit AT&T may earn. Investment in satellites does not.

Yet in spite of the preference of the established communications authorities for cables, it is conceivable that by the 1990s, if not by the 1980s, the capacity of satellites to offer ten and twenty times as many circuits – and to offer them to all parts of the world – will relegate submarine cables to an importance comparable to that of the spare tire.

Satellite Rates

The charges for using Intelsat satellites are based on an odd measure called a unit of satellite utilization. The unit represents the price charged by Intelsat for the use of a half-circuit, which is a ride between a ground station and a satellite. Obviously it takes two rides – one up and one down – to get a signal from a sending station to a receiving station. The Intelsat satellite unit price reflects the costs of building and operating the satellite part of the system, as well as the administrative costs of Intelsat and the compensation paid to investors for the use of their capital.

In fact, the price paid by the user of satellite communication has two other components – the rate charged for the ride from, say, New York City to the ground station at Andover, Maine, and then from the Goonhilly Down earth station in Cornwall into London. So the cost to the user has four parts: two satellite units, plus ground transmission at both ends. One of the headaches in planning for the use of satellites is that the European telecommunications authorities have charged more for their end of the line than the Americans have charged for theirs. In April 1970 the charge for a ten-minute television transmission across the Atlantic was $3,290; of this, $890 represented the American share, $2,400 the European. Some on the American side have accused the Europeans of keeping their satellite connection charges with the satellite high on the old philosophy of 'soak the rich'. The international communicator is a rich customer and presumably can afford to pay the bill. Yet the Europeans argue that their costs for television reception and transmission are not covered by current revenue. The increased capacity of the succeeding generations of satellites has brought about several reductions in the rates. But television broadcasters are pessimistic. Under existing international arrangements they cannot see any hope of a significant reduction in costs in the next ten years. A day may come when rates plunge so that international communications will really flow like water. If computers could exchange data across the Atlantic at about three cents a minute, then the world's libraries and laboratories (and perhaps police files) would really be open to all comers, as the futurologists predict.

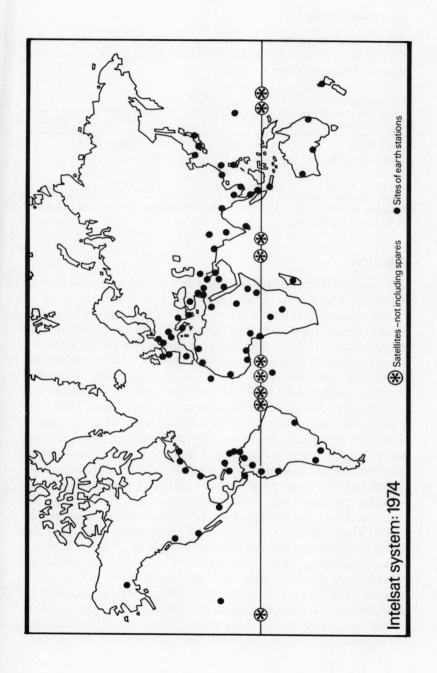

Intelsat system: 1974

⊛ Satellites – not including spares   ● Sites of earth stations

But if the slim experience of the past few years is any guide, the increase in the circuit capacity of satellites will come faster than a dramatic drop in prices.

Intelsat's rates*

Date	Satellite	Unit of Satellite Utilization
June 1965	Early Bird	$32,000 a year
January 1966	Intelsat II	$20,000 a year
January 1971	Intelsat IV	$15,000 a year
January 1972	Intelsat IV	$13,000 a year

* Lease of one-half voice circuit for one year. Television rates are calculated differently.

The Others

All communications satellites now in the sky do not belong to Intelsat. The Soviet Union has its own Orbita system of communications satellites based on a satellite called Molniya, which means lightning. The Orbita system does not use the synchronous orbit, for two reasons: the Soviet Union does not have launching sites in the tropical regions, which are best for launching satellites into the difficult high orbit over the equator, and, moreover, an elliptical orbit (in which the satellite dips low over the far side of the world and high over the Soviet Union) best suits the Russian needs at the moment. The Orbita system involves two transmitting stations – one near Moscow, the other near Vladivostok – and more than thirty receiving stations. It is used largely to distribute television but also some telephony over Russia's vast area.

NASA, the American civilian space agency, has perhaps the most technically sophisticated communications satellites in orbit. They perform experiments in meteorology, mapping the earth from space, and astronomy as well as communications. NASA's satellites carry the label of ATS (for Applications Technology Satellite) and will provide, if there are no more drastic cuts in NASA's budgets, experimental broadcasts in educational television for India and Brazil in the mid-1970s.

An odd thing about the world's communications arrangements is the polite convention which ignores what the military are doing. For example, the chart purporting to show the progress of satellite communications used by the United States Congress and others does not list the operational satellites put up by the US Department of Defense. Yet there were more of these sooner than of any other kind. In 1965, when Early Bird was stealing the headlines, the Defense Department put seven satellites in orbit slightly below synchronous altitude. Its Initial Defense Communications Satellite Network had twenty-six satellites in orbit not long after. The British Ministry of Defense has, in cooperation with the US Air Force, put up its own Skynet system of synchronous satellites, and NATO has some in its own name.

The existence of these satellites is hardly a secret. It is not possible to keep launchings from being detected by spy satellites, and NORAD, North American Air Defense Command, tracks all objects in space, as do astronomical observatories. Moreover, the ITU publishes a list every month of all objects launched into space, including some mysteriously labeled 'no name', with unspecified radio frequencies and unspecified purposes. Quite often, in the United States and Britain, the launching of a military satellite is accompanied by a flurry of press releases, just as if it were a commercial satellite. But after that, silence. These satellites are treated like celebrities' bodyguards – hulking presences that the photographers ignore. To mention military satellites at the ITU or at a conference about the use of satellite communications for the good of mankind is a breach of good manners.

But they cannot be ignored. It is military development that has forced the pace of satellite technology. It was the military investment in satellites, followed by the American space programe (both prompted by the Cold War), that gave Hughes and TRW Inc. the know-how to build communications satellites which enabled the Intelsat system to succeed. The demands of American defense gave American industry a reservoir of experience which the many countries that would like to develop their own satellite expertise find it difficult to duplicate.

Yet military satellites are important to civil communications planners for two reasons, which have nothing to do with national defense. They are the avant-garde of the technology;

what the military are using today is what will be available commercially in a few years' time. (Right now the largest military satellites, modifications of the Intelsat IV, are being used to send signals to very small antennae indeed – three feet in diameter. They are also being used to communicate with small and large stations at the same time and with antennae on the move.) In the second place, the military satellites are occupying space in the synchronous orbit.

Squatters' Rights?

The synchronous orbit, or geosynchronous orbit, as purists like to call it, is like the equator – an imaginary line which arouses strong feelings. The path along which the satellites travel, west to east, 22,300 miles above the equator, is 165,000 miles in circumference. To ask how many parking places for satellites there are along this line is like asking how many points on a piece of string. The answer is: it all depends.

There is at the moment a great deal of anxiety, especially in countries that do not have anything floating through the synchronous orbit, that it may become full, that it will not be able to accommodate all the communications satellites that the countries of the world may in future want to put into it. They feel that the best places will be taken by the early comers and they would like some to be reserved, like seats in a theater, for their late arrival.

It must be said, however, that there is virtually no chance at all of satellites bumping into one another. The synchronous orbit is not, as many people imagine, a narrow track. It is deep and wide, a tunnel rather than a path; there are perhaps 100 miles from top to bottom and several miles across in which a satellite can wander while remaining for all practical purposes 'fixed' over a single degree of the equator's 360 degrees. Two or three satellites could occupy the same position – measured in degrees longitude along the equator – without ever getting near one another.

The real problem is radio interference. If they get too close, their signals interfere with one another. As a result, the current practice is to keep satellites separated by more than a thousand miles. As satellite techniques become more and more refined, it begins to look as if this distance can be reduced. Now that beams can be focused more precisely, it is possible to think of allowing two satellites using the same radio frequency to be placed no more than two-tenths of a mile apart. There are a number of other technical choices that also make it reasonable to hope that the synchronous orbit can accommodate all the uses that can be foreseen for it.

But the anxieties about the scarcity of orbital space will not be easily dismissed. The fact is that there may be a hundred or more objects in synchronous orbit and they will never leave it. They stop sending signals when their power is exhausted, but while they can be nudged out of the way into a less desirable position, they do not have the fuel to be flown up or down to another orbit. At the end of 1970 there were, according to Plessey Radar Ltd., twenty-six active satellites in the orbit. Neither the ITU nor any other international organization is rationing spaces or giving permission for the use of the synchronous orbit. Those who have satellites there – the United States, Britain, NATO and Intelsat – have taken, in effect, squatters' rights in the sky. Moreover, all spaces are not in equally desirable positions. Canada and Latin America both have been uneasy about the growing interest within the United States for a number of commercial communications satellites (see Chapter 6), especially as much of the same segment of the orbit seems best suited to their needs. The day may come when there is an international dispute about places in orbit, and the ITU, strengthened or not, may be forced to deal with it.

Whatever the future holds, the present realities of satellite communications are harsh. As long as satellites need to have such a powerful, expensive ride to get into orbit, there will be only a few countries that can put them there. Even if this number is extended by three or four, the fine-sounding words of President Johnson about satellites having no political allegiance will remain not quite true.

Chapter 5
Lament for Intelsat

I

Let it never be said that communications satellites lacked the advantage of a fresh start. The United States Congress created a new kind of corporation to exploit them, and that corporation in turn brought about a novel international organization to spread the benefits of space communication quickly to the whole world.

But there were congenital contradictions in Comsat, the Communications Satellite Corporation, as it was established by Congress in 1962, and these contradictions were swiftly transferred to Intelsat, the international consortium that Comsat initiated. Intelsat, under the management of Comsat, has brought about a commercial and global network of communication by satellite faster than anyone had thought possible in 1962. It has dramatically increased the capacity of the world's international communication channels and it has made possible live international television. Yet it might have done much more.

Intelsat might have led the world in the planning for the use of satellites for education and for the exchange of television programs. It might have become a single system serving the whole world, which could have been a model for international commercial cooperation as well as a unique partnership between East and West. It might have encouraged developing countries to feel that satellites were an invention which allowed them to come late but equal to the feast of international communications.

Yet Comsat and Intelsat, which are not quite separate (Comsat being the dominant partner among the nearly eighty members of Intelsat), have so exhausted themselves in fighting each other during their formative years that these opportunities which existed in 1964 have been lost.

Perhaps Intelsat was blighted from the start. From the first moment that President Kennedy broached establishing a global communication satellite system, the idea was ridden with contradictions. In June 1961 he asked that the United States develop satellites 'for global benefit at the earliest practicable time'. Enlarging on a suggestion made by President Eisenhower in December 1960, just before he left office, Kennedy proposed that the new satellite system be run by a private company, in the American tradition of having communications in the hands of private enterprise, yet he invited the other nations of the world to participate. He asked that it serve parts of the world where service was un-economic, yet also that it operate economically enough itself to reduce overseas communications rates. Kennedy hoped that a 'constructive role' for the United Nations would be found. And he hoped that there would be foreign ownership in the system, while at the same time he expected that it would be subject to the regulation of the American government.

In other words, the new satellite system was to be both American and international, both commercial and altruistic. It was to make money for its investors while fostering, to quote Kennedy 'world peace and closer brotherhood among peoples'. It was to find a way, to take a phrase from Tom Lehrer's song, of 'doing well by doing good'.

Woolly ideas are understandable in the early days of bold new ventures, but Kennedy's ambiguity turned out to be expendiency in disguise. There was an unbridgeable political gap between those who felt that satellites should be absorbed into the private telecommunications industry and those who felt that satellites should be owned by a public corporation because they were an offshoot of the space program, paid for by $60 billion of taxpayers' money.

The Comsat Act

Needless to say, the American Telephone and Telegraph Company favored private ownership, especially as its own satellite candidate, Telstar, was ready to be launched. AT&T proposed that the new satellite enterprise be created as a closed corporation, with the ownership of shares restricted to communications carriers like itself. Senator Robert Kerr of Oklahoma, chairman of the Senate's committee on aeronautical and space sciences, obligingly introduced a bill into the Senate, embodying the AT&T proposal, and the FCC gave it its blessing. As a Democratic President, however, Kennedy was shaken by the arguments in favor of public ownership – not enough to endorse it fully, but enough so that the bill finally submitted by his Administration contained a compromise. The proposed corporation was to be half public, half private, with public investors holding voting shares and the carriers non-voting shares. The result was to be, as the Senate Foreign Relations Committee was told by Secretary of State Dean Rusk:

Another evidence of the pragmatic ability of Americans to devise new institutions, new techniques, and new organizational forms to meet the practical demands of new situations.

The battle in Congress was fierce. Five separate committees of Congress worked over the bills in hearings. AT&T engaged in such lobbying as had not been seen in many years (souring some who might have voted for private ownership). During the long wrangle some Senators worried that the new corporation might infringe on the prerogatives of the President and the State Department when it went about enlisting international partners. But Secretary Rusk assured them that these fears were groundless. The President would have the authority to control international negotiations over satellites so that they would be consistent with American foreign policy. To most. Congressmen, however, the fight over public-versus-private ownership was of much greater concern, and even that secondary to a greater anxiety.

Congress wanted the United States to get a satellite system up and working before the Soviet Union did. The shock of being surprised by Sputnik had not worn off. There was a feeling that time was slipping by and that a private company could get moving faster than a government-owned company could. The bill that headed toward passage was roughly the Kennedy version – half of the new company for the carriers, half for investors from the public, nothing for the American public in general.

The final battle over satellite ownership was staged on the floor of the Senate in August 1962. Liberal Senators, led by Estes Kefauver of Tennessee and by Wayne Morse of Oregon, were desperate to have the full government ownership of the new corporation. They were so determined to prevent what they saw as a surrender of the public's enormous investment in space research to private interests that they adopted the despised filibustering tactic used by conservative Southern Senators and began to monopolize the floor, talking without stopping. Senator Morse vowed to hold on 'as long as God gives me strength'. Finally the Senate itself found the strength to shut off debate, using a procedure (comparable to the British parliamentary guillotine) so unpopular that it had not been used for thirty-five years. The Communications Satellite Act was passed, and Comsat, the hybrid corporation, was born.

Half of Comsat's shares were to be owned by the communication carriers. The other half were to be sold to the public. Comsat was to have fifteen directors – six appointed by the carriers (of whom AT&T was far and away the largest shareholder), six by the ordinary investors and three – to represent the public interest – by the President. What this patchwork meant, among other things, was that AT&T was shut out entirely from communications satellites except for the influence it could exert on Comsat's board.

Comsat therefore started life with its biggest competitor on its back, and the President, the State Department and the FCC, watching it. Thus hobbled, it set out to find some international partners – fast.

The Partner Hunt

Now there may have been men in the United States who had the imagination, the vision and the tact to persuade foreigners that there was nothing alarming in joining a game with such crazy rules. But they were not the men chosen to lead Comsat. In fact, it could be argued that most of the subsequent troubles of Comsat grew as much from the miscasting of its top jobs as from its contradictory charter. The chairman of the board, Leo Welch, had just retired as head of

Standard Oil of New Jersey. The president, Dr Joseph Charyk, was an aeronautics professor who had come to Comsat from the Department of Defense, where he had been Under Secretary of the Air Force. The vice-president for international affairs, John A. Johnson, had been counsel to the National Aeronautics and Space Administration.

When they set out abroad for informal talks with a number of European telecommunications officials, they were accompanied by advisers from the State Department. But the Comsat team did most of the talking. Tall, abrasive men, inexperienced in diplomacy and eager to get their satellite business started, they did not conceal their impatience with foreigners who, far from being grateful for the invitation to participation in an American-run satellite system, wanted to haggle about the details. Dr Charyk, a handsome, uneasy man who still is Comsat's president, believes even now that there was no necessity to take outsiders in. 'We could have put up a 100 percent US system,' he says.

The organization that is now Intelsat was created almost inadvertently. The Comsat team intended to keep the talks bilateral, between itself and various telecommunications authorities. They even tried to keep different national groups, when they came together, in separate rooms. What they expected to produce was not a new international body but rather a series of agreements like those which govern international telephone calls or civil aviation. To draw in higher levels of government (especially its own) was the last thing the Comsat team wanted. And at first governments kept out. There certainly was going to be no shortage of partners. The external communications men of the British Post Office (then called the General Post Office) were interested; they had built the Goonhilly Down earth station in order to participate in the early experiments with Telstar and Relay – but they were in no hurry at all. Unlike Comsat, they had no vested interest in satellites – quite the contrary. They had invested a great deal in undersea telephone cables – the Commonwealth Cable System, linking Australia, New Zealand and Canada with Britain was near completion – and they had no desire to see traffic diverted through satellites before the cables were full.

But the British Foreign Office saw larger implications in

satellites, and the Foreign Office, in the end, and not the Post Office, determined Britain's policy toward Comsat's overtures. Early in the 1960s Britain and other industrial European countries realized that they stood in danger of being left out of space altogether. The British, moreover, were still eager to join the Common Market, in spite of President de Gaulle's rebuff in January 1963. One result of these frustrations was the decision of Western European countries to negotiate with Comsat, not country by country, but as a group. In May 1963 the European Conference on Satellite Communication was formed (called CETS, the acronym formed from its French title) to coordinate the views of European governments in preparation for negotiations with what was considered to be not a private American company but the United States government. Comsat had lost its bid to keep governments and politics out of the talks.

The Interim Arrangements

But what form of partnership were the Americans offering? The haggling went on in Rome, London, Montreal, and Washington. The Europeans wanted to have some power to sway decisions, even if the Americans unquestionably were going to be dominant. Formal accord was reached in August 1964. There were actually two agreements, reflecting right at the start the profound difficulty of balancing politics with communications. One agreement was signed by governments, another by communications authorities. Twelve countries signed them in August 1964, and several others added their names shortly after (see table p. 88). These temporary agreements are important for they set the basic pattern from which Intelsat, as it emerged as a separate personality, tried to escape and, in the end, failed.

The terms of these agreements were perhaps Comsat's first major mistake. They do little credit to the State Department either. The terms, while not as favorable to the United States as Comsat had hoped, were unnecessarily harsh. They antagonized the foreign partners right from the start.

A consortium was set up. The countries that were members were allowed to contribute a share toward what was expected

The Original Pattern of Ownership of Intelsat

Country	Designated Operating Entity	Quota
1. United States	Communications Satellite Corporation	61.00%
2. United Kingdom	Her Britannic Majesty's Postmaster General	8.40
3. France	Government of the French Republic	6.10
4. Germany, West	Deutsche Bundespost	6.10
5. Canada	Canadian Overseas Telecommunications Corporation	3.75
6. Australia	Overseas Telecommunications Commission	2.75
7. Italy	Società Telespazio	2.20
8. Japan	Kokusai Denshin Denwa Co., Ltd	2.00
9. Switzerland	Direction Générale des PTT	2.00
10. Belgium	Régie des Télégraphes et Téléphones	1.10
11. Spain	Government of the State of Spain	1.10
12. Netherlands	Government of the Kingdom of the Netherlands	1.00
13. Sweden	Kungl. Telestyrelson	.70
14. Denmark	Generaldirektoratet for Post og Telegrafvaesenet	.40
15. Norway	Telegrafstyret	.40
16. Portugal	Administracăo Geral dos Correios, Telégrafós e Telefónes	.40
17. Ireland	An Roinn Poist Agus Telegrafa	.35
18. Austria	Bundesminsterium für Verkehr und Elektrizitatswirtschaft	.20
19. Vatican City	Government of the Vatican City State	.05
		100.00%

to be the cost of putting up a global satellite system – $200 million. Together they would own the system. Yet the amount that each country was allowed to invest was determined by the amount of international traffic that it expected to have in 1968 (when the satellite system was expected to be operating). This provided a rough formula: there was a lot of bargaining back and forth about such intricacies as whether traffic between the

United States and Hawaii counted as international traffic for purposes of investment (it did).

As the quotas worked out, the United States, which would be represented by Comsat, held 61 percent of the vote. The others held very small shares; Britain had 8·4 percent; the rest far less than that. The United States clearly held the veto power over its partners. Yet Comsat's influence was to be far greater than that of dominant shareholder. The interim agreement made it manager of the satellite system. Comsat would keep the books, deal with the aerospace industry and prepare the decisions about contracts and all other matters on which the consortium would vote.

At this point the consortium had no name. The word Intelsat does not appear in the 1964 agreements. But it did have a governing committee, Interim Communications Satellite Committee, (ICSC). Interim was the key word, for the Europeans, joined by the Japanese, Australians and Canadians, had swallowed the American conditions only by making one of their own – that the arrangements would be temporary and that permanent arrangements would be drawn up at an international conference to be called in five years' time. By 1969, they hoped that their own industries would be more advanced in space technology and that their bargaining position would be better.

The ICSC's job was to act as a board of directors. To have a seat on it, a country had to have an investment quota of 1·5 percent. Smaller countries could pool their shares to acquire a seat. Some countries were not represented at all. At its outset the committee had twelve members.

Yet obviously there would be new members joining in the future. For them, a pool of 17 percent of investment quota was to be kept available. The implications of this percentage were profound. It meant that as new countries joined, the quotas of the original signers would drop – but not below 17 percent of what they had in the beginning. None of the original members could lose his seat on the ICSC. Much more important, the United States could never drop below a quota of 50·63 percent. In other words, it would never be less than the dominant partner. Dr Charyk explained this to Congress in 1964: '. . . let me also say a more or less obvious thing, namely that the corporation [Comsat] in any event has a veto over all actions [of the consortium].' In any event, no matter how many countries joined Intelsat, they could not upset the arrangements very much, for the original partners accounted for 90 percent of the world's international communications traffic.

The View from Outside

Membership in the consortium was open to any member of the International Telecommunication Union. That requirement excluded such countries as the People's Republic of China, East Germany, North Korea and North Vietnam. The idea of a private corporation staking out an American claim in space antagonized many who chose not to join, and even some who did. There had been some complaint at the ITU's Extraordinary Administrative Conference in Geneva in 1963 when the delegation from the United States (which included Dr Charyk) asked that certain portions of the radio spectrum be made permanently available for space communications. The Israelis protested against the reservation of part of what was a natural resource, the spectrum, solely for the use of countries which had the power to launch objects into space. But two were set aside none the less.

The sharing of influence according to international traffic was (and has remained) the dominant characteristic of Intelsat. For one thing, it has relegated developing countries to a permanently minor position in satellite communication. They might spend a lot of money on earth stations, but they will never catch up to the amount of telephoning which the big countries carry on among one another. For another thing, the traffic formula has made it unlikely that the Russians would ever join Intelsat. The Russians have relatively little international communications traffic. In 1964, as now, they were unlikely to be tempted into an American-controlled organization in which they would rank below Switzerland. But they were included in the informal early discussions about a satellite system. The Russian reaction to Comsat's proposals was unclear until after the interim arrangements were signed. Then Guennadi Stashevsky, a member of the permanent Soviet mission to the United Nations, lashed out at the UN and in a Russian law journal. In his article he said:

In establishing the space communications system, the US has practically ignored the UN and ITU. Behind the backs of these organizations, it arranged with a small group of Western countries for the sharing out of the profits from the operation of the system on American terms.

In 1965, Russia launched its own communications satellite called Molniya. It was the first of a series designed largely for domestic television, in which the satellites travel in an ingenious high elliptical orbit and give coverage over Russia of about eight hours a day. In no sense was it a competitor for the Early Bird synchronous satellite, which had just been launched, for in 1964, even before its international negotiations were concluded, Comsat had taken the plunge and signed a contract with the Hughes Aircraft Company for the first commercial communications satellite, as a sign to the world and to Congress that it was not wasting any time.

II

New Recruits

From mid-1965 there was a third force in the satellite consortium. The developing countries of Africa, Asia and Latin America began signing up. Some pooled their shares to get onto the ICSC. There was an Asian group representing eight countries, an Arab group representing thirteen countries and four Latin American representatives. Even this change was not accomplished without a row. The Europeans resented what they considered Comsat's finagling to get Argentina a full seat to itself on the committee because its international traffic did not justify the minimum quota of 1·5 percent.

There is no doubt that the Latin Americans and other developing countries were pulling on Comsat's side. The Latin Americans in particular had no passion to make communications satellites, nor were they keen to protect any established interest in undersea cables. What had cables done for their continent except ignore it? With no good communications links to the outside world, Latin America had been isolated. It was not news. Few European or American newspapers dignified it with a permanent correspondent. The Latin American members wanted what satellites promised – instant international contact – and they wanted it fast.

The spectacular success of Early Bird in the summer of 1965 encouraged more of the smaller countries to join Intelsat. Most of them had only minimal investments – they didn't expect to secure a seat on the governing committee. But their growing numbers intensified the pressure on Comsat to get a truly global system working as soon as possible. Until there were satellites over the Pacific and Indian Oceans, many investors could get little use from the new system.

Comsat, therefore, was caught between two opposing forces – the desire of the industrial nations to share in the profits and the experience of satellite contracts and that of the developing countries to acquire satellite communications quickly. That conflict was quickly appreciated on the ICSC, but what was not realized was the intensity with which the smaller investors felt excluded from the decision-making. Yet they were to build up a head of resentment which exploded into a demand for a share of real power when the permanent arrangements came up for negotiation in 1969.

Life on ICSC

Life on the ICSC was not very happy. The foreign members representing the major investors came to Washington roughly every eight weeks for meetings of the committee. But they were irritated by their lack of status and felt themselves at even more of a disadvantage in relation to Comsat than they had anticipated. They were living in hotels. Comsat was on its home ground. They never (at least not until 1967) chaired the meetings. The permanent chairman in the early years was Comsat's vice president international, John Johnson, the archetypal all-American boy grown up to be bank president. Tall, brusque, with fierce blue eyes, and what seem to be more than the ordinary number of teeth, he held what was probably the most delicate job at Comsat: that of helping the foreign partners exercise their allotted voice in making decisions about the satellite system while preventing them from interfering with anything that Comsat wanted to do.

Under Johnson's thumb, the committee grew petulant and complaining. The word 'consortium' was awkward; could it not have a real name? Someone suggested Telsat and then Intertelsat. Finally the icsc hit on Intelsat. Once they had named it, the foreign partners began to ask that it be treated as an organization in its own right. Could Comsat not send out press releases in Intelsat's name? If it were an international organization, why should the staff be composed almost entirely of American citizens? Did the representatives to the icsc have diplomatic immunity? What if they were involved in a car accident on the way to an icsc meeting?

Their anxieties were met with varying remedies. In 1965 President Johnson declared the icsc a recognized international organization; its members were entitled to certain modest diplomatic privileges. Then it was decided that all satellites should carry the family name of Intelsat. Early Bird was renamed Intelsat I, and thoughts of calling the first Pacific satellite, Lani Bird (because it would connect Hawaii to the mainland United States), were dismissed.

Furthermore, Comsat began a halfhearted program to 'internationalize' its staff. According to one British observer, most of the foreign participants did not take it seriously either. 'We sent experts,' he said, 'the French sent spies, the others sent trainees'. But Comsat did little to publicize the existence of Intelsat. The press releases about satellite launchings continued under Comsat's name, even though Intelsat, not Comsat, was their official owner. Intelsat did not even appear as a separate entry in the District of Columbia telephone book until 1969.

A Matter of Contracts

The most important decisions that the icsc had to make were to approve contracts for the building of satellites. It was over these that the most serious rows took place, and that Comsat revealed its staggering insensitivity to the delicacy of its position.

As an American international communications common

carrier, Comsat was subject to the Federal Communications Commission on certain matters. It had to ask permission, as does RCA or AT&T or Western Union International, to add new capacity to the American international communications facilities. On the other hand, as manager for Intelsat, its duties were to act as a leader, to prepare recommendations for the ICSC as to what contracts should be approved for Intelsat's purchase.

In February 1966 Comsat asked the FCC for permission to give TRW, Inc. a major American aerospace company, a contract for building the third generation of satellite, the 1,200-circuit Intelsat IIIs. Yet without waiting for a reply from the notoriously slow FCC, Comsat in April 1966 went ahead and asked the members of the ICSC to approve the contract. Approval was not hard to get, the voting arrangements being what they were (Comsat, as the representative of the United States, casting more than half of the vote). But then there was a snag. The Hughes company, which had made Early Bird and the second generation of satellite, the Intelsat IIs, was angry at being deprived of the next big contract, and complained to the FCC. The FCC then reminded Comsat that it had not given Comsat its permission to move ahead with the contract. Comsat was then in the awkward position of having to tell the ICSC that the contract would have to await the FCC's approval. The international partners were furious. What kind of international organization was it that owned the world's satellite system, yet could not act without the consent of a domestic agency of the American government?

The Intelsat III incident was an international embarrassment, beyond a doubt. The State Department called the FCC's attention to what had happened, and then the FCC commissioners became cross. They gave their approval but scolded Comsat for creating an unnecessary furor. 'There are established procedures,' wrote Commissioner Kenneth Cox, who gave his consent to the contract reluctantly, 'which, if Comsat had followed them, would have permitted the Commission and other agencies of our Government to discharge our respective statutory responsibilities as to this application without becoming involved with international aspects of this matter.'

After a round of letters, it was agreed that Comsat would tell the State Department, the FCC, and the Director of Telecommunications Management (which regulates the governmental and military use of the spectrum) what was to be on the ICSC's agenda well before the committee's meetings began. Haste such as was seen over the Intelsat III was not to be repeated.

Then Came Intelsat IV

But it was. Not long after the Intelsat III was in production, the members of the ICSC began arguing over the kind of satellite to come next. Comsat wanted Intelsat to invest in a radically new 6,000-circuit satellite. But a number of the others on the committee thought that the Intelsat IIIs would see the consortium through until 1975. It had ordered six and taken options on an extra eighteen of these satellites. The ICSC had considered having a series called Intelsat III½ (a 2,000-circuit version of the Intelsat III) with directable antennae before it invested in a completely new model. In spite of opposition to the larger contract, Comsat decided that it wanted to press on with the much more sophisticated and capacious next generation, and one that might be useful for an American domestic satellite.

Here is the way Comsat went about it. On May 15, 1968, Comsat sent an alert to the FCC. At the next ICSC meeting, Comsat wrote, a substantial majority of the committee might want to decide to go ahead with an Intelsat IV satellite. Such a decision might be taken, although the subject of a new contract was not even listed on the agenda. 'If this occurs,' Comsat wrote to the FCC, 'it is essential that the United States representative be free to participate in such a decision.' Comsat requested an answer straight away.

The FCC commissioners did not object this time – none that is except Commissioner Nicholas Johnson. His specialty at the FCC has been the stinging dissenting opinion and, on this occasion, he was livid. He wrote:

The FCC has today accepted its role as the forgotten man in the international satellite policy-making arena.

Comsat has presented the Commission, at 3:00 p.m. this afternoon, a proposal which would allow Comsat to abandon its

Intelsat III½ program and go directly to an Intelsat IV – if, during upcoming international negotiations Intelsat wishes to take such a course. This proposal involves the future course of man's greatest breakthrough in communications technology in recent years; it involves investments of over a hundred million dollars. . . .

We could have been presented opportunities for review of this decision weeks or months ago in a time frame which would have enabled us to give it reasonable consideration. But this is not the first time we have been overwhelmed into providing our rubber-stamped imprimatur in the face of a last-minute Comsat rock slide. And what may have started as a special request for prompt consideration under emergency conditions has now become standard procedure.

The ICSC itself felt that Comsat rushed it into decisions. At the thirty-fourth session of the ICSC in September 1968, when the final decision on awarding the Intelsat IV contract was due to be taken, Comsat did not distribute a summary of the contract until the day after the session began. Then it asked for what was in effect three decisions in one: the confirmation of the Intelsat IV program, the number of satellites to be ordered and the choice of a contractor. In fact, two offers had been made: one from Hughes, the other from Lockheed. Yet Comsat, on the whole, was disposed toward Hughes, and the Lockheed proposal, for an even more advanced kind of satellite, was dismissed. The final text of the proposed contract, worth $73 million, was not even handed around until the same day that the vote was to be taken. It was small wonder that some on the ICSC became suspicious to the point of paranoia about what their manager was up to.

Sharing the Wealth

The Intelsat IV contracts, the biggest prize yet to come out of Comsat's larder, also provided a fertile field for fights about what was called 'international participation'. This high-sounding principle was embodied in the interim agreement to answer the specific worries that the Europeans had. There was an undertaking to share the contracts among the international partners, if they could offer as low prices and as swift delivery dates as the American companies could. On the early contracts, there was little chance for participation, but a genuine beginning was made with the Intelsat IIIs. Small shares of the work were given to six foreign aerospace companies. The actual monetary value of the contracts was not very great. The British in particular were very conscious of this: they had put in around 7 percent of the investment in Intelsat but were not getting anything like 7 percent of the contracts.

But at the time when the Intelsat IV contract was being considered, the deadline for the end of the interim arrangements was drawing near. There was a need to placate the restive Europeans. For the first four satellites in the new series, the proportion of international participation was considerable. About $19.4 million of the $73 million contract was spent in ten countries outside the United States. One of the satellites was to be assembled entirely by the British Aircraft Corporation in Bristol, the contract being worth $7 million to BAC. The countries involved were pleased; their newspapers boasted about their industries' ability to turn out satellites and components to American standards. Then it was the turn of the representatives of the smaller investor countries to get angry. How much was international participation costing, they wanted to know. How much was the subsidy they were paying to educate European industry? The fact that the answer to the question was given alternately as $9 million and $4 million only served to increase the irritation of the ICSC. The members could not question Hughes directly and were asked to accept that the actual financial negotiations between manager and contractor were confidential. The result of the controversy about the cost of participation was that when the second series of four extra Intelsat IV satellites was ordered, the foreign subcontracts were reduced considerably. Thus, when in December 1970 the British Aircraft Corporation produced the Intelsat IV that had been assembled in Britain, the satellite was described as 'the first satellite ever made entirely outside the United States'. There was no mention of the fact that, because of the tensions among the members of Intelsat, it might also be the last.

The foreign partners were also cool to Comsat's plans to build its own laboratories. Comsat said that it needed them in order to have 'in-house capability' – to have, as NASA has, the ability to do some of its own work and to check on the work of suppliers. But Comsat's motives looked different to its partners. They knew that Comsat wanted to increase its capital investment in physical facilities. The satellite system had been built so much more cheaply than had been expected in 1962 that much of Comsat's own original $200 million, the amount put into it by American investors in 1964 remained in the bank. For several years, Comsat earned more from its bank deposits than from the rental of satellites circuits. So it was eager to build all kinds of things – labs, aeronautical satellites and, most of all, a domestic satellite system, to build up its 'rate base' – the investment in plant and equipment by which the FCC judges how much communications carriers are allowed to earn.

The foreign partners had no such desire. By and large they were government-owned. Rate base was nothing to them. And they realized that Intelsat would be paying for nearly half of the research and development work done at Comsat labs. They would get little advantage from this additional investment; on the contrary, they would be reinforcing the American lead in technology. Why could they not set up an international satellite research center, if the object was not to be overly dependent on Hughes Aircraft?

But Comsat labs were opened in September 1969 on a site about thirty miles from Washington in the Maryland countryside. In that year, Intelsat paid Comsat about $4 million for research and development and other work done at the corporation's laboratories, and its share is expected to increase in the years ahead.

Domestic Troubles

Had it not been so brash, Comsat might have been pitied. Its strength on the international scene was counterbalanced by its weakness at home. The new corporation was a gnat compared to the giant AT&T, which was pressing relentlessly on with its expansion of submarine cables. Comsat's public shareholders, who had snapped up the stock in 1964 when it was offered for sale at $20 a share, wanted some dividends from their investment in space technology. Yet as Comsat struggled to strengthen itself, it lost round after round at the FCC. The last thing that the provincial FCC could appreciate was that if Comsat were in a stronger position in relation to the other American commercial communications carriers, it would not have to bully Intelsat.

The FCC dealt Comsat several mean blows. First the FCC ruled that Comsat could not sell satellite circuits directly to broadcasters and news agencies and other customers for overseas communications. It could only sell circuits wholesale to the other communications companies and let them resell them. Comsat was to be a carrier's carrier – a status with about as much potency as a gentleman's gentleman.

Comsat asked to be allowed to own the American earth stations which worked with the satellites. After all, the foreign telecommunication authories owned their ground stations; they were an integral part of the satellite communications system. But the FCC said no. Comsat had to share ownership with the carriers: temporarily at least. Then Comsat was forced to give up the lucrative business it had with the Defense Department, furnishing thirty satellite circuits to the Far East at a third of the cost of what the other carriers were charging the department for cable circuits. And the FCC, over Comsat's most bitter protest, granted AT&T's wish to be allowed to build a new telephone cable across the Atlantic. TAT-5 opened in 1970, bringing 720 new circuits to the transatlantic market place just a year before the 6,000 circuits of the new Intelsat IV opened up on the same route.

None of these slights would have hurt, had Comsat been allowed to become the operator of an American system of national communication by satellite. The United States, spread over thousands of miles of land and water yet having only one language, might seem to be the ideal territory for satellite communications. Yet the political obstacles were formidable.

In 1966 Comsat applied to the FCC for permission to build a domestic satellite system. Actually, Comsat's hand had been forced. Some months earlier, the smallest of the television networks, the American Broadcasting Company, had asked the FCC for permission to put up its own satellite to transmit television programs across the country. The ABC's petition was not taken seriously in itself; what it did suggest was that the television networks were dissatisfied with having to pay AT&T

increasingly high rates of $65 million or more a year for the national distribution of their programs. They wanted an alternative source of transmission, and thought satellites offered a cheaper one.

What was taken seriously, and did spoil Comsat's chances, was the bombshell dropped by the Ford Foundation in 1966. The foundation, in a plan prepared by Fred Friendly, the amiable giant who had quit the largest of the television networks, the Columbia Broadcasting System, because of his disenchantment with its commercialism, suggested to the FCC that a domestic satellite system should be publicly owned. The old 1962 row over public versus private ownership was revived in a new form. Under the Ford scheme, a public domestic satellite organization would earn money by transmitting commercial television programs across the country and then would spend it on giving a free ride to non-commercial and educational television, a cause dear to Ford's heart. Space technology would provide a people's dividend at last.

As a stimulus to new thinking, the Ford proposal was brilliant. As a stimulus to the creation of a domestic satellite system, it was a disaster. At that point in time the United States was unlikely to put a domestic satellite into orbit for use for television only. The practical effect of the Ford plan, in fact, was to paralyse the FCC by making the issue seem even more complicated than it had originally. As far as Intelsat was concerned, it meant that Comsat was more jealous of its power than ever.

The Discontents Grow Louder

The French were getting restive within Intelsat. They wanted to be able to put up a satellite to link the French-speaking countries of Africa, and perhaps Quebec as well, with France. The Europeans, as a group, moreover, banded together in ESRO (the European Space Research Organization) and ELDO (the European Launcher Development Organization), were pressing on, although without much success, to develop their own ability to produce and launch satellites. The Canadians and Japanese were also interested in having satellites of their own. Just how these schemes would fit into the future organization of

Intelsat was anybody's guess, and all parties were careful to avoid the critical question: Would NASA launch their satellites for them?

NASA is proud that it has never refused to launch anything for anybody. It has launched a great number of scientific satellites for other countries, and it performed launchings for Intelsat on a cost-reimbursable basis. But the formal decision taken by the French and Germans in 1967 to proceed with a joint communications satellite project called *Symphonie* backed NASA into a corner. Would NASA launch *Symphonie*, the question came from Europe, if a European rocket were not ready to do the job? NASA gave a cautious 'yes'; it would launch any satellite that did not cause economic harm to Intelsat. This answer was interpreted in Europe as a thinly disguised 'no'. NASA could hardly have dared to be less delphic. On the one hand, the space agency had to observe the State Department's policy of supporting Intelsat. But Intelsat's policy on independent satellites was vague. It was certainly becoming clear that Intelsat could not expect to outlaw independent satellites if it was to hold onto all of its members. Whatever the brave words 'single global system' meant in the interim agreement, they did not mean that Canada and France would give up their ambitions for satellites with their national names on them.

The Approaching Deadline

While the Europeans were panicking about the thought of being refused NASA's favors, the ICSC was beginning to think about the new definitive arrangements that were to be drawn up by 1970. The ICSC was supposed to make its own recommendations for the permanent shape of Intelsat, but if there was not unanimity, the committee's mandate was to compile recommendations that represented all shades of opinion within its ranks. The possibilities ranged from making the interim arrangements permanent to setting up an entirely new international organization.

Until 1967 the troubles of Intelsat had been kept out of the world's press. The ICSC's meetings were secret and Comsat assured the world that Intelsat was thriving. But the enterprising space reporter for *Aviation Week and Space Technology*, Miss Katherine Johnsen, was determined to find out what was happening on Intelsat's international governing committee. As her requests for interviews with John Johnson got nowhere, she wrote letters to all the foreign representatives, asking for an interview. She expected to be granted none. Instead, she got seventeen. The ICSC's men were willing to talk. They were not content at all with the way that Comsat ran the consortium, and they wanted big changes. The Johnsen story, which appeared in *Aviation Week* on February 13, 1967, let the cat out of the bag. Under the headline, 'France Backs UN Intelsat Control,' it revealed that there was considerable support on the ICSC for an international organization on the lines of the ITU to take over the control of Intelsat. The alternative, said the French representative, with some prescience, 'is an Intelsat global satellite communications system and an anti-Intelsat global system, dominated by the USSR, and then, perhaps a proliferation of systems.'

By August 1967 even the British had stopped being polite about Comsat in public. H. G. Darwin, the British legal adviser to the United Nations, speaking at an international legal conference at Stanford University, described Comsat's position in Intelsat as that of 'Lord High Executioner and Lord High Everything Else'. The same month, another Johnson, President Johnson, had recognized the incipient rebellion at Intelsat. He made a declaration which was in effect an answer to the critics and a call for a return to the original ideal of a single global satellite system. He said:

'We seek no domination of satellite communications to the exclusion of any other nation – or any group of nations.'

The President urged the Russians to join Intelsat and to combine their Molniya system with it. He also suggested that perhaps Comsat's weakness in relation to AT&T or, as he put it, 'the division of ownership of international communications carriers,' was not in the public interest. 'We must be prepared to act,' he said. But instead of acting – introducing a bill into Congress asking for the merger of the international communications companies so that they could speak with one voice in international negotiations – Johnson called for a study. And not just an ordinary study but a task force to conduct a thorough re-examination of all aspects of communications policy.

A sweeping assignment, and one so well carried out that many of its major recommendations, which seemed radical at the time, have now become national policy. But it took time. By the time the report of the President's Task Force on Communications Policy, headed by Professor Eugene Rostow – then Under Secretary of State, and now of Yale University's law school – had finished its work, it was late in 1968 and a new President had been elected. Many of the Rostow report's recommendations were anathema to AT&T, which, as the richest corporation in the United States, has plenty of political weight. The Rostow report dared to recommend that Comsat be allowed to put up an experimental domestic satellite system. It also suggested that all the American international facilities be merged in a single organization involving Comsat; this implied taking ownership of the international telephone cables away from AT&T. President Johnson greeted the report with cool silence. Before he left office, he might have given his support to its recommendations, but he did not. And if the outgoing Democratic President did not want to offend AT&T, the incoming Republican certainly did not. For a time it seemed as if the Rostow report might actually be suppressed but President Nixon finally allowed it to pass quietly into print and the hands of the public in the spring of 1969. Its lack of presidential endorsement left the United States without a strong policy either for domestic satellites or for the future of Intelsat.

The ICSC Recommends . . .

As 1968 drew on, the split in the ICSC was grave. By the end of the year the committee was supposed to suggest a permanent structure for Intelsat. The full conference of all Intelsat's members scheduled for February 1969 would use the recommendations as a basis for negotiations. The ICSC had come to a few basic shreds of accord. They all agreed that the future Intelsat should consist of 1) an Assembly of all members; 2) a Board of Governors (the successor to the ICSC); and 3) a management body.

All agreed too that the United States should surrender its position as majority shareholder. Comsat itself had offered the suggestion that no country's representative in the future Board of Governors have more than 50 percent of the vote. But that amounted to no concession at all. As the world's traffic through satellites increased, the American share was falling proportionately. The American part in Intelsat was bound to drop to around 40 percent, no matter what happened.

A related suggestion of Comsat's was laughable. Comsat proposed that on the future Board of Governors all matters be settled by a straight two-thirds vote. One hundred percent minus 40 percent equals 60 percent – less than two-thirds. Comsat was suggesting that it, the representative of the United States, retain the power to veto the rest of the board. 'Why do they do things like that?' asked a foreign diplomat after watching Comsat in action during the long negotiations over a permanent agreement that followed. 'The United States delegation offer these outrageously transparent schemes, clearly designed by Comsat, and then the State Department people withdraw them apologetically, as if to say to us, "We told Comsat you boys would never buy it." '

The ICSC, therefore, agreed on the bare bones of the Intelsat structure but they disagreed about every inch of the flesh. There were conflicting opinions on international sharing of contracts, on the powers of the Assembly, on the powers and the composition of the Board, on the formulae for weighted voting on the Board, on how telecommunications representatives should be worked into the structure – in other words, on all the issues that had caused argument back in 1964.

There was, however, one matter on which there was almost unanimity – that Comsat not continue as manager. The question came before the ICSC in December 1968: should the manager under the interim arrangements continue under the permanent arrangements? There was no doubt about the position of the United States. According to one of those present, John Johnson's hand shot up. He looked slowly around the table. There were no others, not the British, not even that of the Italian representative, who had often taken Comsat's side. The vote was seventeen to one against Comsat's continuing. In a strictly commercial organization, a chairman who drew such a vote of no confidence after five years' work might have felt obliged to resign. But John Johnson stayed on as Comsat's vice president international as Comsat went on to try to win from the full membership of Intelsat the job for which its closest partners refused to commend it.

III

The long-awaited international conference to decide on permanent arrangements for Intelsat opened in Washington on February 22, 1969. It was the biggest international conference ever held in Washington, and it was a festive occasion. Intelsat by then had grown from the original fourteen to sixty-eight members; the Russians and other Eastern Europeans had come along to watch, and the American aerospace and electronics industries dispensed hospitality in Washington's hotels. The head of the American delegation, Leonard Marks, who had been recruited from the United States Information Agency, where he had served a short time as director under an appointment from President Johnson, believed that the conference could be wrapped up in the few weeks for which Intelsat was booked into the State Department's large auditorium. He was wrong.

The gathering of representatives of all the members in one room merely revealed the depth of the disagreement about what Intelsat was and should become. The United States delegation itself was split. Its official position was that Comsat must be appointed the exclusive and permanent manager of Intelsat. The FCC's representative to the conference was just as determined as were Comsat and Senator Pastore over on Capitol Hill, that the Americans should insist on control over the system that they had created. On the other hand, the State Department's men, notably Frank Loy, the Deputy Assistant Secretary responsible for Intelsat, were prepared to be more flexible, but they were not forceful enough to take the rest of the delegation with them. Things were hardly more unified on the European side, where the members of CETS, in spite of five years of preparation, could not agree on a common European policy. They all wanted Comsat to surrender the management of Intelsat to an international directorate, but did not agree on how much authority the new organization should have over its members. The French, with their firm plans for a French-speaking satellite system, wanted a less powerful Intelsat than the British, with a large investment committed to Intelsat, felt was desirable. The occasion of the conference, moreover, provided all the smaller investors which had not been represented on the ICSC with a forum in which to air their discontents. The seeds of an agreement were not there. The conference broke up a month later, little having been decided.

It was clear that the new Intelsat was not going to spring out of the ashes of the old by January 1970, as had originally been intended. Some countries began to wonder if the interim arrangements were going to stay in force forever. Perhaps, they suspected, Comsat would not mind. After all, the interim arrangements were more favorable to Comsat than anything that succeeded them would be. Long negotiations, they believed, only strengthened Comsat's hold over Intelsat.

The United States delegation, on the other hand, believed that the French, West Germans and Swiss were trying to forestall the day when their influence would drop. By 1969, the terms of the 1964 agreement made these and some other countries larger owners than users of Intelsat. That is, their communications traffic had not risen to the expected volume on which the original investment quotas had been based. As a result, they were getting more money out of Intelsat than they were putting in. The Americans were bitter about what seemed to them to be greed. As one of their delegation sourly put it, 'People like the French are renting ownership space, profiting from their investment of other people's money. It's not what you'd expect from civilized people.'

In April 1970, France, for example, had an Intelsat quota of 5.27 percent. That entitled it to roughly one-twentieth of Intelsat's profits. Yet it generated only 2.32 percent of the communications traffic sent through the satellite system (largely because the French PTT preferred to send traffic over the telephone cable, in which it had invested). Japan, in contrast, was getting less than 2 percent of the profits, all that its original quota allowed it. But, because of the tremendous surge of traffic that satellites had brought to the Far East, Japan accounted for more than 5 percent of the use of the Intelsat system. This disparity between ownership and use seemed to the United States delegation, and to Dr Charyk and Johnson of Comsat in particular, clearly to explain why the Europeans were being so troublesome. They believed that the French, Swiss and Germans wanted to wrest the maximum political advantage out of their original quotas before these dropped, as was inevitable under permanent arrangements, to something more in line with their real use of satellites.

At the end of more than a year, the full conference trooped back to Washington for another try. Work had been going on backstage all year, in small groups, but there was little to show for it. The same issues were dragged out, over and over again, making a tedious litany which went from management, contracts, weighted voting, power of the Board of Governors, the authority of the Assembly. Of all these, the management issue was unquestionably the most divisive. The industrial nations would not accept Comsat. They wanted an international directorate to handle the day-to-day running of Intelsat. The American position too was firm, and it was supported by Australia, Brazil and a number of countries with no ambitions in space. Comsat had to remain the manager.

For Comsat, much more than the immediate sums it was paid by Intelsat every year for management and other services was at stake. Of greater concern to its executives was the fear that an international management would take Intelsat down what one called 'the UN path' – jobs filled according to national origin and a general listlessness in the air. Comsat felt that it alone could provide the brisk day-to-day management that was needed to extract from Intelsat in the 1970s the financial rewards promised by the investment and experiment of the 1960s. And above all, people at Comsat believed that to be compelled to surrender its control over its own creation was unfair. Their attitude was: 'We built it and now they're trying to take it away from us.' (To which the corresponding European argument was: 'We're not dependent on Comsat for a satellite system, we're dependent on NASA and the Hughes Aircraft Company.')

The impasse over the management seemed insoluble. Many delegates openly expressed their country's bitterness at having an aspect of its international affairs in the hands of an American private company. Some criticized Comsat by name, not even bothering with the euphemisms of 'the manager' or 'the representative of the largest investor.' Comsat, for its part, was less

inclined to loose its hold on Intelsat than ever. The Nixon
Administration's statement of policy on domestic communications satellites had just been issued and it was a stab in the heart
for Comsat. Let the sky be open to all qualified applicants, said
the White House in a memorandum to the FCC in January 1970,
and let competition decide who the survivors shall be. Thus
ended Comsat's claim to a right to a monopoly on American
domestic satellites. If Comsat then surrendered management of
Intelsat, what would it have left but a dull role as seller of
satellite circuits to AT&T and other carriers?

Suddenly a solution appeared. It was designed by the representatives of Australia and Japan, two remote and prosperous
countries who shared few of the prevailing grievances against
Comsat. They had benefited greatly from the advent of
satellite communications and did not want Intelsat's progress
to be interrupted by prolonged bickering. Their compromise
began with a proposal that Intelsat be managed by Comsat for
six years after a permanent agreement were signed. After that
Comsat was to turn the management over to a Director General
and an international staff. And during the transitional six
years, Comsat would not continue unsupervised but would
have a Secretary General to monitor its activities on Intelsat's
behalf. The Secretary General would not have much power but
he could assure the non-American members of the Board of
Governors that their interests were being safeguarded in
Comsat's dealings with manufacturers. He could also prepare
the ground for the transition to an international directorate.

Just as suddenly Comsat accepted it. The State Department
finally persuaded it to compromise. The length of the negotiations was getting embarrassing; the United States delegation
was on its third ambassador and Congress was becoming restive
about handing over more than $200,000 for conferences which
produced nothing. And all considered, the terms were not too
disagreeable. A six-year transition period would take Intelsat
nearly to 1980. Comsat would still be manager therefore when
the next big round of contracts for the Intelsat V was handed
out. And after that Comsat's 40 percent vote on the Board of
Governors would probably suffice to allow it to steer Intelsat
as it thought best.

With the issue of the management settled, a final agreement

seemed near. On March 13, 1970, the *Washington Post* reported: 'After a year of stalemated negotiations, an agreement for permanent operation of the world's international communications satellite system appears imminent.' But the good news was premature; fighting broke out anew over the fundamental, persistent and unresolved question: What is the role of national governments in an international commercial organization?

National governments were to be represented in the Assembly on an equal basis; each was to have one vote. But for what? The smaller countries demanded a strong Assembly that could give orders to the Board of Governors. Britain and some of the other larger investor countries sympathized with this wish, for they could foresee satellite developments in which governments would not want to leave their national interests in the hands of the telecommunications man who was their representative on Intelsat's Board of Governors. The problem of the Assembly was the problem of Intelsat itself.

As John Killick, head of the British delegation (who was knighted in 1971 and made British ambassador to Moscow) said in a speech to the Paris Space Assembly in June 1970:

'Governments must approach the problem not just as a commercial one but as one in which new means have to be found of reconciling the commercial aspects of an international enterprise with equitable participation for all its participants and a suitable role for governments, who would be failing in their duty as parents if, having given birth to a child, they were to do no more than to pat it on the head, and to put it away to play and take no further interest in it.'

But to the United States delegation this fresh controversy was the last straw. A powerful Assembly meant a weak Intelsat which would transform Intelsat into a debating society.

The struggle over the powers of the Assembly was the major reason that agreement on the definitive arrangements for Intelsat was not reached for more than another year. In the end, the United States won on the issue when its partners agreed that the Assembly would have powers to recommend – but not to determine – policies for Intelsat. They gave in only in exchange for a concession from the United States (forced upon Comsat by the State Department) that the Assembly would at least have the power to amend the permanent agreement by an 85 percent majority vote of all its members. Comsat had been holding out for the power to veto amendments virtually by itself. The vote finally approving a permanent structure for Intelsat was taken on May 21, 1971; it showed seventy-three in favour, none opposed and four, including France, abstaining. The new arrangements were to come into effect soon after approval by a combination of two-thirds of the members and of big investors.

In its final form, therefore, Intelsat has an Assembly of Parties (governments), a Meeting of Signatories (telecommunications entities), a Board of Governors and an Executive Organ, which will at first be led by a Secretary General and, six years after the agreements come into force, by a Director General. It also possesses, as the interim Intelsat did not, juridical personality. It can conclude agreements with governments or international commercial organizations and be a party to legal proceedings.

For all the length of the deliberations, the Intelsat conference avoided settling the main issue of the management. The new Director General, when he assumes power around the end of 1978, must not, under the terms of the agreement, build a large staff of his own but must make contracts with 'competent entities' to perform as much of Intelsat's technical and operational work as possible. And before the Director General takes over, the Board of Governors must obtain reports from at least three professional management consultants from various parts of the world. They should recommend how Intelsat should be managed and then, one year before Comsat is to hand over the management to the Director General, the Assembly can vote on what kind of management the organization is to have. In other words, five years after the new permanent arrangements come into effect, Intelsat will be riven all over again over the question of retaining Comsat as manager.

Has all the talk been worth it? Is Intelsat a model for other forms of multinational cooperation which must come – the international commercial exploitation of the seabed, for example?

Hardly. Intelsat is overstructured, overdefined, and underpowered. The scope of each layer of the organization has been so rigidly limited that Intelsat will find it difficult to make any dramatic changes of direction or to do much more than to sell telecommunications circuits to those who have the money to pay.

All sides lost what they wanted most. Comsat will not be manager forever. Yet by the time Comsat is replaced, the formative years of Intelsat will have passed; a Director General will not be able to change very much about the organization. He will be restrained by the Board, which will be dominated by Comsat.

The Europeans lost their wish for some kind of commitment by Intelsat toward the international sharing of contracts. All the years of maneuvering since the formation of CETS in 1963 were rewarded with the following lines in the final agreement.

If there is more than one bid offering such a combination of quality, price and most favorable date of delivery the contract shall be awarded so as to stimulate in the interests of Intelsat world-wide competition.

As it is unlikely that two identical bids would ever be submitted, this final clause on procurement in the Intelsat agreement means that if European aerospace firms want Intelsat contracts, they will have to underbid their American competitors. By the end of 1970 there was little pretense that industry outside the United States had benefited to any substantial degree from the contracts awarded under the interim arrangements. The State Department told the House Appropriations Committee in December that 92 percent of the $323 million that members of Intelsat had invested in satellites and related equipment had been spent with American companies. American companies, moreover, had provided more than half of the earth stations built to work with the Intelsat system.

For the developing countries, the final shape of Intelsat is a disappointment. Many of them have been induced to invest in earth stations but they have little international communications traffic. Morocco's station, for example, is far from being economical. Yet having spent several million dollars on an earth station does not help them toward a seat on the Board of Governors. The kind of investment that puts a member on the Board is based on the volume of international communications traffic that a country has. And that is principally in the countries which have been the biggest consumers of telecommunications since the turn of the century.

To put it bluntly, a country cannot buy influence in Intelsat, even if it were willing to invest a very large sum. It can acquire it only through the kind of international public communications traffic through satellites which fits Intelsat's definition. And that restriction is the hallmark of Intelsat. The Russians are unlikely to want to join under those terms, and the developing countries have been made cynical. As one of the Mexicans said in 1970, 'Intelsat is not the organization of seventy-nine countries. It is a club. It doesn't serve the needs of a majority of its members but simply protects the interests of the original investors.'

Intelsat could not even design an arrangement to give the United Nations favored status among satellite users. The United Nations had hoped that Intelsat would let it use a few satellite circuits free of charge. During the sessions of the conference, the UN's representatives patiently waited for an answer to their request for free circuits. They hoped that the Intelsat delegates would take pity on it. The UN, too poor to buy satellite circuits, has had to keep in touch with its peace-keeping forces by unreliable short-wave radio. But the Intelsat negotiators ducked the issue. To give a free ride to the UN would set a bad precedent for a commercial organization; besides, many members of the UN are not members of Intelsat. Intelsat did not want to do favors for non-members. The UN request was not actually refused ('Who wants to vote against motherhood?' asked one delegate). It was just put on the shelf.

Intelsat makes no provision for helping poorer countries plan for the most effective use of their satellite connections. In fact, it disdains involvement in such broader questions. When the Twentieth Century Fund suggested, in 1969, in a report on the future of satellite communication, that Intelsat take in as members users of satellite services, such as the BBC, people at Intelsat derided the suggestion. There is virtually no one connected with Intelsat who cares that satellites are little used for television. Telephone authorities present so much more desirable a customer, not rushing in out of the blue like television men, and asking for great slices of satellite time, but instead soberly renting circuits on a yearly basis.

Intelsat, in the words of Abram Chayes, professor of international law at Harvard Law School, who was legal adviser to the State Department when Comsat and Intelsat began, is 'a hope lost'. Chayes told the Zablocki subcommittee in April 1970 that Intelsat had settled for a role as a relatively conventional long-distance communications carrier. He criticized the State Department and Comsat for lack of vision in dealing with Intelsat.

We were too much concerned with our power to get the result we wanted, and our freedom of action, and we didn't give enough weight to the values of international cooperation and activity in this area on their own.

An American official who is too close to allow his name to be used believes that the United States overprotected its interest both in Comsat and Intelsat, thus frightening the Europeans into unbalancing their own space efforts by reducing the scientific programs to concentrate on satellite communications. Once committed to their own satellites, he contends, European governments became tense and alert to the political problems of Intelsat, and from then on each detail of the organization was disputed.

Yet the Europeans hardly acquitted themselves well either. All along they tried to have their cake and eat it too. They wanted to enjoy a share of the benefits of American technological leadership, yet at the same time to narrow the technology gap and to improve their competitive position in relation to the United States. The developing countries too were more obstinate than they needed have been. Were it not for the established traffic among developed countries, the global system which takes them in would never have been set up in the first place.

Perhaps the European ambition could have been accommodated within Intelsat if Comsat had been allowed to have a domestic system satellite and was therefore more generous. Perhaps the negotiations would have been smoother if there had been men of sweeter temper at Comsat. Perhaps the fault for the blighted promise of the venture must really be traced back to President Kennedy. He had no need at all to propose that satellites be run by a private corporation. As a Democrat, he could have looked to the tradition of the publicly owned Tennessee Valley Authority for a model if one were needed.

It is a great irony – considering the battle over the Comsat Act in 1962 – that AT&T and Comsat have joined hands and want to put up a domestic satellite system together, and that there have been suggestions in the Senate and at the Justice Department that AT&T and the other communication carriers should be forced off Comsat's board of directors altogether.

Intelsat, for all its obscurity, is a badly bungled international opportunity. It was a chance to go beyond Babel, to use the new technology of satellites to create an organization in which governments not particularly friendly toward one another might have worked together. Instead, Intelsat, by its commercial orientation and American dominance, has encouraged the proliferation of other satellite systems and has created the real possibility that there may some day be international disputes about places in the synchronous orbit. It has made the work of the weak ITU even more difficult, for the ITU will have to coordinate the interests of Intelsat with those of countries which either cannot meet or will not accept its conditions of membership. Intelsat is the triumph of the past over the new technology, a narrow commercial organization with an accountant's mentality.

In the unlikely event that there is ever a child who asks, 'What is Intelsat, Daddy?' the answer can only be, 'It is the big telephone company in the sky.'

Chapter 6
Coming Attractions

I

While the second decade of satellite development should be as dramatic as the first, it should not be quite so unpredictable. Enough plans have been announced to give some idea of what the satellite services of the 1980s will be like. It is clear that the synchronous orbit will be a very busy place.

Well before the end of the 1970s, satellites should be playing an important part in air traffic control, keeping aircraft in touch with airports even while they are flying over mid-ocean. The major business of international satellites will still be telephone traffic. They will be providing direct dialing among most telephones in the developed world. They will also be linking computers continents apart, transmitting information at around 50,000 words a minute, perhaps at a few pennies a minute.

Yet the biggest change in satellite communication will be the move from the general to the particular, from satellites that offer many services in combination to those that do specific tasks, from satellites that cover many countries at once to those that aim at a particular country or region. This increasing specificity will be a direct result of the greater power of satellites and of the greater precision of their beams.

Concentrated beams will enable communications of all kinds to be brought to remote areas, and they will also enable satellites to send signals to moving receivers. The receivers will diminish in size until they are nothing more than a kind of dustbin lid on a rooftop. What this will mean in practice is that buildings can install the kind of antennae that suits the type of communication the people inside want from a satellite. Blocks of apartments may have receivers for electronic letters; newspaper printing plants may tune in to satellites for electronic instructions for the paper they are to print and to distribute locally, offices and laboratories will look to the sky for data transmission. The trend toward cheaper, more portable receivers will mean that the concept of wilderness will fade. Satellites will be able to keep in touch with the oil prospector in the field, the journalist in the jungle, the survivor in the lifeboat.

Yet there are some disadvantages that accompany the increasing simplicity of satellite receivers. The whole process – the satellites getting more powerful and the receivers getting smaller – is what Americans call a trade-off. Each added advantage carries a corresponding penalty. The smaller the station, the cheaper it is in every way but also the fewer the number of communications circuits it handles. The more power that a satellite radiates, the greater the likelihood that its radio signals may interfere with those of other satellites. And the more dizzying variety of special purposes that satellites can serve, the greater number of claimants there will be for places in the synchronous orbit.

The logical result of this line of technical development seems to be the satellite so powerful that its signals can be received by a plain cheap television set. For many people, this kind of satellite, called a direct-broadcast satellite, seems to combine the best and the worst that the new communications technology has to offer.

Television from Space

To broadcast means to scatter as seed. The ITU defines a broadcasting service as one intended for direct reception by the general public. It defines space broadcasting as broadcasting that comes from an object in orbit. So far there has been no broadcasting – scattering signals at large – from satellites. The Intelsat satellites have provided television services just as they have provided telephone connections – on a point-to-point basis between large earth stations.

The Russian Molniya satellites have gone one technical step beyond point-to-point service by providing television to a number of medium-sized ground stations which then broadcast it over ordinary transmission links. Satellites used in this way are called distribution satellites. What they do is shunt television around a large land area, which is just another way of saying that they provide a television networking service. In the next decade, many countries, the United States, Canada and perhaps even Britain, plan to use satellites to distribute television. But the distribution is effective only if there are sizeable receiving stations dotted around the landscape. An ordinary television set could pick up nothing of these transmissions on its own.

The stage beyond distribution is broadcasting straight from satellites to sets. The important question here is: what kind of set? The United Nations' working group on broadcast satellites divided them into three kinds. The first are 'community receivers' especially designed and centrally placed for viewing by large numbers of people at the same time. The second are 'augmented' television sets, the kind that can sit in a home but need special equipment in order to tune in to the satellite. The third are 'unaugmented' – ordinary television sets with no extras added.

These distinctions may seem pedantic, but they have helped the orderly discussion of an issue loaded with political implications. Few people are worried about direct broadcasting to community receivers; presumably the hand that turns the knob on a community set is an official one. The specially equipped set presents slightly more problems. Who – the government or the consumer – is going to pay for the equipment and then what will the government do if the set owner then chooses to tune in to a broadcast that is not on the national television menu? But what really threatens national sovereignty over communications is the satellite that can broadcast straight into the unaugmented set, bypassing all the institutional and mechanical apparatus that almost every country uses to control what its citizens see on their television screens.

Exactly what governments will be up against was displayed very well by Congressman James Fulton of Pennsylvania in 1969 at congressional hearings on the subject of satellite broadcasting, when he said:

Maybe the citizen of the world has a right to choose what broadcasts he wants to listen to, without national interference. Maybe I am much more a citizen of the world. If I want to listen to something,

I am going to listen, whether it is the foreign policy of the United States or not. How about that? Even if it is Castro.

Such a free-wheeling selection of programs from space may not be economically or practically possible for a long time. Wilbur Pritchard, the director of Comsat's laboratories, told Mr Fulton and attendant Congressmen in 1969 that a satellite powerful enough to be received directly by 'a portable TV set with rabbit-ear antennas located inside someone's apartment in a concrete and steel building in downtown Manhattan where there is a good deal of radio interference' would require a launching rocket the size of the Saturn V that sends men to the moon. The UN's working group did not see such forcible direct broadcasting to be even technically feasible until mid-1985 or beyond. And no one can point to any national government or commercial company which, even by 1985, would think it worth $100 million or $200 million to force television signals into other countries.

Yet broadcasting from other satellites to people in many countries at once need not wait for such unreal conditions to be met. The kind of satellite than can broadcast into a modified television set is already on the way, and the kind of equipment needed to equip a television set for satellite reception now looks to be both cheap and easy to make. Satellite broadcasting, therefore, is imminent, and suddenly the practical problems that it will present have seemed to require urgent solutions. The International Broadcast Institute, an organization founded in 1967 to stimulate international thinking on problems presented by the new communications technology, has sponsored a study by French, British, Japanese and American legal experts of the complexities that broadcasting from space will create in the fields of copyright, spectrum management, and protection from defamation and from the invasion of privacy.

There will be some tough questions to be answered in the next few years. What about advertising from space? Everybody can think of a few soft drinks or varieties of motorcars that might be advertised to an international audience. Perhaps those countries with the power to launch satellites might use them to advertise their own national products to a multi-national audience. Who is to decide? What about satellite signals which (accidentally or not) waft over borders to places where they are not wanted? The ITU cannot prevent that from happening in conventional television distribution on the European continent now.

Most of the anxieties now being expressed seem to center on fears of cultural and political invasion. Latin Americans, for example, worry about the day when their citizens might be able to tune in freely to a satellite broadcasting program from stations in the United States. Their fears were delicately expressed by Edgaro Galli of the Argentine office of the Secretary of State in the ITU's *Telecommunication Journal* of May 1970:

The possibility of broadcasting to vast multinational regions entails the possibility that some of the countries in the area may receive educational or other programs which do not take their true interests into consideration or may even exert a harmful cultural influence or some form of ideological pressure, thereby infringing the sovereignty of some or all of the countries in the region.

The desire to be armed against the direct broadcasting of the space powers is perhaps the main force behind the proliferation of national and regional plans for communications satellite systems.

The French were alarmed enough about the prospect to have proposed at the 1963 World Administrative Radio Conference of the ITU a total ban on broadcasting from space altogether. Since then, under the influence of the UN's working group on direct broadcasts, they have moderated their hostility to the extent of proposing no more than a code of content for programs transmitted internationally from space. The French would like to have forbidden any programs containing insults to heads of state, attacks on the dignity of the individual, threats to the physical, intellectual, psychological or moral development of children. The Soviet Union, also extremely apprehensive about direct broadcasting, would like to have a general code of principles adopted internationally before any direct broadcasting can begin. These principles would state that no broadcast be sent into a country without the consent of its government and that a government should be free to use any means available to counteract unwanted broadcasts.

The mere suggestion of such rigid regulation of television programs alarms broadcasters from many other countries, including Britain and the United States. There has been no such restriction in the history of broadcasting, and many broadcasting organizations are looking forward to space transmission as a new technique that will permit a flourishing international exchange of television programs, as well as much more live coverage of news events from the remote and untidy corners of the world where they choose to happen. Too strict a set of rules for space broadcasting and nobody will use it.

The UN's working group produced a set of carefully ambiguous recommendations in favor of regional broadcasting organizations. What the recommendations meant in effect was that questions of television programing were best left to professional regional organizations like European Broadcasting Union and the Organization Internationale pour Radio et Television (OIRT), the Eastern European broadcasting association, which have considerable experience in negotiating program exchange without drawing governments into it. This solution may be the practical as well as the tactful one. Broadcast satellites, for sheer technical and commercial reasons, are going to aim their beams only at specific geographical regions. There will be very few, if any, broadcasts to the whole world.

The controversy over the form, the content and the financing of space broadcasting will continue for many years. While the World Administrative Radio Conference in 1971 made temporary allocations of frequencies for broadcasting to community receivers, it could not reach an agreement on the more troublesome question of broadcasting direct to home receivers in several countries at once, and postponed any decision until a later conference, not to be held before 1975. Yet at least preliminary approval has been given, and the possibility no longer exists that satellite broadcasting will be banned before birth.

Yet there are dangers, real but more subtle than many people realize. They might be summed up in the words: 'Eurovision Song Contest'. It is not what might be done by force that is worrying but what might be done by regional cooperation. The programs prepared so far for multinational distribution – or even the joint productions of British and European television organizations – are sickeningly bland. Allusions to places and politics are kept to a minimum; every statement is overexplained, the comedy is slapstick, the smiles too broad, the whole program having been designed to give a minimum of offense to a wider than usual number of people. This may be the real danger of broadcast satellites – to broaden the base of the pyramid of taste, making television more of a mass medium than it is already.

II

India and Canada

One of the many ironies of the Intelsat saga is that two of the most dramatic new satellite projects of the 1970s will have nothing to do with either Intelsat or Comsat. The Canadians are on their way to a national satellite system that will put Eskimos on the telephone. The Canadian satellite will also distribute television, in both English and French, all over that enormous country. What India has in mind is in a much more preliminary stage, yet it is breathtaking in its audacity and its promise. India plans to begin about 1974 with the world's first demonstration of the reception of television direct from a satellite and to wind up, at the end of the decade, with its own home-made satellite system, distributing television to half a million villages, teaching them literacy, birth control, nutrition and modern agriculture.

India will have its experiment in space broadcasting, courtesy of NASA. The American space agency's next applications technology satellite, the ATS-F, scheduled to be launched in 1973, will be powerful enough to be received by small antennae ten to twelve feet across. The satellite itself, which will be used for some twenty or other experiments as well as broadcasting from space, will have a huge parasol of an antenna which will unfold like a Japanese water flower once the satellite is in orbit. This antenna of the ATS-F, will receive programs sent up to it from the Indian earth station at Ahmedabad and beam them down again for reception by 5,000 villages. NASA will provide only the satellite. The programs and the operations of the system on the ground will be entirely in Indian hands, as will be the expense of providing them. Project SITE (for Satellite Instructional Television Experiment) is expected to cost India about $1·5 million. It will last for one year.

Already there are those who are starry-eyed about the Indian experiment in mass education by satellite and who are willing to say, as Lincoln Steffens did, returning from the Soviet Union in 1919: 'I have seen the future and it works.' There are also those who feel that such euphoria will once again be proved to have been premature. But for the Indians involved, the question of success or failure is irrelevant. Come what may, the country is set to continue with a domestic satellite development program after the experiment with NASA is concluded. It intends to cover the country with television from satellites by 1980, and sooner or later it plans that the system shall depend entirely on equipment made in India – satellites, launching rockets, television sets and all. These ambitions, while bold, are not impossible. India already has its own electronics and radio manufacturing industry, which has made India's two earth stations and which can supply the national needs for satellite receivers. It has plans for a new launching base on Sriharikota Island in the Bay of Bengal from which it expects to be able to launch small satellites by 1974 and large communication satellites by 1980. This is part of an ambitious space program on which more than $90 million will be spent by 1980.

It is not strange that the Indian space program is run by the Indian Atomic Energy Agency. The same man runs both, for one thing. Dr Vikram Sarabhai is on his way to becoming the same kind of legend as was his brilliant predecessor, the late Homi Bhaba, killed in a plane crash on Mont Blanc in 1966, who blended the two programs in the first place. Space and atomic energy are not unrelated for another thing. Both are devoted ostensibly to peaceful purposes such as nuclear power and communications satellites, but, as India's unwillingness to sign the treaty against the proliferation of nuclear weapons shows, the two programs will also produce the plutonium and the rockets which are essential ingredients for any credible nuclear deterrent.

Perhaps because of the ambiguity of its space efforts, perhaps because of its unashamed dependence on NASA, the Indian satellite experiment is regarded with slight coolness by some quarters. India's long-range plans mean one more claim staked out in the synchronous orbit. India did not ask Pakistan's permission before deciding to embark on the experiment with NASA, even though the radio signals from the satellite will spill over into Pakistan (not that it matters in practise; they will be broadcast in FM, frequency modulation, on frequency bands not receivable on Pakistani television sets). And even the project's well-wishers are dismayed by the bureaucratic in-fighting going on in India among the various governmental ministries involved.

Why India? Arnold Frutkin, NASA's hawk-eyed administrator for international affairs, had to explain to Congress that India is not only uniquely suited to participating in an experiment with the ATS-F but that it was the first country to have come forward with a request to do so. The geographic shape of the subcontinent suits the antenna pattern of the satellite very well. Moreover, India has next to no television at all. It is really *terra nova* as far as television is concerned, while at the same time, as the most technologically advanced of the underdeveloped countries, it has the skills to conduct its end of the experiment. NASA was quite concerned to have as little to do with the program and other operations on the ground as possible. Yet these persuasive arguments did not stop Congressman Clement Zablocki from criticizing the way the project had been arranged. 'It is disturbing,' he said, 'that the negotiations were handled almost entirely by the technical agencies involved – NASA and the Indian Atomic Energy Program, and that the result was presented as a *fait accompli* to the State Department.'

Political tensions apart, the Indian experiment will be extremely interesting. It will show a satellite used both for the distribution of television by medium earth stations (which will broadcast the programs to some 3,000 villages) and also for the direct transmission to specially equipped sets (see Chart 4). About 2,000 villages – selected for their remoteness – will receive their programs straight from the satellite on the kind of specially equipped television set that heralds the world of tomorrow in satellite communications. The fact that the

Project SITE

India's Satellite Instructional Television Experiment planned for ATS-F spacecraft

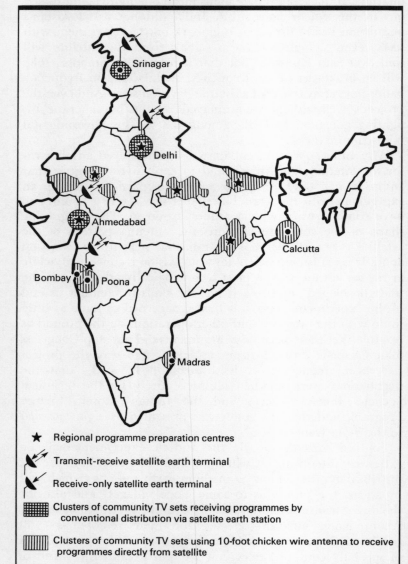

★ Regional programme preparation centres

Transmit-receive satellite earth terminal

Receive-only satellite earth terminal

Clusters of community TV sets receiving programmes by conventional distribution via satellite earth station

Clusters of community TV sets using 10-foot chicken wire antenna to receive programmes directly from satellite antennae for these sets are made of chicken wire only makes the experiment more exciting. These antennae, simple to make, will cost only about $25. The television sets – capable of receiving the satellite broadcasts only – will cost about $50. In between the two, there will be a converter (to change the incoming signals from UHF to VHF) that will cost about $75. The hopes of all those around the world who think that communications satellites may be able to cure illiteracy are riding on the paltriness of these sums.

Canada First

The Canadians were propelled into their domestic satellite system by both politics and geography. It has been clear for a long time that some of the places in the synchronous orbit most suitable for Canada were also desirable for the United States. When RCA Space Systems of Canada outlined its plans in 1968 for supplying Canada's satellite, it announced that 'the challenge is to stake out these pieces of the sky for Canada's use.'

Canada is doing just that. It won Intelsat's blessing because its proposed domestic system clearly was not going to siphon any business away from the international satellite system. Satellites do look like the answer to Canada's communications problems. There are 3·8 million square miles of territory in Canada most of it untouched by the two microwave communications links that can carry telephones, data and telex messages from coast to coast along a relatively narrow east-to-west strip bordering the United States. Satellites can not only encompass these vast distances but can provide television and radio in both French and English. Canada has already made a satellite of its own – Alouette, which was launched by NASA in 1962. But its dream of having its own home-made communications satellite has been dashed. RCA's costs looked to be rising so much beyond original estimates that in October 1970 the contract for the actual satellites was finally awarded to the American Hughes Company. About one-fifth of the work on the $31 million contract has been handled by Canadian subcontractors, however.

The system will be run by Telesat Canada, which was

established in September 1969 as a result of legislation passed by the Canadian Parliament three months earlier. The corporation looks like a modified version of Comsat. Its money comes from the Canadian federal government, as well as from communications companies and ordinary investors. If all goes well, the Canadians should have their system up and working by 1973, well ahead of any American domestic system south of the border. The Canadians will deliver twelve television channels or 960 message circuits to earth stations of varying sizes. In the Arctic regions, some of the stations will be able to send and receive telephone and telegraph messages, but they will have television on a receive-only basis.

Intelsat's Rival

Intersputnik looks good on paper. In 1968 the Russians proposed, together with Cuba, Outer Mongolia and six Eastern European countries, an international satellite system based on their own satellites and since then they have been polishing up the details. So far the most conspicuous feature of Intersputnik has been its organizational principles. These seem to have been designed to appeal to those countries which are discontented with Intelsat. In Intersputnik, for example, all member states will have equal rights in the governing body, irrespective of the capital they have invested. Any country of the world may join, whether or not it belongs to the ITU. Voting on the governing body will be on a one-country, one-vote basis, and the day-to-day administration of the system will be in the hands of an elected directorate.

But Intersputnik seems to have stayed on paper. By early 1971 the Russians still apparently had not launched a communications satellite into the synchronous orbit, and although they promised that Intersputnik eventually would have two synchronous satellites, one over the Atlantic, one over the Pacific, there was no sign of them. Neither were there signs of any new recruits.

The final Intelsat agreement did leave a loophole to allow Intelsat members to join other satellite systems provided that these do no economic harm to Intelsat. But any prospective members of a rival system would have to expect to build another kind of earth station (although a cheaper one than that needed to work with Intelsat's satellites) and also to have to make another substantial investment. Intersputnik will not admit members free of charge. In fact, if and when the system gets working (something to watch for in the years to come), it will run into many of the same problems that have hamstrung Intelsat: how to reconcile the interests of the largest and smallest investors. It will be interesting to see how Intelsat and Intersputnik arrange the technical coordination of their two systems.

Others into the Act

If current plans are to be taken at face value, satellites will be on their way to becoming national symbols, like airlines or world's-fair pavilions. Brazil hopes to have a full-fledged national satellite system in operation, and, like India, it is getting a boost from NASA. Brazil seems set to get a turn on the ATS-F satellite, along with India, and the director of the Brazilian National Commission on Space Activities, Dr Fernando de Mendonça, is extravagantly admired in Washington, both at NASA and by Congressmen who have visited Brazil. There may be still another satellite system at work in Latin America, if Argentina, Chile, Colombia, Ecuador, Peru and Venezuela make their wish come true to have a regional satellite, broadcasting educational television programs in Spanish. The Japanese, for their part, do not want to interrupt their smooth relations with Intelsat, but they are going ahead with synchronous satellites on an experimental basis, and they have begun to make their rockets work. The French and Germans, working on their separate versions of the joint project called *Symphonie*, hope to have launched the first of these by a European rocket in 1973. If it works, French-speaking African countries might be interested in participating in a *Symphonie* system that would give them telephone circuits, as well as television in French. (In addition to the African beam, *Symphonie* would have another sending television broadcasts to the Caribbean and Quebec.)

It would be rash to predict that the European Space Research Organization would actually have its long-proposed telecommunications satellite up and working by 1980. The unfortunate European space program has become so divided as to be comic, with the ten member countries unable to agree on what they want a communications satellite for. The current plan for a combination telephone, television and telex satellite would, if realized, be too heavy for the European rocket that is being developed as part of the same joint program. It is even more unlikely that there will be an all-British satellite, which could beam to the British Isles only, but if there were, no doubt the British television services would be glad to have it in order to send programs to the remote areas where their transmitters will never reach.

By the end of the decade the United States should be trying out a fair number of special-purpose communications satellites, perhaps even using them to deliver letters and almost certainly to interconnect computers and cable television systems. Rumors of satellite ambitions abound – Iran, Indonesia, even parts of Africa have been mentioned as candidates for their own satellites. The next decade will show whether all these ambitions can coexist in the same orbit and whether, if they cannot, the ITU can help them arrange mutually satisfactory compromises. It will also show whether so many satellite systems were necessary.

Chapter 7
Satellites and Sesame Street

Satellites, said someone at the BBC's further education department, are a snare and a delusion. Satellites, said an American adviser to the Organization of American States, are an 'attention-grabber. By offering a clear, compact solution they pull us off our target.'

A very august official of the BBC went so far as to express doubts about the validity of the Indian satellite television experiment. The BBC's experience, he said, is that the most successful educational television programs are made locally, about particular subjects, directed at particular audiences. Once the BBC did believe that it was possible to make generalized programs to teach broad subjects such as literacy, but it has learned that these are ineffective.

'But it is difficult to tell that to a developing country,' he said. 'They feel that there is no alternative.'

Indeed they do. The rush of enthusiasm for education by satellite-distributed television among underdeveloped countries has many causes, of which the principal one is the symbolic power of the satellite.

'It is almost poetical,' said a Brazilian diplomat about his country's plans for a national satellite system. 'A satellite will treat all parts of the country equally. That is important in a federalized country such as ours. All the politicians feel that their states are getting an equal share. And it will provide a dramatic symbol that we are taking the problem seriously. Those illiteracy figures – you have no idea how guilty Brazilians feel about them. And besides' – he was a very candid diplomat – 'Brazilians love gadgets.'

The illiteracy figures and the drop-out rates are formidable for the entire have-not portion of the world. The number of illiterates increases every year, and in Latin America, at least, it is not because there are not enough schools. The school enrolement in Latin America has increased appreciably in the past twenty years, faster than the annual rate of growth of population. But the schools are failing to teach and the teachers are worse than inadequate; they are wedded to old, classical methods of learning by rote. In Brazil the great mass of those who do get to school never advance beyond the first year because the teachers make them repeat it again and again, considering it their job to weed out poor students. These methods are, to say the least, unproductive.

The fact that the present teachers need retraining, fairly well accepted in Latin American ministries of education, has contributed to the allure of the satellite. A satellite beaming down at classrooms could both expose all students equally to the best kind of teaching and it could give lessons, on a national scale, to teachers wherever they are. The discrepancies between urban and rural areas would be ironed out, without bringing teachers from the backwoods to the cities, where they are then tempted to remain. Such retraining must be undertaken before there is any possibility even of dreaming of educating the children of the seven-to-fourteen age group whose numbers will rise from forty million to seventy-two million by 1980. There is no way of reaching the teachers – except by television – and there is no way of getting television into the wilderness except by satellite. In other words, as satellites seem to be the only alternative to despair, they must be the answer to the problem.

Such desperate wishful thinking is understandable in the countries concerned, but it is less forgivable when indulged in by UNESCO. UNESCO first endorsed the idea of using satellites for education in 1960 – two years before Telstar. Its general conference (all member countries meeting together) accepted by unanimous vote the 'obvious impossibility of eliminating mass illiteracy through the use of traditional methods alone' and at the same time recognized that satellites could permit the dissemination of educational programs over vast areas. Since then, UNESCO has encouraged India, Brazil and a group of Latin American countries to go ahead with satellite education projects, even though its own publications are full of dire warnings of the disappointments that lie in wait for countries which rush into satellites unprepared.

In the late summer of 1969 a team of experts from UNESCO

spent one month visiting Spanish-speaking Latin American countries. Upon their return, they effusively recommended a regional satellite, devoted entirely to education and public information:

> The demands that are and will be made on the educational systems of the countries visited cannot possibly be fulfilled through the traditional methods . . . the conclusion seems inevitable that the methods to be used must be as massive as the changes required.

For a massive problem, a massive symbol. One might just as well recommend trying to cure illiteracy by sticking dollar bills on a plaster Madonna, or buying a satellite to cure cancer. There is nothing massive about a satellite except the range of its coverage. It is no more than a technique for distributing television, and educational television is, the world over, a massive problem in itself. The world is littered with failed educational television projects. Latin America itself has a large number of educational television stations which have not succeeded in bringing about any appreciable rise in the general level of education. Satellites will not make these programs more effective. In fact, as had been said earlier, they will simply broaden the base of the audience so that the program becomes more homogenized in content, more diffuse in aim.

A Pedagogical Spectacle

Satellites are the most expensive tool in the kit called 'educational technology'. Some people at UNESCO tend to be passionate enthusiasts for the lot – satellites, television, teaching machines, radio, films, tape recorders, computers. On the other hand, in Britain and in the United States, the fervor for mechanical teaching aids has faded. President Nixon's Commission on Educational Technology reported in March 1970 that the American federal government had spent billions of dollars since the late 1950s to finance innovations of all kinds in schools and yet 'the outcome of much of this endeavor and expenditure has been, to put it mildly, disappointing'. The Midwest Airborne Television Experiment on which the Ford Foundation spent $18 million was one of the notable disasters. An airplane flew over Illinois daily, beaming down television programs to the schools, but many of the teachers did not even bother to turn on the sets.

In Britain, Professor John Vaizey of Brunel University, an educational economist and member of the Inner London Educational Authority, which uses a system of closed circuit television for its schools, says flatly that 'educational television by itself is inefficient and ineffective'. Britain's Centre for Educational Television Overseas (now absorbed into the Ministry of Overseas Development) reported in 1969 that its officers serving in a great number of projects overseas had, in country after country, encountered disenchantment with educational television. According to the CETO report, 'All too frequently, programs are produced which meet no defined need and which are not educationally valid. This devalues the service, disappoints the teachers in the classroom and the service eventually falls into disuse.'

Those who believe that educational television, preferably by direct broadcast satellite, will be the salvation of the under-developed world are not deterred by what they concede to have been the discouraging experience of the richer countries. They believe that the underdeveloped countries have a positive advantage in starting from scratch, and they express their belief in a special kind of internationally shared jargon. Television, for them, will not be 'an additive to the curriculum' but must 'bear the main instructional burden'. The whole educational system must be built around television, and the programs must be especially designed for television. They must be no less than *un spectacle pedagogique* (which a UNESCO bureau-crat translated as 'you must not see the bloody face of the bloody teacher').

Can television carry this burden? Can the content of the basic years of schooling (or of the basic facts about birth control or eating a proper diet) be made into an entertaining series of television programs?

The evidence that it can is so frail that to build whole national educational systems around it is like deciding to build a skyscraper because you have made a matchbox stand on end.

The two magic words are Samoa and Niger. In American Samoa, the entire educational system was rebuilt around television, starting in 1963. Old textbooks were thrown out. So was the job of classroom teacher. Instead there were teaching teams brought in from the United States, trained to use television as the central ingredient in the teaching process. There were new buildings, new administrative procedures, new curricula, all designed around television.

The Samoan experiment worked – but at a very high cost, both in terms of people and of money. The ratio of pupils to teachers was very low – hardly an advertisement for the teacher-saving new technology. What disappointments there have been were duly aired before congressional hearings in 1970. In American Samoa, there is still too much learning by rote, some of the older students have been inattentive, the training of teachers by television has been particularly unsatisfactory. But the use of television in American Samoa has succeeded in changing the form and content of an archaic educational system in a very short time. (It also succeeded – because President Lyndon Johnson was impressed by the project – in elevating the former Governor of Samoa, H. Rex Lee, to a seat on the FCC.)

Niger excites the educational planners even more. (It would be callous to remark that Niger is even more remote than Samoa to the casual visitor). This new nation, landlocked north of Nigeria, enormous in area and sparse in population, turned to France for help in developing a program of televised instruction after it became independent in 1962. French is the official language of Niger, yet many of the children there had hardly heard it spoken, while the primary object of the televised lessons was to teach French; arithmetic and writing were also included.

After a year the statistical results were dazzling. Nearly 90 percent of the students who had had television lessons read French better than the national average. Nearly 80 percent spoke it better, and more than half were better at writing and arithmetic.

The joy of the partisans of educational television is not dimmed by the fact that only 1,000 students were involved in these original experiments in Niger. Instead they point to the exhilarating fact that almost no teachers at all were involved. The instruction was conducted by television monitors, young people with an average of only four years of schooling themselves. This lack of trained teachers, if anything, is proof that television can teach, they say. Currently Niger's program of televised teaching is being extended to reach really large numbers of students, and its results over a longer period will be interesting to watch.

One of the most notable facts about educational television of one kind or another is how little measurement there has been of its effectiveness. There has been (as President Nixon pointed out in 1970 when he asked Congress to establish a National Institute of Education) insufficient research into how people learn and how much of what kind of instruction. It is one thing to set out to teach 'literacy'. It is another thing to know whether literacy has been taught. How much literacy – and for how long? Some people may lose it after a year or two. That raises the even murkier question of what, given limited resources, should be taught? UNESCO is wholeheartedly committed to the value of literacy, but there are some educationists who deal with the underdeveloped world, and who call themselves radicals, who say that literacy is an absurd goal. They would work toward giving people a sense of mastery over their immediate environment and would use television to teach skills and diet and birth control and would forget about the printed word. Until these questions are answered, satellites will be a risky investment.

One drawback about doing proper research into the efficacy of televised teaching is that research can cost almost as much as making the programs. For example, all the BBC can show, when asked about the results of its school broadcasts, is statistics on how many schools say they have tuned in. Whether the programs have achieved their objective of transmitting certain information or supplementing classroom work is simply not known.

The television program which boasts of certified proof of its ability to teach is the American children's program, *Sesame Street*. The Children's Television Workshop, which prepared *Sesame Street* and subsequent educational series, set itself the difficult task of catching, holding and teaching a random audience of children – not at school, where the teacher would control the set, but at home, where they are at liberty to switch to a less didactic program the minute their attention wanders.

Sesame Street worked. In its first season it captured an average audience of seven million children a day. The Educational

Testing Service of Princeton, hired to measure the show's results, found that it had imparted the ability to recognize the letters of the alphabet, the numbers from one to ten, and certain basic concepts such as the similarity and dissimilarity of objects. Better still, the ETS found that the program was not (as its critics charged) reaching only middle-class children whose mothers were keen that they watch it but also children from much poorer homes, who were presumably less supervised. The results showed that the children from slum homes who watched *Sesame Street* frequently learned more than middle-class children who watched it infrequently. The conclusion was 'that such television programs can reduce the distinct educational gap that usually separates advantaged and disadvantaged children even by the time they enter first grade (at the age of six)'.

But *Sesame Street* achieved its results at a price. An enormous amount of professional television expertise went into the making of the show. Scenes, characters, cartoons that did not hold the attention of children in test groups were ruthlessly discarded. 'If we can't hold their attention,' said a producer, 'we can't teach them anything.' A great deal of effort was also put into drumming up the audience – sound trucks blaring through city slums, posters put up in nursery schools and day care centers. The potential audience had to be informed about the time the show would go on. The price for the first season of the series, which ran an hour a day, five days a week, for twenty-six weeks, was $8 million. Those were American costs, to be sure, but they also amount roughly to the price of one satellite.

It is possible that the price paid in intellectual terms was too high. *Sesame Street* has been called the children's *Laugh-In*. Its pace is frantic. The blur of human characters and jumping letters and talking animals and bursts of rock music almost, in effect, tell a child not to bother to concentrate, that something new will be along in a minute. The theories behind the programs draw heavily on Marshall McLuhan and the behavioral psychology of B. F. Skinner, as well as the techniques of the commercial advertisements of the other channels with which they compete. (It was all too much for the BBC, which declined to buy the series on the grounds that it was too American for British audiences, but one of the commercial companies has arranged to show it regionally.) The president of Children's Television Workshop, Mrs Joan Ganz Cooney, herself wonders whether their sights should not have been set higher. With hindsight, it seems as if much more could have been taught. Nonetheless, the program was an enormous achievement and the Workshop has now moved into the heart of the educational problem and prepared programs to teach reading to the older children, already in school, already soured on education because they have failed at it from the start.

The lesson of *Sesame Street* is not that the underdeveloped countries should buy the program (which is what they are doing). It is that a great deal of money, intelligence and care are needed to find out exactly what excites and informs a particular youthful audience, and the expense is no less because the audience is unsophisticated, unaccustomed to spending several hours a day in front of a television set. If anything, the task is harder when the audience is unfamiliar with the conventions of the television idiom and the secret of holding its attention must be found. The other lesson of *Sesame Street* is that even after the money has been spent and the audience loved the show and learned a little into the bargain, there is no clear answer to the question: was it worth it?

The Basic Ingredients

It will be a long time before educational television can take its place beside educational radio as a medium for teaching people out of sight of a teacher. In the first place, the potential audience for radio is larger; there are three times as many transistor radios in the world as television sets. It is cheaper than television to produce, both in terms of money and professional talent. It can find the listener wherever he is. He does not need to sit in a special place. Radio lessons can be illustrated by colored slides, shown in the classroom on a slide projector. These move more slowly than television pictures, which is often desirable, and the slides can be transmitted by mail, which is somewhat cheaper than by microwave or by satellite. The chief advantage that radio has over television for teaching is that a broadcast can be tape-recorded and played back at the teacher's convenience. Video tape recorders may some day become cheap and widely available, but they seem certain to remain more expensive than sound tape recorders. And until the technology of storing television programs reaches the underdeveloped world, any educational television program that is not heard by its intended audience at the time of its transmission is lost.

What educational television by satellite would require is that thousands of people be assembled in front of television sets at the same time of day over an enormous geographic area. If the broadcasts are directed at schools, the pressure will then be on the teachers to organize their day around the television broadcast time. Teachers, who are not among the leading enthusiasts for educational technology, prefer to have machines, if at all, as aids like radio, not as masters. It is possible, of course, to repeat educational television programs at regularly stated times. Yet that will be difficult to organize if, as in the case of the Indian satellite experiment, the programs will be broadcast several times in a number of different languages and if the set is in a central place, to which the audience must be drawn.

The sets themselves present another formidable obstacle to the smooth working of national educational television in the underdeveloped world, whether distributed by satellite or not. What if they stop working? Nothing is more infuriating than to lose the picture in the middle of a program. The small cheap sets planned for the underdeveloped world will be (to borrow more of the educational technologists' jargon) 'ruggedized'. They will be designed to perform in primitive conditions with a minimum of tuning. But ruggedized or not, they will not work forever. An entire course of study could be ruined because a remote village's set packed up.

Then there is the enormous problem of getting students to participate actively in their televised lessons. To have them sit there passively watching flickering screens is just as bad as learning by rote from a repressive teacher. The British Open University, originally called the University of the Air because it would reach its students by television, is relying as much or more on paper and pen as on the video screen; it demands that students do written exercises, which are sent by mail to a tutor, who then returns them through the mail, with his written corrections on them.

UNESCO's own satellite sage, Dr Wilbur Schramm, director of

the Institute for Communication Research at Stanford University, wrote in 1968 that underdeveloped countries should not think of using satellites until instructional television has been made to work. The curriculum must be prepared and the teachers trained to encourage children to prepare them for the broadcast and to conduct demonstrations and discussions after it. Otherwise 'if a country hurries into satellite communication without adequate preparation, it is likely to find itself making false steps, wasting resources, and risking a failure when and if it actually comes to the satellite stage'.

Such preparations cannot be made in the short time before the ATS-F Satellite is launched and the experiments in India and Brazil begin. There has been so much disagreement within India about the programs to be shown – the ministries of agriculture, education and family planning at odds with All-India Radio, which is coordinating the project – that the Indians were actually happy when NASA, because of budget cuts, had to delay the satellite launching for a year. Even at UNESCO some people are now saying that the Indian program should not be judged by the content of its programs but by whether its technical arrangements work.

In Brazil, plans for the experiment to be held in schools in the remote and impoverished Rio Grande del Norte region with the ATS-F satellite, are full of American aerospace jargon about parameters and interfaces. They are also full of lists of new equipment that will be needed and the various tests which computers will perform after the experiment to measure its results. But the plans are very vague on the crucial question of preparing the actual teachers in the classroom to cooperate with the experiment, not to fight it. The Brazilians are adamant that they are paying sufficient attention to the problems of 'software', and they have carefully drawn up schedules to show that the satellite will broadcast mathematics lessons first thing in the morning, to be followed by Portuguese, social studies and science, with radio broadcasts for later in the day for the training of teachers, as well as for the teaching of literacy and vocational skills.

But, as in India, the whole program is in the hands of the space agency and, as in India, it has made up its mind in advance to go ahead with a full-scale plan for satellite education, no matter what happens in the ATS-F experiment. The space agency is convinced already that 'educational television is cheaper and more efficient when directed at large masses'. Presumably if the results of the experiment are inconclusive, Brazil will go on to direct centrally prepared instruction at still larger and more diffuse masses of people. And, as in India, the worksheets and test papers will still have to go to the inaccessible areas by mail. ('It is no good telling them to eat protein,' said one Indian space researcher, 'if you don't get the proteins to the village.') The satellite, in other words, cannot be a real teaching instrument in any place where the mail does not go.

The nagging feeling that satellites *must* be useful for education has even reached Europe. Projects are already under way (with the BBC a reluctant participant) in designing the kind of academic course that might be taught through the proposed European television satellite. To find a subject and an approach on which there is common agreement is not easy, the language problem quite apart. Then there is the not inconsiderable matter of deciding when to broadcast it to thousands of schools in a number of different countries which have different timetables. The subject chosen for the first experimental course was physics (everyone believes that science, at least, can be taught from a neutral multinational point of view), but few broadcasters can see a pan-European satellite instruction program being of much practical use.

Pressured into Satellites

For all the pious talk about paying attention to 'software', countries are rushing headlong into plans for education by satellite not because the software is ready but because the hardware is ready. The pressure of the advance of technology apparently cannot be resisted. Nor can the commercial pressure of the big companies which now know how to make satellites and would like to make them for the underdeveloped world, for otherwise their market for satellites is limited. Intelsat and the military can take only so many. In Britain in 1971, the British Aircraft Corporation told the House of Commons' select committee on science and technology that it had hopes of selling satellites to underdeveloped countries. BAC has also quietly asked questions of the BBC about what constitutes good educational television programs. ('It makes me shudder,' said one BBC man. 'The idea that education is just a matter of getting up in the sky and sprinkling the stuff around.')

A thorough plan, admired by UNESCO, outlining the costs of educational television by satellite was prepared for Iran by Hughes Aircraft. According to the Hughes estimate, a satellite with two television channels and four sound channels would cost Iran nearly $30 million, launch included. The earth segment, including 10,000 television sets equipped for direct broadcasting and 23,000 ordinary television sets, would be $51 million. The annual operating costs, *including program material* would be $22.6 million. It all works out to an average cost per student year of $3.10 compared to $19 per student year expected in Iran's future educational budgets. Similar cost-effectiveness schemes for satellite education have been worked out for Latin America by Telespazio of Italy and Page Communications Engineers, Inc., of the United States.

How can such hard and clear statistics help but be attractive to a country overwhelmed by overpopulation and poverty? If UNESCO, NASA and the space industries keep up the pressure, these countries may soon be setting up ministries of aerospace education, while the big space manufacturers will be peddling satellites around the underdeveloped world, throwing packages of educational film into the bargain, like a free month's supply of soap powder.

That there are political advantages in extending technological patronage to countries like India and Brazil is obvious. The visiting congressional mission from Washington which so admired the Brazilian space program in January 1970 was also alarmed to find, in the rest of Latin America, that the influence of European industries and broadcasting organizations was on the increase. The members of the mission reported to Congress that they discovered, among other things, British-made films teaching English and the gift of television equipment from Philips of Eindhoven in Peru. 'This attempt at penetration from out of the hemisphere is not to be taken lightly,' they wrote in their report. NASA clearly is willing to make the kind of friendly loan of a bit of a satellite that Intelsat might have made had it not been so commercially preoccupied. Yet the experiments with India and Brazil undeniably serve to woo two very important, influential, technologically sophisticated, underdeveloped countries to the side of the United States.

What it all adds up to is a formidable campaign to persuade countries which have little money or time to waste that satellites are a short cut to education. Satellites are expected to succeed where past reform programs, and educational television efforts have failed. At best, satellites will be for the underdeveloped world what computers are for much of the developed world today – expensive underused status symbols. At worst, they will increase despair by absorbing vast time and energy in distributing bland programs that few people want to watch. Boredom is boredom the whole world over, and until there are some startling improvements in the techniques of teaching by television, satellites can only increase the scale of failure.

Part Three

Cable Television

Chapter 8
From CATV to Infinity

I

An almost religious faith in cable television has sprung up in the United States. It has been taken up by organizations of blacks, of consumers and of educational broadcasters, by the Rand Corporation, the Ford Foundation, the American Civil Liberties Union, the electronics industry, the Americans for Democratic Action, the government of New York City and – a tentative convert – the Federal Communications Commission. The faith is religious in that it begins with something that was once despised – a crude makeshift way of bringing television to remote areas – and sees it transformed over the opposition of powerful enemies into the cure for the ills of modern urban American society. The intriguing thing about cable television is that this faith may be in no way misplaced.

Cable television brings television signals into a television set by means of a coaxial cable rather than by an aerial on a roof top. It gets these signals by taking television-carrying microwaves from the air from a conveniently high point with a tall tower or antenna. In many parts of the United States cable television is still called community antenna television, or CATV, and it has prospered chiefly where over-the-air reception is poor. Yet a coaxial cable has so much capacity for carrying signals that a dozen television programs occupy only a fraction of it. The potential of cable television lies in that surplus capacity. Like the telephone line, the cable is a physical link between a building and the outside world. Yet the cable, which is no thicker than a pencil, can carry at least a thousand times as much information in the technical sense as the telephone line can carry. Cable television already reaches about 7 percent of American homes and, while five to a dozen channels are the average, in a few places it carries as many as twenty-seven channels. Systems with forty, fifty-seven and sixty channels are on their way. Within two decades cable television could be the medium through which most American personal, scientific and financial communication will flow.

In the more immediate future, cable television offers a way out of the vast wasteland of American commercial network television. It does so for several reasons. Because its cables extend out relatively short distances from a center, it can be used to carry local original programs and to reach specific audiences in a small geographic area. Because its revenues come direct from subscribers who choose to pay a monthly fee (about $5), the system offers a new way of paying for television, one that resembles that of publishing. Because it carries so very many channels and because its income does not depend on attracting a large audience for any particular one of them, cable television can offer programs of interest to all kinds of minorities: the jobless, the voters of a particular political district, the Spanish-speaking, the medical profession.

What if these minority audiences were linked together nationally by a satellite connecting their local cable companies? Then a particular local program could be transmitted from a neighborhood studio to a selected audience across the entire country. Idiosyncratic chains of viewers could be formed and reformed at random. All the owners of Doberman pinchers could tune in to their television program on Channel Thirty-seven once a month and no one else's television choice need be the poorer. Cable television could even provide television as a raw, empty medium, a service for hire, a common carrier for the public's televised messages.

But these are no more than socially interesting new ways of using television. The excitement about cable television arises from its potential in the more distant future for uses quite beyond television. It could, quite without interrupting its television pictures, print out quantities of material in rolls of paper in the television set. It could even act as a television-telephone, for the coaxial cable can carry information in two directions. If coaxial cable were threaded throughout American cities and fashioned into a national network, then it could deliver letters, library books (printed at a rate of more than a million words a minute) and instructions for university courses to accompany televised lectures. It could print newspapers in the home and act as a computer terminal. Its screen could display information about the contents of warehouses, shops, ships or aircraft. What such a network (called a broadband network, because it would use a broad band of radio frequencies – 300 million cycles wide) might mean is that people would no longer need to work near their offices. The population could become more dispersed. All forms of social organization – commercial, social, intellectual – could be conducted over a much wider geographic area than is possible under today's conditions for exchanging information and ideas.

If the development of technology really unfolded as many people believe that it does, according to a prepared script, the emergence of cable television at this point should be the signal for cheers and stamping feet. Cable television is almost too good to be true, a *deus ex machina* to rout the McLuhanites. The medium of television need no longer be the message; it can be split into dozens of different kinds of message, some visual, some printed, some personal, some (when satellites feed into cables) international. Television need no longer mean a few channels feeding the millions. The exclusivity of the television studio would disappear if there were one in every neighborhood, and to appear on television would be no rarer than to be mentioned or to place an advertisement in a local newspaper. And among the lesser, more prosaic benefits of cable television might be the disappearance of ugly forests of television aerials on rooftops. Meter readers could disappear too. The coaxial cable can read gas and electric meters automatically, and it can also act as a burglar or fire alarm by linking the home or the office with police and fire stations.

There seems to be little doubt that the United States will have this kind of network, that it will become wired for television as it was wired for telephone and electricity. The question is when? As will be discussed in Chapter 9, the difficulties of integrating it into the existing communications industry and regulatory framework have been almost insuperable.

Sol Schildhause, the head of the Federal Communications Commission's cable television bureau, expects that cable television will fulfill its promise, but not very soon: 'Cable is going to be big, but slow,' he says, whacking his leg with a length of it as he talks. A brash, good-looking man, more carnival barker than bureaucrat, he was in charge of the FCC's task force on cable television during the lean years when it was still called CATV, and is somewhat amused at its sudden glamor. 'The intellectuals have discovered it,' Schildhause says. 'The anti-TVs, the people who boast that they've never owned a set. They love cable. There's an awful lot of garbage written about it. But it's going to happen – delivery of letters, newspaper print-out, local television – all that stuff. But a new technology has a terrible time unseating the old. Don't underestimate the difficulty. The power is weighted with the investment of the past.'

Where the Channels Come From

Cable television, as it now exists, is not very complicated. The millions of viewers who would describe themselves as 'on the cable' know that their television reception has little of the snow or interference from aircraft passing overhead that spoil the television picture produced by an aerial receiver. The superiority of cable television is even more pronounced in color than in black and white. In mountainous eastern Tennessee, where ordinary television reception is poor, motels advertise 'Color Cable TV' on their marquees.

There are twelve channels in the VHF band on which the bulk of American television programs are broadcast. Yet sets dependent on aerials can receive at most seven, and these not of equal quality. Adjacent VHF channels in the same broadcast area may sometimes interfere with one another. For clear television reception, program-carrying channels are best separated by empty channels, with the result that there is an enormous waste of the VHF. Viewers in many American cities and towns receive no more than two or three programs.

Cable television is under no such limitation. Television signals confined in a cable do not spread outward; one channel does not blur into the next. Not only can the better cable television systems use all twelve VHF channels, for separate and clear programs, they can squeeze in six channels below Channel 2 and fit in nine separate programs between Channels 6 and 7. Over-the-air television can do neither; the part of the radio spectrum below Channel 2 has inferior carrying capacity

Growth of cable television in the United States

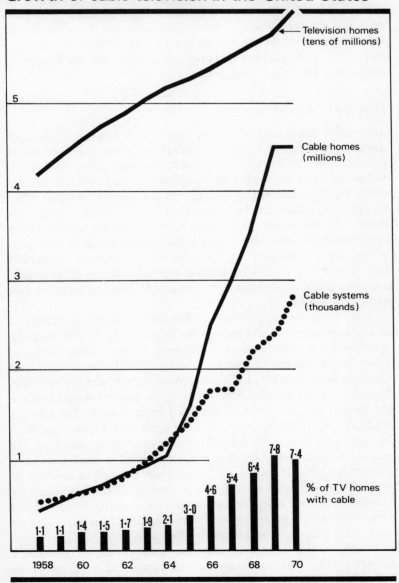

through the air (the signals are easily lost), while the gap in the spectrum between Channels 6 and 7 is reserved by the ITU for other kinds of radio communication. Because cable television does not scatter signals to the public at large through the air but directs them to the sets at the end of its wire, it no more interferes with radio communication than an underground train interferes with road traffic.

Humble Origins

To receive radio and television over a wire instead of through the air is by no means uniquely American. Homes, hospitals and parts of cities in Britain and on the Continent have had wired radio since the beginning of broadcasting and when television came along in the 1950s it acquired the same customers. (See Chapter 10.) But the CATV business in the United States has been unique in its challenge to commercial broadcasting organizations and in the hopes it has aroused. Cable television is now most extensive in Canada, where private companies have flourished, chiefly by offering the importation of American network television shows from broadcast stations in cities just across the border.

Already there are several versions of the birth of American CATV. Legend generally names the father as L. E. Parsons, the operator of a radio station in Astoria, Oregon whose wife, in 1949, had a craving to watch television. The difficulty was that the nearest station was in Seattle, Washington, 125 miles away. Undeterred, Parsons searched the region around Astoria where the Seattle signals could be detected most clearly. True to the traditions of folklore, he found them right on his doorstep, or to be more precise, on the roof of his own apartment building. He put up an antenna, fifty feet high, obtained a clear television picture for himself and his wife, and then decided to extend the service, by means of a cable, to the lobby of the building. By lengthening the cable, he then acquired customers around the neighborhood. For each connection they paid him $100 and he sold them television sets into the bargain.

Pennsylvania, however, was the real cradle of the CATV industry. The first company formed to sell cable television in the United States seems to have been the Panther Valley

Television Company, located in a mountainous region about sixty-five miles from Philadelphia. For an installation fee of $125 – and a monthly charge of $3 – the company offered its subscribers better reception than residents of the suburbs of Philadelphia were getting. For a long time, cable television flourished in the mountains and hollows, in the so-called 'white areas' where it was the alternative to no television at all. Rural appliance dealers, delighted to have a way of selling television sets, found that there was nothing technically complex in placing an antenna on a hill or mountain top and to catch television microwaves as they floated through the air. They ran the signal along a cable down the mountain to a central station where, using not very complicated procedures, they removed the interference and strengthened the signals. The station was connected by a web of trunk cables to the various streets in town, from which smaller coaxial cables were strung in to the individual homes. The cables were usually hung on the telephone or electricity poles, and the whole procedure lumbered along, and was fairly well ignored, under the label of CATV.

Yet two new possibilities soon became clear. One was that cable television could provide something more than better reception. It could provide more programs. Because of its high antenna, it could bring in clear signals from television stations in distant cities, in contrast to television sets dependent on aerials, which tend to be limited to the output of the nearest city or cities. The other was that cable reception could be as useful in cities as in the countryside. Tall buildings can block microwaves in the same way that mountains do, and a television picture can be as shaky in parts of Manhattan as in the hills of West Virginia. In the 1950s cable television companies began to spring up in some cities (New York and San Diego were the only large cities to have substantial systems), using both clarity of signal and diversity of programs as selling points. In order to win more monthly subscribers, cable operators next began to search for uses for the spare capacity of the cable and found that it was simple and cheap to point a camera at a clock or a weather map or at a news or stock market ticker so that subscribers could get some information instead of a blank screen on the idle channels. Cable television had been expected to fade away as more and more American cities acquired their own television broadcasting stations and did not need to depend on imported signals to receive any television at all. But CATV continued to expand, and as it did it began to encounter the legal obstacles which have persisted to the present day. Nonetheless, between 1952 and 1958 the number of CATV subscribers rose from 14,000 to 450,000. By 1971 there were approximately 5.3 million, served by 2,385 systems. The Stanford Research Institute estimates that subscribers will increase by 12 percent a year through 1975, and the National Cable Television Association predicts that its industry could have from twenty-five to thirty-two million subscribers by 1980.

II

At the present moment, long before cable television fulfills any of the futuristic fantasies held out for it, it can offer local television. This is the prospect on which the social planners are basing their hopes. If there were a city-wide system or interconnected systems, there could be centrally prepared lessons sent to all the schools within a town. There could be coverage of local political meetings. There could be channels of information about local welfare and housing services. A study done for the Rand Corporation envisages no less than the 'Wired Ghetto' to give people who live in slums the kind of immediate information about jobs, schools, health clinics, housing applications that others get from reading newspapers. The Rand study considers that community television in the ghetto could offer pre-school education, literacy training for adults and even a kind of secondary school of the air, enabling people willing to watch the courses and to meet occasionally with tutors to get that American necessity, a high-school diploma.

These are big dreams indeed, and perhaps as poorly founded as those of the underdeveloped countries which expect more from satellites than they can possibly deliver. But there is a difference. These American slum homes, however poor, have television sets already and the cable television networks are in the actual process of forming. The physical plant is on its way, in other words. It is only the use to which it will be put that is uncertain.

The government of New York City takes the potential of cable television very seriously. It had its own task force to study the phenomenon and recommend what the city's long range policies should be. When in 1970 its Board of Estimate gave twenty-year franchises to the TelePrompTer Corporation and the Sterling Manhattan Cable Television Company, it required that they expand from twelve to twenty-four channels by 1973, and that they reserve some channels for the use of the city government, others for the use of the community, and another for programs originated by the companies.

There are some modest grounds for believing that cable television can offer the kind of local service which is a social asset. Several major metropolitan Canadian systems devote one of their eight to a dozen channels to locally originated programs, which include foreign-language broadcasts of news and information for immigrants. At Oregon State University, lectures are carried by television into the surrounding community where people can either use them for learning or simply for seeing what goes on at the university. The cable system provides a common channel for town and gown. In the northern part of New York City, where TelePrompTer, America's largest cable company, has one of its main bastions, the cable system won critical applause for carrying a program about heroin and heroin-takers. Produced on a bare stage in Harlem, it was both too controversial and too unpolished to have been put out over either the commercial stations or the public broadcasting station. (The program, 'King Heroin', was also cheap to make. Whether cable operators will be interested in investing in the kind of daring program which costs a lot of money remains to be seen.) Also in New York Sterling Manhattan Cable offers its subscribers telecasts of the kind of sporting events, such as professional basketball and hockey, which appeal to much smaller audiences than those which follow baseball and football. It also shows foreign films. Several cable systems present regular local news programs. But all these are just sketchy beginnings of what might develop.

Cable television eventually may provide the best, most pleasant and efficient way of using video cassettes. The system can keep a library of video recordings of not only television programs but films of entertainment or instruction. Then the viewer will not have to fill his home with stacks of tapes, discs or spools. He can, after consulting the directory channel which cable television needs to carry, so that people can find out what is on its many channels, instruct the cable center, either by telephone or by a dial, which program he would like to see. (The British version of this service has already been developed and is discussed in Chapter 10.)

Prospect for Politicians

Cable television has, in general, cheering implications for politics. It could, by using filters, send programs to specific political districts within a city. The cost of an hour's time on such a channel might be as cheap as $20. As things stand, the costs of appearing in American commercial television, either to deliver a sober speech or to advertise one's candidacy, form the highest part of the great costs of running for office in the United States. It is not only irritating to watch most candidates making their pitch to a great many people who could not vote for them if they wanted to, it is also wasteful of the airwaves. The advertisements for a candidate from a small congressional district in New York City are sprayed all over northern New Jersey, southwestern Connecticut and parts of New York state.

Televising politics in Britain also remains an unsolved problem, even though political broadcasts are allowed on the air free of charge and the expenses of campaigning are infinitesimal compared to those in the United States. The boredom of the public and the inequality of access to the medium are no less. Only those candidates with a national political reputation get to use the national airwaves, and most members of Parliament, unless they manage to associate themselves with some controversial cause, will never see the inside of a television studio.

Local television through cable could allow lesser politicians – from national representatives down to mayors and school officials – to address their particular constituencies. It could give every politician the opportunity Senator Edward Kennedy enjoyed when, in the summer of 1969, he bought time to appear on television to tell the voters of Massachusetts his version of what happened at Chappaquiddick. Why should not the head of a school whose contract is not renewed do the same? He could – if there were inexpensive local television.

Political meetings at all levels of government could also be opened to television if the price were low. There would not need to be much more than a camera – an eye on the meeting – if there was a channel that could be tuned in by those who were interested. It is certain that there are more people who would like to know what goes on at council meetings and other forms of political assembly than ever bother to go and attend.

Through cable television they could not only watch, but vote. The simplest form of two-way transmission will be available to cable subscribers soon – a button which allows the viewer to send a simple signal to the station (or to a computer, or to a voting machine). It would be very easy to collect and count the number of responses sent in electronically from homes. Voting by cable television will not be useful in political elections, however, until a way is found to establish identity electronically, perhaps through a number or, in the longer run, a voice print.

Clearing the Air

If all television were sent underground, the portion of the electromagnetic spectrum most desirable for radio communication, the VHF and the lower UHF frequencies, would be cleared for other uses. In the United States television now absorbs the major share of the parts of the spectrum that are ideal for two-way radio, car telephones and policeman's walkie-talkies. Mobile communications of all kinds must go through the air as they cannot go about the world dragging a line with them. Eventually portable telephones will be creating a demand for the use of these frequencies. The world is spectrum-hungry and television is now the greediest consumer. Cable television offers a way to clear the air.

Nothing is perfect. Cable television has several unpleasant drawbacks. The worst of these is the monthly fee. The social planners who dream of wiring the ghetto and inspiring slum dwellers to perform on television have not yet solved the problem of payment. One of the obvious reasons why television is so popular in slum homes is that it appears to provide free entertainment. The poor are unlikely to be eager to commit themselves to $5 or more a month, with all the unpleasant connotations of falling behind in the payments, just to see their neighbors and local welfare workers on television. Old-age pensioners too will resist the recurring expense and even the middle class will not be immune. 'A monthly television bill for the rest of my life?' speculated an executive of the new non-commercial Public Broadcasting Service, 'I'm not sure I want that.'

Another worrying aspect of cable television is its particular suitability for pay television. Pay television, often confused with cable television, is something much more limited: a means of sending television signals in scrambled form so that only those who pay, by dropping coins in a box or by arranging to be billed, can see a particular program or channel. While pay television can be sent through the air, cable transmission is far more convenient. It does not consume a valuable broadcasting channel and the wired connection with the viewer offers a means of automatic billing and measuring the size of audiences. When two-way transmission becomes a standard part of cable television, pay television will be even more easily accommodated, for viewers will be able to instruct the cable center electronically about what they wish to see.

As cable systems expand in capacity, the temptation to cable operators to fill several of the forty or sixty channels with pay television will also grow. The danger is obvious, and if it were not the broadcasting and film industries will not cease to repeat it: what if all the best programs were gradually shifted onto the scrambled channels so that the public would eventually have to pay for what it now sees free of charge?

The FCC is alert to the threat and has imposed on cable television the same kinds of rules that it has made for pay television in general. No charge may be made for viewing a sporting event which has been televised on free channels within the preceding two years. Moreover, no films less than two years old may be shown, and no programs which are part of a series.

The existence of so many different kinds of television program on cable television may eventually lead to selective pricing of channels, a practice which may be to the public's advantage.

If viewers want to see, for example, the live performance of a play or a concert in a distant city, they would probably rather pay something akin to a box-office fee (but smaller) rather than do without the program entirely. If they want a special televised course of instruction or programs in a foreign language, possibly they should be required to bear some of the cost. It has been suggested to the Canadian Radio and Television Commission that an extra charge, comparable to an import tariff, on American television programs might help to reduce the disproportionate amount of American material viewed on Canadian television.

Solutions to the various problems concerned with the fees of cable television are feasible, but they do require the regulation of television to take on a new dimension. New York City has already established an Office of Telecommunications to supervise the cable television rates. It has also banned pay television on cable systems unless specifically authorized by the FCC. Other cities and states and perhaps other countries may have to establish similar authorities to monitor cable television and to restrict the amount of advertising if it is allowed at all. It may be necessary to use public money to provide television service free for those receiving welfare assistance, to require that television cable be installed along with the electrical and water supplies in new buildings, and to insist that some part of cable television's revenues be used to subsidize the supply of service to areas where it is uneconomic. Some form of protection for the poor is needed, in any event, if cable is to be useful to them. To have a constant unthreatened supply of television might encourage slum dwellers to use the local television studio. The burden of another monthly bill would not.

Censorship by Cable?

American enthusiasts for cable television have said little about its sinister side. They see it only as a new medium for political and cultural expression. Yet cable television cannot only create special audiences; it can also exclude them. It is closed-circuit television on a broad scale. Two of the countries most interested in the possibility of wiring cities for television are Spain and South Africa. In South Africa, for example, if black townships were to be wired, then they could receive quite different programs from those broadcast to white audiences. Cable television would be particularly advantageous to a government worried about space broadcasting. If the national television system were wired, and the government controlled what went out over the wire, then the inhabitants need not be troubled by the sight of Lucille Ball's refrigerator or other disturbing influences from foreign television. The only foreign signals that could be fed into the cable would have to be caught from the air by the government's antennae.

The Real Danger

The real danger of cable television for the United States is that it could be forty times as bad as American television is now. The FCC, gingerly testing its powers to improve the quality of American television programing, tried to compel large cable systems to originate some of their own programs only to have the requirement overturned by a federal court. But in any event, to compel originations to be truly original would take more courage and attention than the FCC has been able to muster in the past.

The program hawkers are at work already. They are offering, for $50 a month, fillers for 'baby-sitting channels', cartoons and films to run non-stop every afternoon from three until six o'clock. They also offer film packages of miscellaneous information – household hints on when to water the plants and how to protect clothes from moths, for example.

The nightmarish vision that arises is almost as bad as if Big Brother could look through the private television screen (he can't – a television set fed by coaxial cable can be switched off like any other). Americans could come to rely on canned television as they have on canned music, as background for everything. (Some bowling alleys already install cable television so that mothers can leave their children in front of cartoons while they bowl.) The programers' sales campaign began almost as soon as the FCC hinted at its rules about origination, scaring cable operators, who are just technicians with no knowledge of show business or television production. When the programers were invited to show their wares in Chicago, in the spring of

1970, the offerings shocked the television critic of the *Chicago Daily News*.

'It's probably already too late to save cable-TV,' he wrote. 'The technological advancement that was supposed to herald the millennium of wonderful TV communications is polluted already.'

What he saw at the so-called 'program origination' convention were 'lousy cartoons, bad movies, silly games, old network shows'. Probably the most ominous offering was cable TV Bingo. Here is how it was described to its potential customers, the cable television operators, as a filler for their 'origination channel':

Every number on the card must be covered. Each day you will play one complete game of Blackout Bingo. The actual calling of the numbers, each repeated three times, requires about 10 minutes of time. In the remaining time allotted, your cable Bingo Show can be taken up with rules, mentioning participating merchants, and, of course, the advantages of subscribing to Cable Television.

Remember, the participating merchants are going to be your salesmen. Mention them as frequently as possible and the availability of bingo cards in their stores.

However, the National Educational Television organization was also at the first programing convention. If there are to be program packages, they could contain some of NET's best shows, including British imports. Perhaps there could be a whole channel devoted to constant repetition of 'The Forsyte Saga'.

III

It is a long way from Blackout Bingo to computer-assisted instruction in the home. Yet the two are not incompatible. The force of the need for communications networks which can handle large quantities of information from computers, and which can overcome the handicaps of the letter-carrying service, will be inexorable. Even were cable television to provide the torrent of tawdry entertainment that is possible, it still would, as it grew from city to city, be forming the basis for the national broadband network of the 1980s.

Irving Kahn, the man who built TelePrompTer into the

largest cable-television company in the United States, in many ways embodies the contradictions of the industry. He may be the world's prophet on the future of cable television. He is short, enormously round, with a leather face and long straight hair. His silk suit is creased by his bulk, his shirt buttons threaten to pop off and little pointed shoes peer out from underneath the mass like cardboard feet stuck on a Mickey Mouse balloon. He wipes his nose with his hand as he discusses the broadband networks of tomorrow, and he refers to the Coast, wherever he is, with the ease of one who was, as he likes to mention, the youngest vice-president ever appointed by 20th Century-Fox. Until his conviction for bribery in 1971, he was the outstanding figure in the cable-television industry, and whatever history's judgment on him he may be its most unforgettable character.

It is the calmness of his conviction about cable television's future that has made him more than the archetypal entrepreneur. Smiling at his challengers, he pours out new ideas for cable television faster than they can suggest reasons why these will never come to pass. He believes that cable television will furnish the fourth, fifth and sixth television networks in the United States. He believes that it will provide socially responsive local television, that it will become both the national highway for communications traffic and the source of detailed information about whatever immediate environment the individual finds himself in.

'I like fishing,' he says. 'If I'm in England, and in the country, I want to know what the fishing conditions are within a twenty mile radius. If I'm in London, I want to know what theaters and restaurants and shops there are right around the hotel. If I want to know the weather, I want to know the weather outside the door, not in Scotland. Cable television – with a studio covering the immediate locality – can give me that information.'

Kahn believes that cable television is going to make its way on its non-television services, that it is the cable, not the television, that counts. It can read the utility meters more cheaply than can a man going around on foot, and more cheaply than can the telephone line. The same cable, attached to electronic sensors placed at strategic points and connected to police and fire stations, can provide burglar and fire alarms in the home, a service that Kahn, like others in the industry, is counting on to increase cable TV's penetration in large cities.

But it is when cable systems work in tandem with communications satellites that he expects their real potential to begin to be achieved. TelePrompTer has anticipated this day by forming an alliance with Hughes Aircraft (which owns 17 percent of TelePrompTer's stock). Together they have drawn up plans for a domestic satellite system for the United States which would allow cable systems to be interconnected into a national network (as well as offering telephone and other communications services).

Once a national cable-satellite system goes into operation, no matter what companies are involved, the entire structure of American communications will be rocked. What once seemed an impossible obstacle – the expense and difficulty of laying cables both in remote areas and in big cities, where the cost of digging up the streets is phenomenal – may be overcome eventually by new techniques of sending microwaves over short distances. Cable television could become cable-less television.

Let a Hundred Channels Bloom

The FCC occasionally shows some vision itself. In 1968 it took a deep breath and asked for comments from all and sundry about the future of cable television. The commission acknowledged that the nationwide interlocking of cable systems might be feasible soon. It observed that chief among the new services offered by a national cable-satellite system would be easier, more widespread and more flexible access to computers. With uncharacteristic boldness, the FCC also raised the possibility that all of television broadcasting might be taken off the air and sent through cables. And it said it could foresee that some day communications networks, whether involving television or telephones, might be formed at random, by users who might be moving as they talked. What did others think?

Two replies offered bold sketches of what cable television could hold in store. Doubtless, the opinion of the industrial electronics division of the Electronics Industries Association may be suspected of being self-serving. It is the electronics industries – the makers of computers and television sets and photo-facsimile machines – who will be selling the equipment to the users of any broadband networks. But the EIA's vision was eloquently detailed and has had a great influence.

The EIA told the FCC that the services to be provided by broadband communications networks in the future were the equivalent of new natural resources. Their development was so crucial to the public, as well as business and industry, that the wiring of the United States with coaxial cable should be undertaken as a national goal. It was a project 'comparable in size and importance to the electrification of the United States at the turn of the century'. The EIA report identified three developments in American life that will force the creation of a system of swift, copious messages in both visual and tangible forms: the move to the suburbs, the social anarchy of the cities and the paralysis of the mails. The EIA predicted that the impact of broadband communications network on the American social system would be profound:

Eighty percent of the people in the United States live on less than ten percent of the land area. No other vertebrate congregates in such masses as man – it's not natural. Man has tended to cluster in cities because at the time of the industrial revolution, these areas were the sources of energy (coal, water and electricity). With the advent of broadband communication networks, man will have the opportunity to live in significantly less dense population centers – in more rural areas and yet have the tools available to communicate for business, entertainment, and sociological purposes. . . .

Broadband communications is the tool not only to provide a means for new styles in human settlements, but also to rebuild, in a sociological sense, the crowded inner core of major cities. Broadband communications systems using cable can be structured to promote small, self-determining communities within the massive megalopolis. Through these, city dwellers can find order, identifiable territory, community pride, and opportunity to participate and vote on matters that can be of local option – education, cultural pursuits, recreational interest, etc.

Such wide-band systems in the 1980s appear to IED/EIA to be an absolute necessity if the nation is going to find solutions to national pollution, urban traffic, and inter-city transportation problems.

The EIA recognized (as it was politic to do) that AT&T had its own plans to develop a broadband national network for its picture telephone system. But this would have two characteristics which would make it quite different from the kind of broadband communications network which could deliver mail, library books and printed information from computers. The kind of video telephone network planned by AT&T will be much narrower in band width (1 megaherz instead of 300 megaherz) than a cable television broadband network, and it will be designed to put any picture telephone in touch with every other; it will be a switched network. The more capacious broadband network could feed outward from centers – it would be like a wheel, rather than a web, a different kind of distribution system entirely. Therefore, the EIA concluded there would be room for two new networks in the United States. It estimated that an investment of $13 billion for the picture telephone network and $11 billion for the broadband network would make picture telephones available at a ratio of one to each 100 ordinary office telephones, and would connect about 50 percent of the nation's homes to the broadband system.

To ensure the full development of all the kinds of communications services that were feasible along the broadband cable system, the EIA recommended that there be a clear distinction between the service (delivery of letters, advertising of merchandise, television entertainment, newspaper printing) and the transmission system. The message, in other words, should be separated from the medium.

The American Civil Liberties Union told the FCC the same thing, but for quite different reasons. The ACLU, a liberal political organization, has been demanding that the FCC compel cable systems to reserve all spare television channels for hire by the public. Everything that is not used for relaying over-the-air television programs should be offered for sale to the public on a common carrier basis, says the ACLU. As a common carrier, the cable system would have no control whatsoever over the content of what was carried through its many channels. These should be open for sale, at uniform, fair and reasonable rates, to anyone who had anything to say over them. The ACLU and another liberal pressure group, the

Americans for Democratic Action, see television as a mass communications medium which must be made as accessible to public expression as print is now. If necessary, they believe, the government should finance broadband public electronic communications so as not only to allow freedom of expression but to allow equality of access to central libraries of recorded information.

As for the programs, the ACLU recommended that they be financed by the monthly fees paid by subscribers to the cable systems. These could be very much like telephone rates, based in part on a basic fee for service plus optional charges for extra services.

The Wired Nation looks splendid in prospect, and there can be little doubt that broadband networks of some sort will come about in cities. But the economics of a national rewiring are far less understood than the technology. To wire all of New York City would cost approximately $1 billion. To wire all of the United States would, according to one estimate of the Sloan Commission on Cable Communications, cost $1.3 trillion. While there has been considerable progress in transmitting wide bandwidths, the equivalent of thirty-eight television channels, over short distances through the air, a truly comprehensive national cable television system would probably have to rely on communications satellites. Yet it will be some time before it is clear whether satellites are a worthwhile investment even for American domestic telephone service.

The appeal of locally originated television is another uncertainty. It may be weak. The Rand Corporation's study of some Canadian cable systems that have presented from ten to thirty hours of local live shows every week for many years found no evidence that local origination in itself attracted enough subscribers to make cable systems profitable. The extent to which cable systems can depend on local advertising revenue is also unknown.

Until now, cable television's problems have been regulatory. Congress has avoided its responsibilities in making a new copyright law for the new medium, and the FCC has been nearly distraught trying to make the old Communications Act of 1934 accommodate the complexities of cable television. Yet, once the legal obstacles are overcome, the economic ones will take their place. Cable television may be the embryonic Wired Nation and the ballot box of tomorrow, but it is still not yet out of the womb.

Chapter 9
Years in the Wilderness

I

One way to stop the advance of a disturbing new technology is to stop it dead in its tracks. This maneuver is easier in Britain, where the Post Office has a monopoly on all forms of long-distance communications, but the FCC, in spite of its feebler powers, has done what it can. In spite of its recent awakening to the potential of cable television, the FCC has in the recent past repressed it, partly at the urging of the commercial television broadcasting industry, and partly because the commission has believed that cable systems had an unfair advantage over broadcasting systems. As a result cable television does not exist today in many of the largest American cities. There has been a greater choice of television programs in northern Vermont or Montana than there is in Boston and Pittsburgh. And if the National Cable Television Association can claim that cable television serves a growing number of American homes, it cannot boast of the sophistication of its audiences. The tough restrictions of the FCC have kept cable television from selling its most desirable product – out-of-town television programs – in the one hundred biggest television markets. Only 10 percent of the American population lives outside the one hundred largest markets. The great information medium of tomorrow, in other words, has been excluded from cities larger than Augusta, Maine.

American television markets are markets for advertisers. Cable television systems have been unpopular with local television broadcasting stations in many parts of the United States because they erode the audience for the local station's shows. By doing so, they cut the size of audience that a station can promise its advertisers. And size of audience, a former chairman of the FCC, Rosel Hyde, reminded Congress (which needed no reminding), is what an American commercial station has to sell.

Perhaps the simplest reason why cable television has been held back in the United States is that no major industry stood to profit from it. The lack of a powerful friend has been perhaps more harmful to cable's development even than the fact that such a powerful industry as that of television broadcasting opposed it. Neither the manufacturers of television sets nor the advertising world were likely to make a great deal of money from cable's expansion. The telephone companies might have done, had they woken up earlier to the potential of cable television. But they did not, with consequences that will be discussed later. Cable television began as a fragmented, small-scale operation, lacking both friends and enemies. In the late 1940s, if small-town television dealers wanted to encourage the sale of television sets by running cables into homes, they caused no more stir than if they gave away pop-up toasters or plastic daffodils.

Those years were the early days not only of cable television but of all television. In 1948 the FCC tried to decide what to do about finding channels for all the television stations that wanted to open. In 1945 it had provisionally allocated thirteen VHF channels for commercial television (while requiring them to be shared with mobile radio and other services.) Yet even then the FCC predicted that this part of the spectrum did not have enough room for the development of the number of channels that would be needed if the United States were to have competitive services available across the whole country. There obviously was much more room for television up in the more commodious UHF band, but in 1945 the techniques of using this higher frequency band had not been developed. It would not have been reasonable to require television stations to use them. By 1948 the overcrowding had become severe. The existing stations were interfering with one another, and the FCC was faced with a surge of applications for licences for new stations. What it did was to stop the sharing of the VHF bands – mobile radio having to yield the use of this desirable part of the spectrum to television. And it stopped granting any new licences.

Between 1948 and 1952 what is referred to as the 'television freeze' prevailed, while the FCC pondered the future shape of American television. The commissioners hoped that during the freeze the technology of UHF transmission would develop, forestalling too heavy an investment in VHF broadcasting.

In 1952 the FCC finally presented its grand design for the development of television in the United States. That it was one of the colossal wrong turns in communications was not to become clear until later. The commission decided that television in the United States should grow along the pattern of radio. The country would be blanketed with small television stations as it was with small radio stations. Such a pattern would draw upon the regional richness of America; it would give outlets for local expression and would prevent the concentration of the medium of television in a few hands. Obviously if there were to be a great many stations, there would have to be a great many channels – and the UHF was the only place to find them. The FCC therefore boldly allocated for the use of television broadcasting not only VHF Channels 2 through 13 but seventy channels of the UHF. Having provided so much raw material, the FCC went further to protect the public interest and reserved a number of channels in both the UHF and VHF for non-commercial educational uses. Then it sat back, pleased. It had drawn up a plan for all foreseeable needs of American television.

The major miscalculation in this plan was the failure to allow for the high costs of producing television. The economics were against strong local television programing, especially by non-commercial stations without advertising as a source of support. But the FCC also ignored some important facts. One was that commercial broadcasters did not like the UHF. It was a far more difficult part of the spectrum to work in; it gave a poorer signal than VHF and it required more expensive transmitters. Another was that most American television sets could not receive UHF. The standard television set as it came off the assembly line had only twelve channels on the dial. And if most people could not receive the UHF channels, advertisers most certainly were not eager to buy time on them.

What happened is history, sorry history that helped to warp the growth of cable television. The VHF television licences were the most sought-after. Because of the problem of interference, there could be only a few in each city. Commercial interests pushed aside educational groups, and those that won the VHF licences went on to form affiliations with the national television networks, which gave them substantial financial support, plus network shows which drew big audiences and therefore large advertising revenues. The UHF stations in most cities could not interest the two biggest of the national networks, the Columbia Broadcasting System and the National Broadcasting Company. If they found a network to take them in, it tended to be the weaker American Broadcasting Company. Because of the scarcity of UHF channels, a fourth network, Dumont, collapsed entirely. The UHF stations with no network affiliation at all had to go it alone, competing with the network-supported VHF stations for local advertising.

Suffice it to say that the UHF has never flourished as intended. Many allocations have gone unused. Many of the UHF stations have gone out of business. Nearly two-thirds of those that were surviving in 1970 were operating at a loss and pulling out schedules that are full of old films with which they try to woo some of the local television audience away from network shows.

The FCC has never recovered from its guilt at having encouraged investment in UHF stations while making it nearly impossible for them to survive against the network competition on the VHF. What the FCC might have done in 1952 is what Britain is belatedly doing now – shifting all of its television broadcasting on to the UHF. Or it might have encouraged regional television broadcasting. Regional stations might have allowed the formation of a greater number of networks around the country. (These could have relayed their broadcasts with powerful transmitters, as is done in Britain, so that rural areas far from any community television station could have picked them up. There might have been little need for CATV at all.) But the FCC remained loyal to its ideal of local television, even though the very opposite developed. Many cities had just one strong station which was little more than a funnel for network programs produced thousands of miles away, and isolated communities had none at all.

Over the years the FCC has made various efforts to strengthen the UHFs. One, an attempt to persuade Congress in 1962 to pass a law requiring all television sets to be made capable of receiving all seventy UHF channels, as well as the twelve VHF channels, has been relatively ineffective. The so-called 'all-channel tuners' do not give satisfying clicks as they turn from one UHF channel to another. They slide worryingly from Channel 27 to Channel 28 in such a way that if the reception is not good (as it often is not on UHF) the viewer is not sure when he has gone past the mark. Undaunted, the FCC is now seeking to have precision-tuners mandatory in all television sets.

Another way of helping the UHF, as the FCC saw it, was to squelch cable television. A great many cable systems had grown up during the freeze and it was not long into the 1950s before CATV systems were identified as threats to the struggling local UHF stations. If a cable company brought in extra programs from another town, the local station most likely to lose viewers was the UHF station without a national network behind it. Any enemy of the UHF was no friend of the FCC's.

Starting in 1954, the broadcasting industry in general began to complain to the FCC about CATV. They believed that cable systems offered them unfair competition; they foresaw that it might destroy not only the UHF stations but the weaker VHFs. As users of the radio spectrum, they had to have licences from the FCC in order to operate; the CATVs did not. Television stations had to hire performers and announcers and to hunt for sources of advertising revenues. The CATV men paid nothing for the signals they took out of the air. But the FCC, although it was sympathetic to the broadcasters' worries, decided in 1959 that it could do nothing to help. The commissioners felt that they did not have the authority to regulate television that did not travel through the air. Cable television, therefore, because it did not fit into the rule-making pattern, was left to grow without guidance.

But the broadcasters were not satisfied, and a year later their grievances against the burgeoning CATV industry had reached Senator Pastore's subcommittee on communications. Pastore himself presided at the bad-tempered hearings at which CATV operators and broadcasters shouted insults at one another. Pastore finally decided to sponsor a bill which he had been led to believe would both please the cable operators and mollify the broadcasters. The bill would have placed CATV under the jurisdiction of the FCC and required the cable operators to get the FCC's permission before going into business, as with the broadcasters. But – and here Pastore's bill was lenient to CATV – they would not have had to ask permission from a broadcaster before retransmitting one of his original programs.

Senator Pastore himself served as floor manager for the bill. He fought hard against a formidable opponent, Senator Robert Kerr of Oklahoma, who took the broadcasters' side. Just before the vote was to be taken, however, the cable industry changed its mind. It decided that it did not want to be regulated by the FCC after all; it did not want Pastore's bill. Pastore was furious. He had antagonized his old friends in the broadcasting industry to no purpose. From the Senate floor he thundered up at the CATV men in the gallery and warned them that they would rue the day, that the time would come when they would be begging for federal regulation. The Senate then killed his bill by sending it back to committee. It is safe to say that Senator Pastore has never forgiven the cable television industry for his humiliation. In American communications, there is no worse enemy to have.

Emboldened by Congress's failure to do anything about CATV, the FCC began to decide that perhaps it did have some authority to control the new industry after all. In 1962 it announced that those CATVs which used microwaves, as some of them did, to carry signals from their high antennae into their local stations, came under its jurisdiction because they used the airwaves. Then it began to tell cable operators what they could and could not do to compete with local over-the-air television stations. For example, it required cable systems to carry all the programs broadcast by television stations in the communities where they were located, so that subscribers to cable television would not be cut off from the output of their local television stations. The commission also forbade cable systems from using out-of-town signals to duplicate any program that a local station had shown or planned to show within a fortnight.

In the early 1960s the owners of cable systems began to be hauled into court with demands for payment of copyright. They became frightened. The early decisions went against them, and while the legal battles went on and on, they realized that they would have to pay copyright fees sooner or later. But how much and by what means? If cable operators had to search out the original author or performer of each program they carried, they would be buried in an avalanche of paper. They toyed with formulas for payment while the broadcasting industry kept on pressing for 'full copyright liability' – payment for each and every program.

In 1966 came the first big blow. The FCC finally claimed jurisdiction over all cable television with a vengeance. It forbade cable television systems from bringing signals from another city into the one hundred largest television markets without getting the FCC's consent. By and large, this order has effectively shut cable television out of metropolitan America because it has prevented the industry from selling its prime service – diversity of choice. New York City is a special case because ordinary reception is so poor that cable television has taken root there simply by offering clear television pictures. But New York's cable companies cannot bring in programs from Philadelphia or Boston, and in most big cities this kind of added attraction would be necessary if cable companies were to win enough subscribers to make a profit.

The rationale for the restriction on imported signals was to protect the weak UHF stations. That has not been done. What happened instead was that cable television was prevented from building up the very large base of subscribers that might have enabled it to provide local original programs of professional quality.

A Churlish Reputation

By 1966, excluded from the mainstream of urban America, cable television had acquired 1·6 million subscribers, nearly 5 percent of American homes with television. (In Canada, it was growing even faster, as Canadians subscribed to cable systems which could bring them American television programs.) Its potential as a general information-carrier was barely considered. There was still something vaguely churlish about CATV. For all the restrictions, some operators were making enormous profits with very little risk.

Many companies began with little capital. Instead they collected it from their customers, charging them installation fees of $100 or $200, far in excess of the actual cost of wiring up. Once they had enlisted a large number of customers and a large pool of capital, the operators often sold out at several times what the system was worth. In 1958, when Senator Pastore's subcommittee held hearings into CATV profiteering, there was one notorious example where nearly one million dollars in installation charges was collected on an initial investment of $200,000. It will take some time before cable television sheds its reputation as a get-rich-quick, shabby business, devoid of responsibility for making programs, for improving technology or even paying for what it sells.

Not only the cable operators were greedy. The city governments which gave them franchises – licenses to operate – are also culpable. In most communities, unless they are as large as New York or Los Angeles, a cable television system must have a monopoly. There can be only one system wiring up a town. Permission to do so must be given by local governments, and they have not been unaware of the prize in their gift. The custom has been for the city fathers to demand a percentage of the cable ˙operator's gross receipts in return for a franchise, and these percentages have not been small. Some cities demanded as much as 11 percent, before the practise was declared unconstitutional by a federal appeals court. With so much money at stake, the question of which company of many applicants is to be awarded a cable television franchise remains one of the most important issues that many American city councillors face in their political careers. Sometimes they have made some money for themselves on the side. Sometimes they have been unable to decide at all. Chicago and Washington, D.C., have stewed over franchises for years without awarding one.

Telephone companies have also fed off cable television. It is a measure of the lack of imagination of the American telephone industry that it woke up so slowly to the latent possibilities of the coaxial cable which is its stock in trade. From the very beginning of cable television, the telephone companies (of which there are a great number in the United States in addition to the regional affiliates of the giant AT&T) often let CATV operators attach their cables to telephone poles. For this favor they charged a fee. Then the telephone companies began to string up coaxial cables themselves to lease them to CATV

operators who wanted to get into the television relay business
but who could not afford the capital investment of buying and
installing cables. Some of the independent companies themselves bought and ran cable systems. Sometimes these leases
cost the cable operators considerably more than building their
own system would have done. But the wiring was done more
quickly and expertly, and in some instances, because the
telephone people already held a franchise for crossing rights-
of-way with their cables, the cable television system was
able to go into operation on the strength of this franchise,
without having to ask the city for a separate franchise
of its own.

Gradually telephone companies began to dominate the cable
television business. Those that were independent of AT&T's
Bell system began acquiring CATV systems themselves. The Bell
telephone companies were prohibited by an agreement with
the Justice Department from engaging in any activities not
regulated by the FCC, so they could not own systems themselves.
But they leased them to outsiders, and Bell inhibited their
performance by refusing to carry the signals of any systems that
originated their own programs. The cable companies felt hard
used by the telephone companies. They complained that
sometimes the installation of cables was delayed until a rival
company had entered a higher bid for the lease.

At the end of the 1960s the FCC, encouraged by the Justice
Department, began to crack down on the telephone companies'
activities in CATV, just as it began to force the television
broadcasting industry to retreat from ownership of CATV
systems. The two industries, both bitter opponents of CATV, had
gone a long way toward buying up the new business which
threatened them. The pattern of ownership shown by the table
below has now begun to be broken.

Cable system ownership, 1969	% of total systems
TV – radio broadcasters	33
Telephone companies	25
Newspapers	15
Other	27

Source: Legg Industry Review, August, 1969.

By 1968, cable television was still fringe television. Senator Pastore was antagonistic toward it, the FCC looked down on it (although it had established a CATV task force to study it), the broadcasters and cinema owners were fighting it hard. Municipal authorities and telephone companies were milking it. Because of the harsh regulatory climate and the provincialism of most cable operators, the technology of cable television atrophied. Other kinds of communication, with industrial research behind them, were improving month by month, but CATV's were still limping along on the technology of the 1950s. What the FCC had achieved in trying to shore up the UHF was to have choked off the growth of the medium that could provide the very localism that the commission had been aiming for.

II

Cable's prospects began to brighten slightly around 1968. First the Supreme Court put the FCC out of its agony by ruling that the commission *did* have authority over cable television. Then the Court overturned the decisions of lower courts and ruled that the retransmission by a cable system of a television broadcast did not constitute a performance within the meaning of American copyright law. This ruling, called the Fortnightly decision, did not mean that cable television was free from copyright forever: it did lift the threat of retroactive payment from the heads of cable operators. If Congress wanted them to pay copyright fees, the Court pointed out, it should put the wish into law. But existing law did not require payment.

As usual, given encouragement, the FCC showed some muscle. First it ruled that cable systems could, if they wished, put original programs out to their customers. Then it ruled, in one specific case, that a cable operator could sell commercial advertisements. Moreover, it began to crack down on the entry by telephone companies into the cable business. And quite contrarily, while it was apparently encouraging cable, it tightened the rules about importing distant signals.

By December 1968 the FCC recognized formally that cable television was more than an upstart method of transmission.

At that point it issued its notice of inquiry into the future of the medium. For the interim, it proposed that large cable systems be forced to originate programs on one channel. Then, to protect cable's independence, it suggested that no cable systems be owned by broadcasting stations and perhaps not even by newspapers.

By 1969 cable had made converts in high places. The FCC's restrictions against importing distant signals began to be criticized sharply. President Johnson's task force on communications policy raised cable television's status by proclaiming it the most promising method of 'creating a greatly expanded multi-channel capability', and it criticized the FCC for its temporizing solutions. The Justice Department reminded the FCC of its responsibility to assure that cable television fulfilled its potential. It urged that no restriction be placed against a cable system unless it were absolutely essential to project some clearly defined interest.

A number of other influential voices blended to tell the FCC that cable television was the foundation for the Wired Nation and that the FCC should bring that wiring about, not stand in the way.

While visions of its future began bubbling up from think tanks and law-school journals, the National Cable Television Association showed in May 1969 how broad the vision of the industry itself was. The NCTA worked out a peace treaty with the National Association of Broadcasters which surrendered the very freedom that made it an exciting alternative to broadcasting. The NCTA was willing to promise never to link cable systems into a national network for broadcasting entertainment programs if the broadcasters would drop their objections to cable's importing distant programs into the largest cities. An enormous outcry greeted this back-room deal. The American Civil Liberties Union repeated its demand that the FCC declare cable television a public utility, required to provide time to any person or organization desiring to hire time to appear on television. The Justice Department also frowned, and the proposed deal collapsed. All it accomplished was to leave another black mark on CATV's reputation for lack of principle.

With the arrival of Dean Burch as chairman of the FCC, cable television's fortunes brightened. Burch, a taut Arizonan who had been chairman of the Republican National Committee in 1964, the year of Senator Barry Goldwater's Presidential campaign, had not been expected to be willing to offend the broadcasters. He was a bona fide conservative, a Goldwater man. Yet he almost immediately revealed a concern to lift the restraints from cable television. He elevated it to the status of a full bureau within the FCC and took himself to address the NCTA annual convention. For the FCC, it was the equivalent of the United States recognizing mainland China. Yet an executive at CBS expressed no surprise. 'Burch is an Arizonan,' he said. 'He has no love for the East Coast media. He saw how they treated Barry Goldwater.'

In June 1970 the FCC, revitalized under Burch, seemed to deliver the news that the cable industry had been waiting for. It released a set of rules and proposals which added up to a blueprint for the long-range development of cable television in the United States. By then, the FCC had recognized three imperatives in planning for cable television: 1) cable systems had to be allowed to import some distant signals into the largest cities if they were to be profitable there at all; 2) the existing industry was in need of some protection, for cable presented a real, if not lethal, threat to its advertising base, and 3) the cable industry would have to be pressured into developing new services. The FCC then spent more than a year trying to find a formula that would accommodate all three. In June 1971 Chairman Burch went before Senator Pastore's subcommittee to describe it.

Cable systems would be allowed to carry at least two otherwise unobtainable channels into the one hundred biggest markets. (Two was the number decided upon as the minimum necessary to allow cable systems to attract new customers without luring away too much of the audience from local television stations.) Furthermore, cable systems could import even more distant signals if the cities in which they operated did not have what the FCC considered to be a full range of choice of over-the-air television. (That was decided to be three network stations and three independent stations for viewers in the fifty largest markets and three network stations and two independent stations in the next fifty biggest markets.)

For these import privileges, however, the FCC set a price.

Cable systems would be required to carry a channel of non-broadcast service (locally originated programs or publicly leased channels, chiefly) for each broadcast signal they carried. Moreover, new cable systems in the large markets would be required to have a capacity for two-way non-voice transmission. Further, to clear away the obstacles in cable's path, the FCC declared that Congress and not itself should deal with the issue of cable's copyright payments. Moreover, the commission declared that it did not seek the power to license new cable systems, as it does radio and television stations. That would be left to lower levels of government.

The FCC believed its formula to be nicely balanced, but others were not so sure that over-the-air broadcasting was sufficiently protected. Senator Pastore warned Burch that the FCC was not to take any irrevocable action. Just about the same time, President Nixon woke up belatedly to the magnitude of the issues raised by cable television and appointed a special advisory group to tell him what the Administration's policy should be.

The White House then proceeded to exert its influence to see that cable television would not expand as freely in America's largest cities and suburbs as the FCC had hoped. Through its Office of Telecommunications Policy, it presented the rival industries, broadcasting and cable, with a new peace treaty solving the troublesome copyright question. Although both the NAB and the NCTA had to make painful concessions, they accepted the compromise in November 1971, largely out of a fear that Congress would deal with the copyright issue itself and do so less delicately.

The broadcasters, for their part, agreed at last to drop their opposition to cable companies importing distant signals into big cities. But the cable industry had to surrender even more. For the first time it agreed in principle to pay copyright owners for the films taken out of the air and sold to cable subscribers. More than that, it conceded that in the fifty largest markets, no cable company should be allowed to import from out-of-town any film or television series to which a local station had bought exclusive rights. And it agreed not to import signals from anywhere in the country but to take them from stations close to home or from relatively small cities. The effect of the compromise was not only to inhibit cable's growth in metropolitan America, but to reduce its chances of interconnecting one system with another, thereby forming a fourth national television network.

Events move rapidly in this new field, but it would appear that cable television will be hobbled for some years to come. Each advance it is permitted to make sets off a new round of legal challenges and administrative maneuvering. For example, one result of the FCC's 1970 proposals was to excite the interest of state governments in regulating cable television. Until then, only five states had done so, but between 1970 and 1971 nineteen legislatures dealt with proposals to give states and not municipal governments the authority over cable systems within the state boundaries. Why should a new service which might turn into a public utility, such as telephones and electricity, be allowed to grow without supervision?

The prospect of a third level of regulation sent the cable television industry into a further orgy of self-pity. It was convinced that it had been unjustly inhibited by the harsh regulatory climate. It was less ready to acknowledge that it was in part to blame for its plight, by trying to avoid regulation and payment of copyright for so long.

Undoubtedly cable television will be hampered in the future until the proper roles for all three levels of government – federal, state and local – have been distinguished, but there is nothing holding it back from developing the non-broadcast services that it can uniquely provide. The challenge to the cable television industry in the next decade will be to resist the temptation to move into the biggest markets without developing the non-broadcast services, to intensify its competition with the existing television entertainment industry and to skimp on its program origination.

Yet in a sense the challenge is unfair. The FCC has been trying to force cable television to turn its back on the cut-throat competitiveness of commercial broadcasting – which has been the American tradition for more than fifty years and which Congress has encouraged – and to invest in services which the public may not want but which the FCC and others believe to be in the public interest. That is a great deal of social responsibility to expect of a commercial enterprise, especially a struggling one with such a past.

Chapter 10
Cable in a Cold Climate

It could well turn out that by 1980 many American audiences will have forty channels of television and the British will have three or four. By then American television may have gone beyond entertainment and be on its way to becoming a multipurpose national information network, while British television remains restricted to a few national programs broadcast at mass audiences through a thin veil of regional coloring. Two Ministers of Posts and Telecommunications, John Stonehouse and Christopher Chataway, although of different political parties, have shown a lively appreciation of the possible advantages to Britain of multichanneled television. But in general there is almost total ignorance that the possibilities even exist. The television critics, the McLuhan interpreters, the sociologists of the mass media, even the television professionals, tend not to know that their intellectual counterparts in the United States are excited about it. 'Cable television?' said an executive of the BBC. 'Frankly, we haven't thought much about it, except to think of it as a bit of a menace.'

Such indifference has respectable roots. When it comes to television, people in Britain are not inclined to look to the United States or anywhere else for models. Britain has avoided the two great traps into which most of the world's television has fallen – overcommercialization and government control. Whatever the imperfections of the BBC and the various companies within the Independent Television Authority, they have managed to remain independent of political control while putting out an impressive amount of instruction and civic information along with entertainment. Moreover, even in terms of transmission, the British television services can feel morally superior to the American television networks. Those who live in rural areas of the United Kingdom, by and large, have had little need to indulge in the snatch-and-grab operation of CATV, stealing television programs intended for cities out of the sky and ferreting them home to the farm. Both the BBC and the ITA blanket the country with their signals at their own expense and have, with their VHF 405-line transmission at least, managed to reach about 99 percent of their entire population.

Yet Britain will be at a great disadvantage in the years after 1980 if it does not have the facilities that cable television brings with it. Authors, journalists and politicians ought to be able by then to use the medium much more freely than is possible at present and the viewing public need a wider selection of programs. As things stand, the BBC in particular turns itself inside out to provide programs for minority audiences but puts them out, as indeed it has no alternative to doing, on its national channels. As a result, a program of interest to only 25,000 nurses is broadcast to thirty million people. A program for mothers of young children, because of the pressure of more popular programs for the peak viewing hours, is shown after eleven o'clock at night when most mothers have gone to bed. This kind of restrictiveness will be even less tolerable as the century gets older. Moreover, without a broadband network for the distribution of electronic information, Britain may fall far behind the United States in its ability to exchange commercial information, to create a sense of community within sprawling urban populations, or even to deliver its letters.

Wired Already

The irony of the prevailing indifference is that Britain has a great deal of cable television already. About 7 percent of all television license holders subscribe to what is variously called cable television, wired television or television relay (because it relays or re-transmits the signal.) This is nowhere near as much as exists in Canada, where about one-quarter of all television comes over wires, but it is nearly the same proportion as in the United States, and the pace of growth may be even faster. In Britain, wire is often the more accurate adjective to describe the method of reception, because there are two different types of relay television in current use, and the more prevalent uses

Growth of wired television in Britain

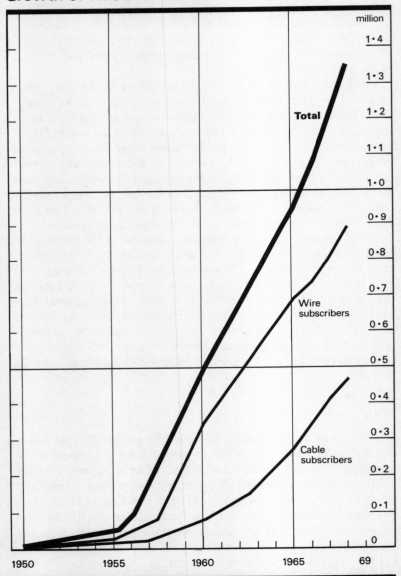

Source: Ministry of Posts and Telecommunications latest figures available in 1971

pairs of wires, like telephone wires. The other, which uses coaxial cable, carries a broader band of frequencies and is more comparable to the American CATV. Much of this cable and wire is old, but there are some cable and wire systems now in operation that could carry a great deal more than the ration allowed them by the Ministry of Posts: three television and four radio programs.

Portions of central London are wired for television; so are parts of Newcastle, Hull, Sheffield, Leeds and many places in the hinterland where there are clusters of people and where over-the-air television reception is poor. The valleys of South Wales, with houses strung conveniently in rows along a few streets, have been ideal territory for wired reception. Yet little is heard about the possibility of expanding this existing network of wires and cables into a national information-carrying network.

Growth of Relay

Anybody who wants to relay television, that is to collect television signals and convey them along a line to specific points, needs not one but two licenses. The Post Office must issue a license because it holds a monopoly over all forms of electrical communication and because it is concerned to prevent the relays from interfering with the telephone service. But the Ministry of Post's license is the more important; it recognizes that television relay is an extension of broadcasting and therefore that the programs that are carried must meet the Ministry's requirements.

The holders of relay licenses range from small groups of families who share a communal television aerial to commercial television relay companies. Of these, Rediffusion Ltd. and British Relay Wireless Ltd. are far and away the largest. These companies trace their origins back to the early days of radio broadcasting, and the shabby, bare office of their trade association, the Relay Services Association of Great Britain, in a pre-war building in the City of London, betrays not only the age of the industry but the apologetic stance it has been forced to assume over the years by the Post Office (which, in its old form, used to have full authority over relay) and by the BBC.

Relay companies have been controversial since the beginning. Their aura, oddly enough, has always been the same as that of American CATV, which developed later – cheeky and vulgar. In the early 1930s they provided radio cheaply for many of the working class who had no electricity and little money.* The relay companies offered programs, not only of the high-minded BBC, then under the austere guidance of Sir John Reith (later Lord Reith), but also from the continental Radio Luxembourg, with its commercials and dance music. Moreover, like relay television later on, relay radio was easier to tune and suffered less from interference than sets which depended on aerial reception.

The secretary of the Relay Services Association, Mr Halden Evans, can remember the early days when the cost of radio relay was less than ten cents a week. 'Relay went like a bomb in the gas towns,' he calls. 'But the BBC never really liked us. Everywhere there was a relay, the inference was that the BBC wasn't doing its job. But they made no move to take us over.'

If they had, Britain might be nearer to a national network of cable television, forty channels and all, today.

The BBC did think about taking over the relay services, and so did the Post Office. Professor Asa Briggs, in his history of broadcasting in the United Kingdom, describes how the BBC first considered then rejected a scheme to use wire as an integral part of its transmission service. The obstacle apparently was the Post Office. According to Briggs, 'the Post Office would not commit itself to the principle of BBC monopoly in the event of the scheme proving a success.' (The same conflict in slightly different form remains to be resolved. If the Post Office itself were to provide wired television on a national scale, could the BBC and the ITA retain their exclusive right of access to the medium?)

It was Peter Eckersley, the BBC's first Chief Engineer, who tried to persuade the BBC to adopt a policy of 'substituting wire

* Radio could be obtained in a home with no electricity by having a loudspeaker from which wires ran back to what was called a wireless exchange. The power to operate the loudspeaker was supplied along the wire with the signal. The first radio relay service in Britain began in 1924 in Hythe, Hampshire, where a wireless dealer named Maton attached wires to his radio receiver and ran them into the homes of his friends so that they could listen in.

for wireless'. In 1925 he perceived that wired broadcasting offered a solution to the shortage of wavelengths and the radio interference that plagued broadcasting through the air. He foresaw that a day might come when wired radio would be the dominant form of transmission, with wireless broadcasting a supplement. In 1931, after Eckersley had parted company with the BBC, he joined Rediffusion, which was already one of the larger relay companies.

In the 1930s the radio relay companies went through many of the same kind of battles that American CATV faced in the 1950s, and they lost most of them. The Post Office kept them on a very short lead. It specified that relay companies could not send out original programs. It forbade them to import foreign programs which conveyed the news of the results of sweepstakes – no Irish broadcasts, in other words. Radio Luxembourg was permitted, however, because it was a program intended by its broadcasters to be received by British audiences, and did not in a sense constitute a foreign program. The Post Office reserved to itself the right to take over the private plant of the companies at three months' notice, and at first it gave them licenses for only one year at a time. In 1932, however, it extended the licenses to 1936, when the BBC's charter was due to expire.

In 1936 the Ullswater Committee, the first of the monumental committees which have periodically investigated the structure of British broadcasting, recommended that the Post Office take over the relay companies. That was what the BBC wanted, for the relay companies had grown to the point where they had half a million subscribers who tended to prefer Radio Luxembourg, especially on Sunday when the BBC was forced to stick to a somber Reithian diet of serious music. The Post Office, however, rejected the Ullswater Committee's advice, largely because of the pressure of the supporters of the commercial relay services in Parliament. But it renewed the licenses for three years only.

The relay companies have all through their history pleaded for a substantially longer license, in order to protect their capital investment, but they have not got it. In 1939 their licenses were extended to 1949, when they again made their pitch for more generous treatment, this time to the Beveridge Committee.

Their result was another three-year extension until 1952 when, with the advent of television, a fifteen-year license was granted.

Television gave the relay companies something new to sell: better reception and the rental of a set. But relay television in Britain has never produced the kind of profit that CATV has in the United States. There are only a very few parts of Britain where relay has been the alternative to no television at all. In some places, relay companies have had captive subscribers because landlords have forbidden aerials on the roof or because ordinary reception is so bad (as in Victoria in London) that wired television is preferable beyond question. Over the same cable or wire that feeds the television set, the relay companies can offer four radio programs. Yet even with this advantage added to that of the guaranteed clear picture, they have not been able to set charges for their subscribers much above those of companies which rent television sets plain and simple. In practice, their prices have had to be nearly the same. In London in 1971 the rental of a television set dependent on a wire for reception, offering superior programs and radio into the bargain, costs about nine new pence a week more than the rental of an ordinary set. The National Board for Prices and Incomes, studying the whole field of television rental and the relay industry in 1968, found that relay subscribers did not have any decided preference for wired reception.

The capacity of television relay to carry more than two BBC and one ITA channels has hardly been noticed. The most notable exception was the pay television experiment of 1966 to 1968. In spite of the Pilkington Committee's firm opposition to pay television even on a trial basis, the Conservative government in 1963 decided to permit an experiment which allowed people in certain areas with wired television to receive special programs (mainly films and sporting events) on an idle channel as long as they put coins in a box attached to the set. The experiment was carried out, by a specially formed company called Pay-TV Ltd. on British Relay's wires, in London (in Kennington and in Westminster) and in a part of Sheffield. Only 10,000 subscribers participated. In 1968 the Labor government refused to allow the experiment to expand when Pay-TV argued that it would need to test the service on a much larger audience, something nearer a quarter of a million people, before it could determine whether the service was wanted and whether it was profitable. The experiment was terminated, the company having lost a great deal of money – around £1 million. The most significant thing about the experiment was its wired transmission. It was the beginning of an official recognition in Britain that the idle capacity of wired reception could be put to work.

The question of importing distant signals – the heart of the American cable television controversy – has never been a lively issue in Britain. British copyright laws are much stricter. Every re-transmission of a performance, even by the broadcasting company which originally paid for it, involves a payment to all the performers. It costs the BBC roughly £110,000 every time *The Forsyte Saga* is shown again. If a relay company were to bring in programmes from abroad and put them out on its idle channels, it would have to pay copyright fees to the original broadcasters. But quite apart from the copyright burden, importing programs from the Continent is no great temptation. How many would subscribe to a service because it offered French, Belgian, Dutch or Danish television? If relay companies are ever to be allowed to fill their idle channels with extra programs, it seems clear that these programs must originate in Britain.

Instead of asking for permission to fill their empty channels the British relay companies have been preoccupied with the introduction of color television and the shift of all the television services from transmission on the VHF bands, with 405 lines to a picture, up to the UHF bands, with 625 lines to a picture, which offer technically superior transmission. The higher shorter waves used for color and for UHF are harder to receive through the air than those of the VHF – a fact which has given the relay companies a stronger selling point than they have had in the past. For the BBC and the ITA, in spite of enormous expenditure and efforts to provide six times as many UHF transmitters as they have had VHF transmitters to get their programmes around the country (and with a UHF transmitter costing about £250,000), have small hope of achieving a nearly complete coverage of the entire population. In 1970 only three-quarters of the population could receive BBC-2 (broadcast exclusively on UHF). All the

UHF transmitters have not yet been built, but even when they are, there will be perhaps two million people who cannot receive the UHF programs by means of rooftop aerials. Many of these will be candidates for relay television.

Yet the relay companies are up against the same hard facts of economics and geography as are the engineers of the BBC and the ITA. It is profitable for the companies to string cables and wires up only where there are clusters of a thousand or more people, about the same density that merits a television transmitter to send programs through the air. Any concentration below that tends to be too costly for either the television authorities or the relays which have not been earning a great deal. The Prices and Incomes Board found that the wired networks were earning less than 5 percent on total capital invested.

In spite of the handicaps, the total number of relay subscribers is increasing steadily. Their very growth, however, at a time when cable television is booming on the other side of the Atlantic, constitutes a challenge to the Post Office and the national television services. The relay networks have latent capacity. At some time or another, the pressure will mount to use them for something other than passing along BBC and ITA programs. It is possible that it will put the companies in peril, for if wired communications came to be seen as essential, the Post Office might try to take them over, or the television services, with their shared monopoly on providing television to the British public, might want to absorb the relay systems into their own physical plant.

The Search for More Television

In 1960 the Pilkington Committee on the future of broadcasting was faced with the duty of recommending how to provide more television channels for Britain, which then had only two. Its decision – that all television service move up to the UHF bands where there was room for four channels with national or near-national coverage – was adopted by Parliament as national policy. But in its search for alternatives the Pilkington Committee did pay serious attention to the suggestion of the British Institution of Radio Engineers that the wired television system which had sprung out of radio relay provided an alternative means of increasing the number of television channels. Nobody then was talking about forty or fifty channels; the idea of six was fanciful enough.

The Pilkington Committee recognized that the television signal that came over a wire was more stable and free from interference than that which came through the air. It also saw, without any particular pleasure, that wired broadcasting offered a convenient way to introduce pay television. But the committee was far more impressed with the disadvantages of wired television:

It would be very expensive to serve rural and many suburban areas. In towns, wayleaves [rights-of-way] would have to be obtained and amenities safeguarded. And, so long as coverage remained significantly less than 100 per cent, it would have to be supplemented by transmission by radio; since, because a wire system must take a very long time to install throughout the country and because large numbers of people would, therefore, have to wait many years for any additional services of broadcasting, it would be difficult to refuse to provide a broadcast transmission of these services in the meantime.

Accordingly, the Pilkington recommendation was that any further extension of the television services should be by broadcasting transmission in the UHF range of the spectrum.

1976 is Coming

In 1976 the British Parliament will have to determine the course that British broadcasting is to take in the years to come. In that fateful year, all the existing arrangements come to an end and must be renewed, abandoned or reshaped: for the BBC's charter expires, the Television Act permitting the ITA also runs out, as do the licenses of the television relay companies. There have been similar watersheds in the past and they have been preceded by the ponderous inquiries which have been mentioned: Ullswater, Beveridge, Pilkington. Since the Pilkington, however, there has been a revolution in communications technology. The very word 'broadcasting' has become ambiguous. The choices in 1976 will be immeasurably wider than they were in the past and the decisions more difficult.

How best to prepare for 1976? In May 1970, the Wilson government, in what it did not realize were the waning days of its stay in office, set up a committee to conduct a broad inquiry in the tradition of its predecessors. The committee on the future of broadcasting, headed by Lord Noël Annan, provost of University College, London, was to have considered a wide range of new possibilities. In the view of Mr Stonehouse, the then Postmaster General, the 'breathtaking technological environment' which loomed in the future might allow the quasi-monopoly of the broadcast organizations to disappear. The Annan Committee, therefore, was to examine the relationship of the BBC and the ITA to Parliament and to recommend whether or not they should be merged or replaced by some other authority. The inquiry had to begin early, Stonehouse said, because the Pilkington Committee had taken two years to do its work and then had complained of insufficient time, and because new legislation would have to be formulated by the end of 1974 and passed through Parliament during 1974–1975 if there were to be an orderly transition in 1976.

One group in particular was delighted with the formation of the Annan Committee. It was the 76 Group, a band of television writers and producers and executives discontented with the management of both the BBC and the ITA. Taking their name from the year of the impending changes in broadcasting, the 76 Group have been demanding that those who are involved in the actual making of television programs have a greater voice in management than the BBC and ITA allow them. The 76 Group, which professes to be interested in all kinds of innovation that might make television a more accessible medium, believed that the Annan Committee would lead to the kind of full-blown national discussion of these innovations that they themselves wanted to initiate.

The man who became Postmaster General after the Conservatives won the General Election in June 1970, Christopher Chataway, seemed to agree with his predecessor about the importance of the 1976 decisions on almost everything except the belief that yet another monumental committee was the right way to approach them. Chataway feared that British broadcasting was falling into a pattern of ten-year cycles in the last few years of which all decisions were frozen. Deciding to proceed in a lower key, he reactivated the dormant Television Advisory Committee to examine and report to him on the new technical choices that now exist: satellite broadcasting, video cassettes, and multichanneled television. Once the purely technical issues were made clear, Chataway reasoned, then the political and social implications of the future structure of broadcasting could be assessed more clearly.

His reasoning may yet be proved to have been false. There is no such thing as pure technology. Each of the technical possibilities, multichanneled or cable television particularly, is loaded with political implications especially for the future of the BBC and ITA. Moreover, the supposedly objective Television Advisory Committee was heavy with representatives of the institutional status quo, including the Directors General of both the BBC and ITA.

Dialed Television

One development forcing British politicans to consider new possibilities for broadcasting is the dial-a-program television system developed by Rediffusion, the largest of the relay companies. Rediffusion has the system working on an experimental basis in Dennisport, a small town on Cape Cod in Massachusetts. That the system, which has had wide publicity in the British press, has had to be demonstrated abroad rather than at home could produce some pressure on the Ministry of Posts (and ultimately Parliament) to relax the present restrictions on television broadcasting.

The dial-a-program system is based on the kind of wire that Rediffusion uses in its British relay services. The wires reach straight from a central exchange to ordinary television sets. When the subscriber comes to replace his receiver or to buy an extra one, he may choose a simpler and cheaper set designed for use only with the dial-a-program system and unable to receive television through the air.

To some critics, the Rediffusion method is primitive because it does not use a coaxial cable. The British Post Office is not an enthusiast, and its planners claim that the kind of communications cable that the Post Office has installed through and around the new town of Washington in County Durham is technically superior. But the Rediffusion management argue that the simplicity of their wired system is a virtue and that, moreover, it can offer at the present time the wide variety of services – dozens of television programs, access to computers, libraries and shops as well as two-way transmission – that most American CATV companies can only dream of. They even claim that their methods ultimately could provide a switched picture telephone network, and go beyond that to combine the national telephone and television networks in single sets of wires. No small order; it would mean the re-wiring of the whole country – but those at Rediffusion consider that the electricity networks have been through similar replacement cycles in their history, that a major national re-wiring is inevitable, and that the decision to be made merely concerns what kind of wire it is to be.

The superiority of one multichannel system over another will be the subject of debate in the years ahead, but the Rediffusion system has attracted attention because it is British and it is ready. These facts alone will inevitably bear on the national debate on broadcasting that is on the way.

The dial-a-program system provides each television set with a dial similar to a telephone dial and several push buttons. At the other end of the wires is a program exchange. The viewer dials a code which tells the exchange what he wishes to see on his television screen. When he wants to change channels, the viewer presses a button, canceling his previous instruction, and on his screen there automatically pops up a listing of the codes needed to obtain other programs offered by the exchange. At its present stage of development, dial-a-program allows thirty-six choices of channel, all of them with clear reception. More could be added without rewiring.

Rediffusion has visions (and brochures to advertise them) of turning dial-a-program into a video network covering an entire city and eventually a number of cities. The subscriber with his dial need not be limited to the contents of his local program exchange. One exchange can be connected to others and could have links to many of the sources of information that a subscriber might wish to see displayed on his screen – banks, supermarkets, libraries, airline and theater reservation bureaus. The program exchange in the Rediffusion system can have on tap a stock of television cassettes into which the viewer can dial by dialing the right code. But none of this can be offered in Britain unless there is a radical relaxation of the restrictions on broadcasting. Rediffusion's chief engineer, R. P. Gabriel, complained about the sorry contrast between wired television's prospects in Britain and in the United States in a speech to the Relay Services Association in 1969:

The broadcasting signals we may carry are strictly regulated, program origination is absolutely prohibited and common carrier services are unheard of. Now you see why the Pilgrim Fathers had to leave this place. We [the relay companies] are not even allowed to distribute the programs from the Irish Broadcasting Authority in parts of the country where we can obtain good reception and have a large number of Irishmen among our subscribers.

Obstacles to Origination

If relay companies offered their subscribers a wider variety of television fare than was available over the air, a fundamental principle of British television would be violated – that what is available for one section of the population should be available to all. Belief in this principle runs very deep and is related to the fact that the major share of the expense of broadcasting is borne by the public in the form of license fees. All pay the same. All should receive the same. Or as Charles Curran, director general of the BBC, put it, 'So far, there has been general assent on the proposition that broadcasting financed by the public should serve all the public.' It would not be fair, according to this argument, for people in London to have a choice of forty channels while those in Scotland have only three, or in places where they cannot receive UHF, only two.

The principle of equality has been breached, of course, in a small way with the pay television experiment and on a large scale by local radio. BBC radio is subsidized by the license fee, but by no means all of the population is within reach of a BBC local station and there has been little objection from the public. Yet it is television, not radio, which accounts for the size of the license fee which is a genuine hardship to many people. If some were to get a greater selection of television than others (even if the extra programs were financed by advertisements) the outcry would be fierce.

Moreover, many people in Britain believe – and those at the BBC are absolutely convinced – that a limited national television service creates a valuable sense of national identity. At the BBC, in fact, diversity is a dirty word. It means quantity, the enemy of quality. Curran has become quite ill-tempered when confronted with the suggestion that a wide choice of channels might be desirable for the viewer. A senior civil servant at the Ministry of Posts also sounded incensed at the idea. 'We believe,' he said firmly, 'that it is a logical fallacy to think that the proliferation of channels has anything to do with extending the range of choice.'

Chataway himself clearly understood the shattering of precedent that would be involved if Britain were to permit the relay companies to introduce original programs over their cables and wires. In 1970 he told the Relay Services Association that he himself sympathized with the arguments that television and radio might some day be as free from constraint as writing and publishing are now. He recognized that governments might some day be able to drop their paternalistic attitude toward broadcasting services. But (and it was not what the relay men wanted to hear) not right away:

So long as it is felt that the Government must have a responsibility for answering to Parliament for the use of scarce frequencies and for the use of the wired services that are akin to broadcasting, then there will be great difficulties in allowing the relay services to enlarge choice beyond that provided by the broadcasting authorities ... If we are to move out some time from the present system, it should only be as part of a coherent strategy and not as the result of piecemeal decision or short run considerations.

Whether 'a coherent strategy' for the future of broadcasting in Britain can be decided by 1976 remains to be seen. The time is short, the new technical possibilities confusing, the general lack of understanding about them among members of Parliament is great. Perhaps the BBC and the ITA may relax. There will be no revolution. In any event, there are two other worries which will weigh against multichaneled television whenever it is raised as a serious possibility for Britain. One is that local television, much more than local radio, might undermine national news papers. No one is happy about the high rate of mortality among the great papers, and the rise of local television stations might persuade some subscribers to give up newspapers altogether. Then too, if the local stations were financed by advertisements, they might cut into the sources of support for the national commercial television channel. A more fundamental anxiety rises from a bewilderment about what so very many television channels might be used for.

Yet possibilities are not difficult to imagine. There could be special channels for Scotland and for Wales (perhaps one in Welsh, one in English) and channels in Pakistani. The Open University could have a whole channel to itself; so could schools television. There could be one channel devoted exclusively to the televising of Parliament, thereby eliminating what has in the past been one of the major objections to televising the House of Commons – that if it were live it would encourage MPs to play up to the cameras, and that if it were filmed it would be subject to the editing and cutting hands of the television broadcasters in ways that might not be impartial. If Parliament were accessible by television at any time, then those who wanted to take pot luck could be bored, just as visitors often are, or those who wanted to watch a particular debate could take pains to find out when it was likely to occur.

There could also be local television. It could be in the hands of the local authority, which could put the costs (which should not be exorbitant) of filling its one channel onto the rates. The local authority could show its own council meetings, local news, performances at schools, or simply – failing all else – a flat printed news sheet of information of interest to people within its jurisdiction – whether there was oil on the beach or where the traffic bottlenecks were likely to occur. All these are fairly straightforward uses for extra channels, quite apart from the more exotic television fare that might become available, if there were international programs available at the flick of the dial, or if there were common carrier channels on which the public or groups of artists could buy time.

How?

There are several ways in which multichanneled television might come to Britain. The simplest would be for Parliament to allow the relay companies, temporarily or permanently, to fill their idle channels with programs not available over the air. A more extreme course would have Parliament nationalize the relay companies and put their facilities in the hands of the Post Office, which could then sell television channels on a common-carrier basis and also develop non-television services requiring a communications cable with greater capacity than a telephone wire. A compromise solution might be to allow the BBC and the ITA to be in charge of the additional programs that the relay companies (or the Post Office) were allowed to put out.

The BBC's dread of more channels is ironic, for it could conceivably become the provider of programs to the majority of these extra channels. Now, under its present restrictions of time and money, the BBC is less and less able to engage in risk-taking and experiment. If it had some quiet backwater channels at its disposal, it might regain some of the adventurousness which the 76 Group feels that it is losing. (The money for these programs could come either from the relay companies, who must pay the BBC in order to have special offerings with which to attract new subscribers, or it could come, in the form of Pay TV, from the viewers themselves.)

Since the BBC already earns an increasingly large part of its income from the sale of programs abroad, and has contracted to make the Open University's television programs for it, its future may, in truth, lie in becoming program supplier to the whole world. To people at the BBC, this eventuality would be surrender and defeat; they interpret their responsibilities as the selection and balancing of schedules, as well as the making of individual programs. But this belief may be a sign of how autocratic they are, for eventually the television viewer is going to make his own schedule with his dial. (He does, in a limited way, even now.) Moreover, the BBC must expect to undergo a drastic change in its means of support for it cannot reasonably expect to live on license fees forever.

Eventually, long after 1976, television will be paid for by the month or the quarter, like electricity and telephone service. People will pay for what they take. Yet there will be no reason to abandon the principle of 'free TV', nor of a national television service of high quality. To preserve these will remain a concern of Parliament and one that will not disappear if all of what is called broadcasting is funneled through a pipe. Perhaps the national programs should be the cheapest to the viewer or entirely free of charge. Programs that were expensive to make or to import and of interest only to small audiences would not be on the national channels but elsewhere on the dial and they would cost more, much as long-distance telephone calls do. There could be a Cable Television Authority to protect the national and the public interest.

The danger is that preoccupation with the issues presented by broadcasting will obscure the fact that Britain needs cable television for information distribution, quite apart from television. Yet the Post Office will not cheerfully let Rediffusion or anyone else wire up the country, and all its capital is tied up in the attempt to give Britain by 1980 the telephone service the country should have had in 1960. The Post Office can hardly begin to think about extending broadband communications until that labor is done. It would be surprising if Britain had a broadband network capable of distributing mail electronically by the end of the century.

Yet there is one disaster that must not be allowed to happen. By 1985 the staggering task of shifting television upstairs to the UHF will have been completed. The VHF, the part of the spectrum most useful for mobile communications, will be empty of television at last. The Ministry of Posts is actually considering putting a television channel back on it. That would be like clearing a slum to rebuild a slum. Britain needs not only cable television and broadband communication but mobile radios and portable telephones and the new devices which make communicating easy. For the country to be without them in the year 2000 would be inconsistent with economic health.

Part Four

Telephones

Chapter 11
Telephones in Transition

I

Telephones, invented nearly 100 years ago, are the basic instruments of the new communications technology. Telephones already can be used for spur-of-the-moment intercontinental conversations, and this facility will gradually be extended to include most countries of the world. Within the next decade, moreover, telephones will begin to perform any number of new services, such as taking messages or ordering theater tickets. Eventually they will become the means through which homes and small offices will have access to computers. While in the long run many of the functions of the telephone may be taken over by the television set, telephones will be ready to move into the territory now occupied very inadequately by radio – that of providing mobile, open-air communications. The telephone's future can hardly stop short of the two-way wrist-watch picture telephone which will allow anyone to talk to anyone anywhere or to dip into many of the world's repositories of stored information.

That the potential of the telephone has been so little publicized is not surprising, for even in the present form telephones are an under-used and unappreciated form of communications technology. There are now well over a quarter of a billion telephones in the world, yet even in the United States and Canada, the two countries which are far and away the most addicted to telephoning, the national average number of conversations is less than two per person a day. Even in countries well supplied with telephones there are large groups of the population who could well use the instantaneous two-way exchange of human voices that telephones provide but who are largely deprived of it: the poor, the very young, the travelers. The extent, moreover, to which quite sophisticated people remain telephone-shy is remarkable. There are any number of tourists who have flown to the far corners of the earth who would not dream of making an international telephone call. Such inhibitions make poor use of the world's telephone networks which are (although few notice) technical miracles. The networks can make millions out of billions of possible connections among telephones thousands of miles apart in a matter of seconds. And they can just as swiftly unmake them and make millions of new paths in quite different directions. On a Monday morning in winter in the eastern United States there may be 30 million people using the telephone network at any given moment.

Telephones are important to the future of communications, not only because of their potential, but also because they already provide the bulk of the world's communications business, and the world's communications networks are planned on the basis of telephony. Telegraph and telex traffic travel over circuits that are derived from telephone circuits; one telephone circuit can yield as many as twenty-four telegraph or telex connections. It is telephone authorities more than any others who have the power to decide whether things like the electronic delivery of printed material or motorcar radio telephones are going to pass into the hands of the public. And when they make decisions affecting the future, their primary concern is to preserve the integrity and smooth-working (such as it may be) of their existing telephone system.

Right now these authorities, whether privately owned, such as AT&T in the United States, or publicly owned, such as the British Post Office, are under enormous strain. (See Chapters 12 and 13.) The number of telephones and the size of the network under their command is doubling every ten years, or faster. The demand for the interconnection of computers by telephone lines is growing even faster – from 30 to 150 percent a year. The men in charge must decide how to expand the present service while introducing the new technology and new services. They must stand still and move forward, and the penalty for failing to do either is an enraged public. In Britain and the United States there is unprecedented criticism about the way in which the telephone systems (and to some extent the computer connections) are performing. The ultimate threat is very real. AT&T and even the British Post Office could lose their historic monopolies.

More Telephones for All

The search for better telephone service is virtually universal. What makes it difficult is that telephone equipment – the subscriber's apparatus, the central exchange machinery and the transmission lines – is expensive and not quickly produced. Only a handful of countries (chiefly the United States, Britain, Canada, Sweden, Japan and West Germany) have communications manufacturing industries of a size which can serve the home market and export great quantities as well. Much of the world is dependent either on exports from these countries or on licenses from them to manufacture their equipment locally. The competitions among these suppliers (which also include the New York-based international conglomerate, International Telephone and Telegraph Corporation, ITT) is fierce. For once telephone authorities in a country have committed themselves to a certain supplier, they must buy equipment in great quantities and they cannot change brands in a hurry.

One of the reasons that much of the world's telephone service is so poor is that there are too many varieties of equipment working together. Insufficient standardization is largely responsible for making the French telephone system so unreliable and it contributes to the legendary troubles of places such as Brazil. (In Brazil, the service is so bad that boys are hired to sit holding clusters of receivers to their ears, ready to signal if a dial tone appears.)

But the picture is brightening. AT&T reported in its 1970 volume, *The World's Telephones* (one of the world's most readable collections of statistics) that the total numbers of telephones rose from 134,600,000 in 1960 to 255,200,000 in 1970. The greatest increase was seen in Asia which, over the decade, went from 9 million to 31 million telephones, largely because Japan increased its telephones nearly fourfold during that time. But Western Europe too showed impressive growth, faster than that of North America, which began the decade (and the century, for that matter) better supplied with telephones. In Europe, Spain went from 1.6 million telephones in 1960 to 4 million in 1970; Greece from 190,000 to 881,000. Almost all the other European countries, including Poland, Czechoslovakia and Yugoslavia, doubled their numbers of telephones in service.

With so much new equipment going in every year, the world's telephone services are rapidly becoming entirely automatic. Less developed countries can join telephony technology at the eleventh hour; they can begin with automatic flexible telephone systems, while countries with older telephone systems must phase out the old-fashioned switchboards and manual telephone operators gradually. Already about 95 percent of the world's telephones can obtain a dial tone without the aid of an operator. Some day international dialing will be just as automatic.

The progress of international self-service by telephone customers is well under way. Since 1952 it has been possible between the United States and Canada. In the 1960s, subscribers in various Western European countries began to dial across their borders and in 1970 the first automatic transatlantic dialing began. Before all the world's telephones can be interconnected, a number of difficulties must be overcome, of which the greatest has been the dissimilarity of telephone numbering arrangements around the world.

The ITU has been hard at work since 1961 to draw up world plans for automatic telephony. It has determined the routes along which traffic will flow and has examined the technical and financial problems involved. Its most important contribution has been the preparation of a world-wide telephone numbering plan, which will accommodate the world's telephones until the year 2000.

A world telephone number will have between thirteen and nineteen digits. Anyone wishing to make an intercontinental telephone call will first dial two or three digits to be connected to his own country's international telephone exchange. Then he will dial one, two or three digits to be connected to the particular country he seeks. The remaining eight to ten digits will take him to the trunk number within the country and then to the particular telephone that he is calling.

As part of this plan, the world has been divided into nine large geographical zones, each with its own telephone number. These are:

1 – North America (except Mexico)
2 – Africa
3 & 4 – Europe
5 – South America, Mexico and the Caribbean

6 – South Pacific
7 – Soviet Union
8 – Far East
9 – Middle East and Southeast Asia

The relationship between poor communications and political isolation has not been sufficiently appreciated. South Africa and Portugal had inadequate radio links to the rest of the world until new submarine cables were completed, giving them telephone circuits of good quality twenty-four hours a day. One of the first signs of the willingness of the People's Republic of China to revive its contacts with the West was the re-opening in 1971 of the international telephone service suspended in 1948. The number and quality of telephone connections between Eastern and Western Europe is increasing, and automatic dialing across borders will inevitably follow. (Think what direct dialing in and out of Czechoslovakia would have meant in the spring of 1968.) It may be that international telephoning will be more effective than satellite broadcasting in creating a sense of world community.

In practice, it will always be possible for any country to sever its telephone connections with the outside world, no matter how much automatic international dialing there is, for all international calls must flow through certain national points called gateway exchanges. But to block the lines would be a serious disruption of the international telephone traffic patterns, which will, on an increasingly automatic basis, flow through one country or another according to the ITU's plans for routing traffic under varying conditions. The more international traffic there is, the more reluctant must be any government to put roadblocks in its way, and the greater the freedom therefore its inhabitants must be considered to have gained when it arranges to allow automatic international dialing.

Even if telephones were to be used only for talking, their future growth would seem to be irrepressible. Millions of people still are waiting for their first telephone; everybody who has one will tend to talk more often for longer periods over greater distances. The only natural limit to the use of the telephone may be the human inclination to sleep seven or eight hours a day. When it is eight o'clock in the morning in Europe, it is five o'clock in the evening in Sydney, Australia. All telephone traffic between

Europe and Australia seems destined to be crowded into the few hours of the day that are convenient on both ends of the line.

II

But telephones are going to change their function. More and more, they will transmit electronic information to computers as well as voices to human ears. To do this, they must have push buttons, not rotary dials, and if they are to display pictures and print, they must have small screens. Of the two, the push buttons are perhaps the most important.

Push-button telephones are already in widespread use in North American and Swedish public telephone systems and in a great many other places in the kind of private automatic telephone systems that large companies use. Their superiority over a rotary telephone dial is obvious to anyone who has tried both. Pushing a dial round and round suddenly seems exhausting, and the wait for the dial to return to position interminable. Push buttons can feed a telephone number into a telephone exchange much more quickly than a rotary dial can; in addition, by getting the number out of the dialer's head more quickly, before he forgets it, they produce fewer wrong numbers.

The order and arrangement of the buttons have exercised the imaginations of the ITU's telephone committee (the CCITT) considerably. Some had argued that the numbers should rise from bottom to top, as they do on most adding machines, so that office workers could have manipulated the telephone buttons with the same fingering that they had learned for calculating machines. But the view which finally prevailed put the buttons in reading order. There are four rows of three buttons each, with the numbers proceeding horizontally from left to right. The bottom row has a zero in the center, and the question of what to do with the two extras – called utility buttons – remains to be decided. Most probably they will be used to convey the end of one series of digits or a change from one set of figures to another or perhaps a currency symbol.

The effect of these changes will be to turn the telephone into a numerical typewriter, a typewriter connected to a telephone line. The buttons will not only feed telephone numbers into the telephone exchange but other kinds of numerical codes through the exchange and beyond to computers at banks or shops or booking offices. Then it will be a swift matter to use the telephone for banking, shopping or making reservations of various kinds.

In the near future the kind of telephone services that children imagine are possible will at last be available. There will be three-way telephone conversations. If a call is made and the line is busy, the telephone will automatically try the number again. Only very short telephone numbers will be needed for places frequently called: to ring home from the office will require one or two numbers, not seven. One will be able, while talking on the phone, to receive a signal that another call is waiting, to interrupt the conversation, answer the second call (without changing to another receiver), and then resume the original conversation. It will also be possible to arrange for the automatic transfer of calls to another number simply by dialing the right codes into the telephone exchange. A doctor going over to the neighbors' house for a drink will not bother to alert his answering service. The exchange will become, in fact, everybody's answering service.

The office switchboard operator, one of the major obstacles in the flow of the world's communications, will disappear (or at least do double duty as a receptionist and flower-arranger) as internal switchboards become automatic and calls from the public telephone network find their way automatically to the desk of the person for whom they are intended. Dialing outward directly without the assistance of an operator would be too prosaic a convenience to be mentioned here, were it not that too many offices, those in Britain in particular, do not enjoy very much of it yet. Anyone who thinks that technology is moving too fast should contemplate the lack of these services that were technically possible years ago.

Pictures Too

If any single piece of the new communications technology has been advertised in advance, it is the picture telephone, yet there is little sign of any demand for it at all. Telephone manufacturers trot out a picture telephone whenever a world-of-tomorrow exhibit is called for, and in the United States AT&T not only has put them into service but expects to have installed one million by 1980. Perhaps the demand will materialize but the picture telephone's future is bound to that of cable television and broadband communications. If one flourishes, the other may not.

An AT&T picture telepone was a curiosity at the New York World's Fair in 1963–64. It was the subject of an experiment among branches of the Westinghouse Corporation in the late 1960s, and AT&T led the world in introducing picture telephones into commercial service in 1970. Ten of them were installed in the White House in 1960, but none in the President's office.

The disadvantages of picture telephones are formidable. They consume as much bandwidth as several hundred telephone calls, a fact that must be reflected in the price of the service for a long time to come. At its outset, picture telephone service costs $100 a month, just for the basic rental of the set. Another disadvantage is that the quality of the transmitted picture is less sharply defined than that of television ; the public may be willing to accept this, and again it may not. The third is that the picture telephone is even more inhibiting than an ordinary telephone, and may be underused, once it is installed.

Picture telephones are unlikely to be used for anything but business communication for a very long time. The price will be a formidable deterrent unless a much simpler system, along the lines of that designed by the Radio Corporation of America, in which pictures can be sent over an ordinary telephone connection as long as the speaker stops talking, comes into use. In any event, picture telephones will probably have to perform some kind of photo-copying service, in which a chart or a diagram displayed on the telephone screen can be reproduced on sensitized paper, before it is in any widespread demand. Conceivably, by the end of the century a call by picture telephone will be no more expensive than an ordinary voice-only call. Price reductions will depend on the introduction of millimeter waveguides carrying a quarter of a million telephone circuits and also on advances in solid state technology to make the apparatus (which is really a kind of small television camera) become lighter and more able to perform under varying conditions of lighting and distance. Its long-term future, if it is not deprived of one by the emergence of the multi-purpose television set, is probably in the graphic display of print-out from computers. One could dial up the inventory of the contents of a warehouse or the flight arrival news from an airport. Its social uses, however – showing off the baby or showing the doctor what the spots look like – must not be dismissed.

Strowger's Invention

The telephone exchange is the heart of the telephone system. It is the place where incoming calls are accepted and sent along their way to their destination. The actual process of accepting and routing is called switching. It may be repeated many times if a call is traveling a long distance: the call goes, like a car on a journey, from a local road to trunk roads and then finally back to a local road again, stopping at a particular building. If too many calls come into an exchange, they cause congestion and the dialer fails to get a dial tone or gets a busy signal before he has finished dialing. This annoyance is increasingly common as the world telephone networks struggle to cope with rising traffic. Yet telephone exchanges cannot be designed to cope with all conceivable peaks of traffic. That would be as inefficient as to design roads capable of carrying all the cars in a country at the same time.

The biggest obstacle to better communications in the world is the antiquated telephone exchange equipment used in 90 percent of the world's systems. It is old but it is still working. Telephone exchanges are the most costly part of a telephone system and the longest-lasting. Telephone authorities are reluctant to scrap technically obsolescent equipment while there is still some life in it and they are also loath to change basic systems too frequently.

If telephony were a new invention, starting out now from scratch, telephone exchanges would be a form of computer. Any computer could get in touch with any other computer in the system simply by reading the code fed in by the telephone number. Instructions about how to deal with carrying patterns of telephone traffic could be contained in the computer's memory. So could all the information on providing special services for customers and even some disservices: computers could automatically disconnect a telephone if the bill were not paid and automatically connect it again when the debt was cleared. Telephone exchanges are, even in their old-fashioned form, a mechanism for storing and transferring information. Computers could combine the whole operation in a single box or row of boxes. They will do so eventually; it is only a matter of time.

And it could be a long time. What the world's telephone systems will depend on for the next decade or two is the automatic telephone exchange, which is a modified version of that invented in Kansas City in 1889 by an undertaker named Almon B. Strowger. Strowger distrusted the local human telephone operators, for he suspected that they were giving telephone calls intended for him to his rivals. So he invented a device to eliminate the operators; he called it a girlless, cussless telephone. (Even so, women's liberation from the menial, tedious job of telephone operator is not yet complete.)

Strowger's automatic exchange takes the electrical connections to all the telephones served by a particular exchange and gathers them into banks of one or two hundred. These banks are curved, in ten rows of ten, around the inside of a cylinder. When someone dials a seven-digit telephone number, the first three numbers usually select the particular local exchange that is being called, and the next four numbers select the particular block of one hundred and send a mechanical arm counting step by step up the cylinder until it finds the right horizontal path, and then in along the row until it reaches the contact which is attached to the telephone of a particular subscriber. An electrical contact is made and then (with any luck) the telephone rings.

The important thing to remember about Strowger switching is that it works step by step. It is slow. There are lots of moving parts which get dusty; the dust introduces noise; maintenance men must go along and clean them. There is nothing wrong with Strowger switching. It is interesting for schoolchildren to see on visits to the telephone exchange, and it will serve many of the world's telephones for the rest of the century. But the switchings are inefficient and they do not store information. As the volume and variety of communications traffic rises, Strowger becomes more and more of an economic drain on the system. The faster that a telephone exchange can connect two parties, the quicker the billing starts, and the more calls that can be made through it, the more money the telephone authority can recover from its enormous investment in the exchange equipment.

Then Came Crossbar

After World War II, the search was on for a faster, cleaner form of telephone switching. In the United States and in Sweden, well before the war, a much lighter and more compact switch called a crossbar had been developed. The contacts are in the open air, but they do not gather as much dust as Strowger switches and are capable of much more flexible operation. The failure of Britain to follow the American and Swedish lead into crossbar switching is the main reason for the sad state of the British telephone system today (see Chapter 12). In the United States, more than 50 percent of telephone exchanges use crossbar. In Japan and in Sweden the proportion is even higher. In Britain, however, more than 90 percent of the exchanges still depend on step-by-step switching, with all the concomitant disadvantages.

Since crossbar, exchange technology has been moving slowly toward all-electronic telephone exchanges that perform like computers. One development has been semi-electronic exchange based on a device called a reed relay, in which two hairlike metal reeds are sealed in nitrogen in a glass ampule. Because the reeds are so tiny, the time required to draw them together and to make the electrical contact is infinitesimal, and the telephone at the receiving end rings as soon as the caller has fed in the last digit. In general, only telephone exchanges built on some form of semi-electronic switching can offer the kind of customer services discussed earlier.

Eventually telephone exchanges will become all-electronic – that is, they will work entirely with solid-state devices and not require even the tiny kind of open-and-shut mechanical operation that occurs in relays. Eventually, too, office switchboards will disappear and their functions taken over by company computers. Before that day, computers will come to work more and more as traffic directors for more conventional exchanges, and there is some hope that their intelligence may be coupled even to Strowger to force the plodding old machines to do new tricks.

III

Computers may be the salvation of the telephone networks, but they are also a threat. The greatest new source of traffic along the telephone lines is data transmission, the stream of electronic information sent from one computer to another. The difficulty is that the world's telephone lines were not designed to carry the digital codes that computers use. They have been made to carry electrical reproductions (or analogues) of the human voice, and the work of many years has gone into making the lines carry voices as efficiently as possible. Yet what is efficient for voice is in many ways unsuitable for computers. The kind of noise produced by Strowger switching can introduce actual errors into data transmission, for a far greater degree of clarity is needed to distinguish the difference between an electrical pulse and the absence of a pulse than to distinguish spoken sounds.

Analogue transmission not only introduces errors, it works too slowly for computers. The fastest data transmission service that the British Post Office carries is 48,000 bits of information a second. Such speed is absurd for the kind of computer that can disgorge and absorb information at a rate of 1.5 million bits a second. What makes the process even slower is that computer signals have to be translated into an analogue before they enter the telephone network and then translated back into digital codes when they come out. They do this by passing through a device called a modem (a short name for modulator demodulator) which is as good a symbol as any for the subordination of the new to the old in communications.

In the beginning, the telephone networks were the only available means for computers to connect with each other. But now, with data traffic growing five times as fast as voice traffic, and the number of computers doubling and trebling every year, a sensible solution might be to allow some other form of network to be used for computers. The telephone authorities, by and large, will fight to the death to see that these new networks are controlled by themselves. In the United States, AT&T has promised an all-digital network by 1975, and the British Post Office hopes to have its own ready by about the same time.

But will these networks be fast enough? Could new private companies serve the special needs of special customers better? These are questions which must be answered in the next few years for the rise in data traffic can make a national telephone service deteriorate, since computers tie up large numbers of lines, and they do not talk for three minutes, they talk for hours.

The conflict between analogue and digital is only temporary, however. There is no question but that eventually all the world's communications will wash back and forth in digital codes and that every country will, in a sense that is both practical and profound, share a common language.

Chapter 12
Life with Strowger

Imagine a restaurant. Imagine that all the tables are filled and that there is a queue outside waiting to get in. Yet those who have been served are picking at their food and some leave it practically untouched. Imagine then a restaurant manager who explains, 'It's something in their national character. They just don't like eating.'

The British Post Office, neither in its old form as a department of state nor in its new form as a public corporation, can understand why so many people want telephones and then use them so rarely when they get them. The Post Office is now embarked on an enormous five-year program to spend £2,700 million on repairing the deficiencies in the British telephone system caused by underinvestment of the past three decades. It is trying to satisfy the pent-up hunger for telephones, which expresses itself in a waiting list that remains at around 100,000 however many new telephones are installed. Yet the Post Office has no confidence that the expanded ranks of telephone subscribers will be any more avid users than those of the past.

Britain's consistently sluggish performance in the world's telephoning league is a constant embarrassment to the Post Office. There are approximately 17 million telephones in Britain, twenty-five for each one hundred people, and yet the national average of telephone conversations a year for each person, taking business and residential use together, is only 174. The British use the telephone less than the people in ten other countries, as the facing table shows.

This under-use makes the Post Office ambivalent to the point of hostility toward the residential telephone subscriber. To install a new instrument in a home or flat which has not had a telephone before costs the Post Office £170, of which a maximum of £25 is paid by the subscriber. And then the telephone sits, hardly touched. Reginald Bevins, who was Postmaster General from 1959 to 1964, has said:

Our customers just don't use the damn thing ... Many thousands of people who would never dream of using a refrigerator as an ornament seem to look on the telephone as one. Why? I don't know.

By 1970, an Act of Parliament had turned the Post Office into a corporation which was supposed to be businesslike and competitive in its approach to industry and to customers. Yet Lord Hall, the first chairman of the corporation, had absorbed his successors' prejudices about the telephone subscriber. He said in September 1970, just before he was forced to resign:

People in Britain look on the telephone as a status symbol. If they can't afford a car, they get a telephone and put it in the window where the neighbors can see it. For some, to be on the waiting list is in itself a status symbol. When their name gets near the top, they take it off.

The heavy telephoners

Country	Telephones per 100 people	Average number of conversations per person during 1969
United States	56	745
Sweden	54	649
Switzerland	45	337
New Zealand	44	*
Canada	44	710
Denmark	32	369
Australia	30	216
Norway	28	220
Britain	25	174
Netherlands	24	196
Finland	23	*
Japan	22	336
West Germany	20	150
Belgium	20	124
Austria	18	*
France	16	*
Italy	16	180
World	7	95

Source: The World's Telephones, AT&T, 1971.
* information not available.

This persistent inability to appreciate why the ordinary user does not pick up his telephone more often is an ill omen for the future. It suggests that the Post Office will not vigorously introduce the new conveniences that are of far more interest to the residential, rather than the business, user. Shopping and banking by telephone, for example, will offer the greatest advantage to those who do both in small amounts. But the Post Office historically has had many more subscribers from the business rather than the residential sector of the population (just the reverse of the ratio in Sweden, Canada and the United States), and it has grown accustomed to looking to the commercial world for its main financial support and tolerating the residential customer as a social burden.

The Post Office has not, in fact, done what it might to stimulate use of the telephone. It has done very little, for example, to discourage the national prejudice that the written letter is a form of communication superior to the telephone call. Even though the Post Office has for years lost money on its postal services and reaped substantial profits from its telecommunications business, it has not deliberately used its pricing powers to shift communications traffic from letters to phones. (The long postal strike of 1971 performed a great service for the Post Office in this respect.)

Neither has the Post Office done what it could to lift the widely held prejudice that the poor do not need the telephone. It has never fought with local authorities to install telephones in the millions of homes built with public money since the war. Only about 10 percent of the people who are considered working class are telephone subscribers. No wonder they put the telephone in the window when they have one; there are too few people whom they can ring up.

Even for the residential telephone users who are better off, there is too little that can be accomplished with the telephone. Shop assistants become confused when an order is telephoned, and sometimes ask for it to be confirmed in writing. Doctors will exchange next to no information on the telephone. It is still extraordinarily difficult to make a telephone call on the spur of the moment, away from home or office. To be sure, the problems of keeping telephone kiosks in working order is severe – and not confined to Britain. But these do not explain the scarcity of public telephones in places like public houses, schools, shops and restaurants where the potential telephone users are and the vandals are not. Nor does it explain the Post Office's reluctance to adopt the types of vandal-proof boxes that designers have offered it.

The reason why the British do not use the telephone more, in short, is because the whole procedure of telephoning is too difficult. The fact that the service is bad (an investigation in 1969 by *Which*, the magazine of the Consumers' Association, shows one out of four subscriber-dialed trunk calls made from London went wrong) is secondary.

What is worrying is that the quaint telephone phobia of the past may be passed on to future generations. The Post Office's plans for the years ahead, for example, are alarming in their modesty. The corporation hopes that by 1980 two homes out of three will have telephones. That is a level of telephone penetration reached by Canada and Sweden in 1960. The Post Office has declined to follow the lead of the United States and West Germany in allowing subscribers to choose and buy their own telephone equipment or other kinds of communications devices that can use the telephone lines. Its policies have discouraged the introduction of automatic switchboards and direct inward dialing, and radio telephones as well. And it has no clear policy for extending telephone service to the poor. In October 1969 John Stonehouse, then the Minister of Posts and Telegraphs, said that the Post Office was working on a plan to sell local authorities the idea of a cheap telephone link to every council house. Yet after a much publicized project in Washington, a new town in County Durham, little more was heard about the plan. The danger in all this is that by the mid-1980s the countries with which Britain compares itself will have turned the telephone system into an information network while the Post Office's idea of 'telephone services' will still be Dial-a-Disc and the Speaking Clock.

The Post Office admittedly is in an unenviable plight. The enormous, almost absurd, rise in demand for new telephones – lately about 40 percent a year – comes at a time of rapid technological change. The pent-up demand cannot be held back any longer, yet the Post Office is committed to paying for half of the cost of expanding the telephone service from the revenues derived from it. The other half must come from the Treasury; the Post Office has not been allowed to borrow capital from the private money market. Worse still, the British manufacturers of telephones and telephone exchanges cannot keep up with the new orders.

Chained to Strowger

If there is one bit of AT&T's Bell system that the Post Office covets to the point of lust, it is not Bell Labs but rather Western Electric, the wholly owned subsidiary of AT&T whose only aim in life is to turn out equipment as fast as the company wants it. The Post Office would like to have its own captive supplier. It has, under the 1970 Post Office Act, the right to do a good bit of manufacturing itself; whether it should try to do so is politically controversial. The Labor Party is inclined to want the Post Office to become more self-sufficient, while the Conservatives would prefer it to lean more heavily on private industry.

Lacking a Western Electric, however, the Post Office as long as fifty years ago tried to create for itself the next best thing. It entered into a relationship with certain British manufacturers of telephone equipment, which has become a loveless marriage providing, for both parties, security without satisfaction. Even when, as part of its metamorphosis into a corporation, the Post Office was encouraged to break loose and find new suppliers, it has been extremely slow to do so. Yet the Post Office has grown more and more shrill in blaming 'the persistent inability of manufacturers to meet orders on time' for the conspicuous faults of the telephone service. The implication is: if the industry cannot do its job properly, why should anyone blame the Post Office? The industry has its own bitter answer. The Post Office's belated decision to plunge into a heavy program of expansion, after years of stagnation, has forced the industry into a hurried expansion of capacity to meet the Post Office's orders for equipment that happens to be unattractive to foreign buyers and consequently has ruined the industry's export performance.

The history of this unhealthy partnership goes back to the early 1920s, when the General Post Office, as it then was, decided to make a version of the Strowger step-by-step switch standard throughout its exchanges. Because the Post Office needed great quantities of Strowger and because it needed the assurance of steady supplies, it gave the five largest manufacturers of telephone equipment – who had been competitors – the exclusive right to make equipment for the Post Office. No one else needed to apply; neither did the five need to exert much imagination. They shared contracts among themselves, according to an agreed formula, and everything that they turned out followed the specifications of the Post Office. No matter from which company it emerged, the equipment all looked the same, down to the last nut and bolt and color of the paint.

The group was cozily known as the Ring. It included the companies which have become, through various board-room convulsions, the three major suppliers to the Post Office today: Plessey Ltd, General Electric Company-Associated Electrical Industries, and Standard Telephone and Cables. STC, the smallest, is owned by the International Telephone and Telegraph Corporation, but it has retained, so far, its separate personality. The Ring supplied all kinds of telephone equipment to the Post Office, including the telephones themselves, but there was no doubt that the Strowger switches that worked telephone exchanges were the most lucrative part of the business. The Ring were also the suppliers to the telecommunications authorities of what was then the British Empire, who had followed the lead set by the GPO and established Strowger, made in Britain, as the basis for their national telephone systems. Until the war, Britain led the world in exports of telecommunications.

The Ring did provide a secure source of supply to the Post Office, but it also encouraged complacency and discouraged innovation. New ideas were of little use to an industry that had no hope of interesting its biggest customer. As a matter of fact, one of the Ring, Automatic Telephone and Electric (since absorbed by Plessey), did invent a variety of crossbar switch, similar to that which the American and Swedish telephone authorities had begun to develop as a faster, cleaner, more flexible replacement for Strowger exchanges. But AT&E did not turn the invention into something it could sell; it simply put it on the shelf.

After the war, when it was clear that the British telephone system needed to be modernized and made larger, an official from the Post Office went off to Sweden to inspect the crossbar switch. He was converted by what he saw and came home to announce: 'We must have it. It does everything!' But they decided not to have it. Neither the industry nor the Post Office was willing to embark on the drastic retooling and upheaval that a fundamental change in switching technology would have meant. They jointly agreed not to develop crossbar. The Ring preferred to go on supplying both home and overseas markets with Strowger equipment. One man who sat in on the deliberations of that time remembers a manufacturer saying triumphantly, 'I've just thought of another reason for selling Strowger to Latin America!'

This disastrous mistake made after the war is to blame, as much as any one thing can be, for the crossed lines, static and dead silences now encountered in the British telephone service. Its effects were compounded by later errors of judgment, but there is no doubt that the Post Office's rejection of crossbar, when the rest of the world's sophisticated telephone systems were adopting it, was one of the classic wrong decisions in telecommunications.

Even to expand at home with Strowger, however, required money. The Post Office did not get it. Telecommunications traditionally ranks very low among nationalized industries and other claims on the public purse. (This is equally true in developing countries, where politicians tend to prefer to spend development funds provided them by the United Nations or the World Bank for roads, electrical power, agricultural improvements or schools rather than on improved communications.) The Post Office pleaded with the Treasury for funds but to little avail. Between 1950 and 1960 the number of telephones in Britain increased from 5·4 million to 8·3 million, but the modernization of exchanges did not keep pace.

Then came the Post Office's next error, so foolish as to be barely credible. Having missed out on the chance to switch to crossbar, it decided to make up lost time by skipping not only crossbar but the next stage of development, the semi-electronic exchanges. It decided to design a telephone exchange that would be all-electronic, that would be, for practical purposes, a huge specialized computer built just to handle telephone signals. The idea was a bold one and, like many bold ideas, ahead of its time. The all-electronic exchange that was built was based on valves, not transistors. To get the signals in and out of the valves turned out to be much slower (and therefore costlier) than the engineers from the Post Office and industry had estimated. The folly was that during the five years that it took to find this out, the Post Office had developed no other exchange as insurance against the risk of failure. And failure there was. The much heralded Highgate Wood all-electronic exchange opened and closed on the same day in December 1962. It was an electronic white elephant which left the Post Office facing the 1960s with nothing but slow, dusty, old-fashioned Strowger exchanges to handle its growing flood of telephone calls.

The story is sadder still. Together, the manufacturers and the Post Office decided to reinvent the wheel. They embarked on a program to develop their very own version of the kind of semi-electronic exchange that AT&T was already putting into operation in the United States. That program too – labeled TXE (for telephone exchange electronic) – was less than a spectacular success. Out of six projected versions of the TXE, on which £25 million was spent, four were canceled. Of the two TXEs which survived to go into production (which means that the manufacturers make more than one) neither is as cheap as crossbar; neither is of much interest to buyers abroad. As the version called TXE-2 deals with only 2,000 telephone lines, it is too small to work as an exchange in most big cities. The larger exchange, the TXE-4, has 10,000 lines but has proved stubbornly expensive to run in its development stage. Nonetheless, in late 1971 the Post Office committed itself to putting a number of TXE-4s into service to help with the modernization of the network in the late 1970s. What the TXE-4 lacked in versatility, the Post Office believed, it compensated in its ability to work with Strowger.

The irony is that these two expensive new creations, the TXE2 and TXE4, cannot work with digital signals. In other words, they cannot work directly with the new pulse code modulation lines, which the Post Office is ordering in increasing numbers, a fact that is one of their proudest boasts. (PCM, as described on page 29, is a digital technique for sandwiching a great number of telephone calls on the same line.) The result is two separate streams of press releases emanating from the Post Office: one boasting that Britain leads the world in electronic exchanges, the other that it is far ahead of most other countries in its installation of PCM. Little is said about the fact that the TXEs and PCM do not work together, that the new roads, the PCM, produce a kind of traffic that the new roundabouts, the TXEs, cannot handle in their present form. And there has been little publicity for the fact that the Post Office is quietly installing crossbar exchanges at the same rate as its much publicized semi-electronic exchanges.

This succession of errors had a disastrous effect on British exports of telecommunications equipment. By the early sixties, telephone authorities overseas lost their awe of the GPO. They too were interested in fast expansion, but they wanted to buy crossbar.

One by one the old markets were lost to Britain. Nigeria went to Canada, Australia to Sweden, Ceylon to Japan. Britain was passed and then left behind by Sweden with Ericsson equipment, and West Germany with that of Siemens, the huge electronics and engineering company based in Munich. And the new markets in Latin America, which Britain might have won, also went to Ericsson, Siemens, ITT and the Dutch-owned Philips company.

Breaking the Ring

The Post Office's major mistakes escaped much public notice because they involved technical details of which people know little and care less. But they were not unnoticed at a higher level and were among the reasons for the transformation of the Post Office into a public corporation. The new Post Office was expected to act more ruthlessly in seeking new equipment. It was to shop around to find the best designs, prices and dates of delivery. One by one the old bulk-supply agreements with the Ring were terminated. On contracts for the all-important exchange equipment, the big three suppliers were still to have a favored position: they were guaranteed 50 percent of the Post Office's orders, to be divided among themselves according to a formula: Plessey and GEC-AEI were to have two-fifths each of the orders and STC one-fifth. For the rest, the Post Office was free, free, free; it could even buy abroad. To import in many ways seemed the logical way out of the dilemma, as the Brookings Institution of Washington recommended when it surveyed Britain's economic prospects in 1967. Otherwise, the Brookings report said, British industry will be forced to expand its capacity to produce Strowger, which not only is of no interest to export but which the Post Office will not need in a decade's time, and the industry will be left with useless production capacity. That is exactly what has been happening.

But like a bird which will not leave the cage when the door is opened, the Post Office did not want to be liberated. It decided not to buy what it needed most – small electronic exchanges from competitors of the big three – until a year and a half after it was free to do so. Worse still, it decided not to buy large semi-electronic exchanges, such as the TXE-4, competitively until after 1974. Such timidity drew a stern rebuke from the Committee on Public Accounts, which has been muttering for years about the wastefulness of the Post Office's TXE program. But the Post Office defended itself by saying that it 'recognized the contribution which the firms in the group had made to electronic development and considered they should be guaranteed continuity of production for a limited period to reap the benefit of their investment'.

In other words, the modernization of the telephone system is being delayed because the Post Office feels guilty at having led its old suppliers into one dead end after another. Yet the suppliers themselves do not deserve a lot of sympathy. Their performance has been lamentable. By 1970 the average contract was running eight months behind schedule, and the newer the type of equipment, the greater the delay. The absurdity goes further. While the Post Office has been unwilling to buy modern exchange equipment from outside the old Ring, it has not hesitated to buy the old-fashioned Strowger from outsiders. It is buying and installing Strowger – which has a lifetime of twenty-five to thirty years – in enormous quantities and will be doing so at least until 1980. Thus, caught between the new technology and the old, the Post Office has decided that it has no alternative but to expand with the old. It is pouring unprecedented capital into outmoded equipment that could condemn the British telephone system for many years to come to the slowness and inefficiencies of the past. In the words of one of the manufacturers who is supplying this outmoded equipment, 'It is really very depressing.'

Where Are the Buttons?

Saddled with Strowger, the Post Office sees no point in putting modern telephones in the hands of the telephone users. It is handing out well over a million new telephone instruments every year; each one has a lifetime of about ten years. Yet all of them have rotary dials, which are about as up to date as legs for bathtubs. The Post Office has its own version of the push-button telephone now in wide use in the United States and even on the Continent, but it keeps it, like its picture telephones, only for exhibitions of the world of tomorrow. For several years the Post Office has deliberated about the best ways of introducing the devices. It also deliberated long and hard to come up with a name – Key-Phone – which did not ape Bell System's Touch-Tone. (Its picture phone, to avoid Bell's 'Picturephone', is called View-Phone.)

Push-button telephones, the essential and basic instrument by which the public can have access to computers, will not be introduced in Britain on even a limited scale until 1973. That means that well into the 1980s the British public will not be able to use the telephone for financial transactions, for the Post Office is unlikely to suggest that they throw away fairly new rotary dial telephones before these are worn out. The Post Office believes that its hesitation over the buttons has been sensible. What is the point of sending streams of electronic pulses into an old-fashioned Strowger telephone exchange which cannot handle them? (The slowness of Strowger is the reason why the rotary telephone dial takes such a long time to return to zero after each number is dialed. The dial could move much faster but the Strowger cannot.)

There are two answers to this argument, neither of them acceptable to the Post Office. One is that manufacturers have in fact developed, and are trying in vain to sell to the Post Office, push-button phones that work with Strowger exchanges.

The other is that some telephone authorities abroad have thought it worth their own money to absorb the extra costs of accommodating old-fashioned exchanges to button phones, simply because the efficiency of the system is increased by doing away with the dial, or have provided button phones to customers for a surcharge.

The main reason, however, why the Post Office ought to start handing out push-button telephones now is to train the British public to their use, so that by the time the electronic exchanges do arrive and push-buttons come into their own, they will be used to good advantage. Push-button telephones are now being used in the United States to convey information from electrocardiograph machines over ordinary telephone wires. It requires no special skill from nurses or medical technicians but is unlikely to be a technique introduced on a wide scale where there is a general unfamiliarity with the instrument.

What will happen instead with Key-Phones in Britain is easy to predict. The Post Office will wait until long past the point where rotary dials have disappeared in other advanced countries and then introduce buttons with a stern educational campaign to inform the public about the things that buttons can do that a dial cannot. Yet industry will not be able to produce great quantities quickly enough. There will be a waiting list for them and a surcharge. The public will take to button-telephoning reluctantly, and Britain's basic information-carrying network will be just as patchy and underused as its present telephone system. Perhaps it is just as well. One telephone connoisseur from industry believes that the kind of buttons that the Post Office has selected for its Key-Phones will produce more wrong numbers, not less, as the moving finger inadvertently depresses two buttons at once.

The Telephone Bill

There is yet another ordinary convenience of which the British telephoning public will be deprived (because of the Post Office's wrong decision) for some years to come. It is the itemized telephone bill that tells what trunk calls have been made to what numbers on what days and how much they cost. When it introduced its STD (Subscriber Trunk Dialing) system, the

Post Office decided to have each subscriber's telephone wire metered by individual meters. All that these meters can do is count. They have no way of recording the destination of the call nor the length of time talked. Telephone bills in Britain, therefore, contain only a tally of message units. There is no way of knowing whether one's child has direct-dialed New York and left the telephone off the hook for an hour; all that the telephone bill will show is an extraordinary number of units. There were complaints in Parliament in November 1970 about alleged errors made by telephone meters. Some people believed that their meter in the exchange did not stop registering, even after they had hung up.

The British Telephone Users' Association, a small organization which tries, somewhat awkwardly, to pursue both the public interest and the advancement of commercial communications interests, keeps a file of quaint anecdotes about people who have been astounded by their telephone bills. The association can tell of Mr J.F.M., a mathematics graduate, who rented (as one may do) a meter from the Post Office after he received a bill much higher than ordinary. When the Post Office, at the association's request, investigated the case, it was found that 11,000 STD units had passed through the circuit as test calls.

To abandon such a system once it is installed on a nation-wide scale before it wears out is next to impossible. The Post Office chose it for cheapness and is now stuck with it. And so is the subscriber, who will be able to dial telephone calls direct by satellite all over the world long before he is able to receive a telephone bill that will report to him exactly what he has done.

A Question of Monopoly

The monopoly powers of the Post Office, as described in Chapter 3, are a particular partisan issue. A minority of Conservative members of Parliament would not mind turning the entire telephone service over to private industry. A larger proportion of the party would like private enterprise to have some share in the profitable work that the Post Office now keeps exclusive to itself – the installation of telephones, for example. And others agree with the view expressed by the conservative *Yorkshire Post* that 'it is difficult to see the tele-communications side of the Post Office ever getting enough capital except through turning partly or wholly to the private market'. (April 4, 1970.)

To many Labor M.Ps, denationalizing any part of the telephone service is as unacceptable as denationalizing the National Health Service. They believe that the current flaws in the telephone service are attributable to private industry and its inability to deliver equipment on time at a reasonable price. They believe that there is a moral for Britain in the collapse of good telephone service in New York City (see Chapter 13). In a pamphlet on the future of telecommunications put out by the Fabian Society, Derek Bourn and Norman Howard, officers of the Post Office Engineering Union, argued:

The real difference between the British and American systems is that the British system recognizes its public and social responsibilities and is not dominated, as the Bell System is, by a motive toward maximizing profit. This gives some clues as to what the real, rather than the stated, motives of Tory spokesmen are when they advocate the handing over of the British telecommunications service.

To see a problem in communications development as such a matter of black and white, or blue and red, is a disastrous oversimplification, one that spoils the Post Office's ability to plan for the future. For it is not the monopoly that is inhibiting the proper growth and enjoyment of communications in Britain but the unimaginative use of the monopoly. The only way that the Post Office corporation can try out innovations and special services is to do so on a small scale. Yet if it relaxes its monopoly by giving limited permissions or licenses, then a first-class political furor breaks out. A step in any direction by the Post Office becomes a victory for one side and a defeat for the other. So boxed in is the Post Office that it is quite grateful that there exists in the city of Hull a small enclave of telephone service that because of a quirk of history does not come under its jurisdiction. Hull is very useful to the Post Office for trials and surveys; it was the first city in Britain to have 'yellow pages', directories of classified advertisements.

It is difficult to see how, in the present political environment, the Post Office could adopt any of the more permissive attitudes toward special communications services which the FCC is taking in the United States. The Post Office seems determined, for example, to hold onto its ban on many kinds of equipment that customers might want to attach to telephone lines. It is worried about preserving the integrity of its network even though there is increasing evidence that if certain technical standards are met by the customers, their attachments will not put electrical interference into the telephone system. The Post Office also seems determined (because of pressure from its unions) to retain its monopoly on the maintenance of all equipment attached to the network. Anyone who designs a new kind of switchboard, or private telephone system for a company, a hotel or large organization for example, must let the Post Office engineers install it and look after it. This is an inhibition on invention which has hurt the British market for private telephone systems. The Post Office itself is the exclusive supplier of all switchboards of fewer than a hundred lines, and these are not as modern or versatile as many businesses would like to buy. There is no chance at all, as things stand, that an all-electronic switchboard, sending both voices and computer data in and out of the public telephone network, will be allowed in Britain.

There also seems to be little likelihood that there will ever be private data-transmission links among widely scattered universities or laboratories or financial houses. They must use the data networks of the Post Office, even if these, which are improving, may be too slow or otherwise unsuited to their specific needs. By the mid or late 1970s the Post Office has promised the ever-increasing numbers of computer owners and users that there will be a special network dedicated to digital transmission. On it, the Post Office can use many of the new techniques such as pulse codes modulation and digital switching that its research and experiments have made available. This new network will hardly touch the conventional telephone trunk networks at all. It will be the new superimposed on the old, without disturbing it. Yet the Post Office keeps shifting the date when the network will actually go into service, and there is nothing that computer owners can do in the meantime but put up with the inefficiencies of the present analogue transmission.

Advice of Friends

The big upheaval of changing from a government department to a corporation has not changed the Post Office very much. The first board of directors was drawn largely from the old Post Office hierarchy, and all through the vast organization the staff remains largely the same. 'It will take twenty-five years, a whole generation, before you see any change in the Post Office,' said one radio engineer. And it will take more than that unless the Post Office can be made open to unwanted new ideas from unexpected sources.

Instead, its principal source of guidance comes from its appointed advisers. It has an Advisory Committee on Systems Definitions to help it face technical decisions of the magnitude of past disasters; yet the members of the group are from the big companies of the communications industry. The Post Office also had what the press described as a 'private think tank' headed by Lord Charles Snow. According to unconfirmed reports, the committee gave the Post Office some of the startling suggestions it needs – for example that it make some money for itself by offering public photo-copying services, coin-operated, in post offices. But the Post Office found such advice of limited value, and disbanded the group. Then there is the Post Office Users' Council, a body created by the Post Office Act, to convey the views of the public to the Post Office. Its members are appointed by the Ministry of Posts. But its main task is to complain about rises in rates, and as the Post Office is committed to generating half the capital for its own expansion, the increase in demand for telephones can hardly help to reduce rates. The Users' Council's role, therefore, is essentially the negative one of asking that the rate rises not be as high as the Post Office would like.

It would be unthinkable for the Post Office to issue notices of inquiry along the lines of those of the FCC. But where else can unexpected – but serious and carefully prepared – new proposals for the use of communications technology come from? The Ford Foundation's plan for the use of an American domestic satellite to subsidize educational television would not have had the weight it did had the FCC not invited comment from the public. In Britain, serious public discussion about communications policy seems to be confined to the letters columns of *The Times* and the *Financial Times*. And even there the arguments seem to focus around the relative culpability of the Post Office and private industry for the sorry state of the telephone service, and whether New York City's telephone service on a bad day is worse than London's on the average.

The comparison with New York City is well worth making. There are as many telephones in the New York metropolitan area as in all of Britain. What is more, New York Telephone, a subsidiary of AT&T, is investing roughly as much a year now to improve New York City's service as the Post Office is investing in the whole national telecommunications system every year.

The sad truth about Britain's telephones is that while £2,700 million is an enormous amount of money by present as well as past standards, it is not enough to do the job of bringing the British telephone service abreast of that in the countries with which it likes to compare itself. The leaders of the Post Office have honest expectations of being able to graft computers onto the old equipment and to install an increasing number of modern exchanges along with all that Strowger and to have a smooth-running telephone system by 1980. At times, in public statements, they have been carried away into making rash promises that by 1980 Britain will have the best telephone service in the world. That is not true, and it cannot possibly become true. What Britain will have by 1980 is a telephone system that works. But whether it will be as versatile and extensive as the country's economic health will require is far from certain.

Chapter 13
Will Ma Bell Survive?

I

To many Americans, it is socially unforgivable to speak a word in favor of motherhood, the flag, or the Bell telephone system. There was a time when the Bell system, which the inventor of the telephone founded and turned into the American Telephone and Telegraph Company, seemed to symbolize the superiority of private enterprise over socialism. 'Look at the mails,' the argument went. 'Government run, terrible service. Look at the telephones – run by a private company, wonderful service.' The sudden deterioration of service in New York and other major cities in the late 1960s destroyed this faith and was as devastating psychologically as the great electrical power blackout of 1965. It was, in its way, one of the series of the shocks of the 1960s which began with President Kennedy's assassination and continued through the war in Vietnam, extinguishing forever the naive and pleasant American sense of living in God's own country.

Shattering illusions is dangerous. AT&T's Bell system lost its reputation just at a point when computers, satellites and cable television were revealing that the existing telephone networks were limited and could some day become obsolete. AT&T now finds itself watching the erosion of its virtual monopoly on the nationwide carriage of public communications traffic. (It has shared the monopoly with the Western Union Telegraph Company, now the Western Union Corporation, only because the federal government kept Western Union alive simply to furnish competition to AT&T.) The challenge and the dilemma facing AT&T is how to restore its monopoly telephone service to its former quality while competing with all the challengers ready to offer the new kinds of communications that technology now makes available.

At present, AT&T is still a symbol of impregnability. It has nearly $50 billion in assets, far and away more than any other private enterprise in the world. Within the United States, it is the biggest employer and the biggest user of computers outside the federal government. Its annual profits are exceeded only by those of the General Motors Corporation. It is also the most popular investment in the world, with more than three million shareholders who can have, if they wish, their copy of the annual report in a foreign language, in Braille or on a phonograph record. Many of them would scoff at the idea that such an institution could be threatened by the rise of broad-band communications networks, communications satellites for American domestic traffic and of a number of far smaller companies offering a variety of highly specialized communications facilities.

Yet the threat is real enough to the executives on the top floors of AT&T's old-fashioned office buildings in Manhattan, where the color of the walls, the gentility of the furnishing, the silver-wrapped chocolates in a glass dish, suggest a company past its prime. AT&T's executives are acutely aware of the fate of the railways. They know that the company's nickname, Ma Bell, is not flattering and that they must do more than modernize the design of the Bell symbol to get a new image. Yet they also know that neither the Department of Justice, which acts to restrain monopoly in business, nor the FCC may let the company venture very far in new directions or even to raise its telephone rates as much as management feels is warranted. Moreover, they know that the company's ability to find $35 billion for expansion in the next few years depends in large part on holding the public's enthusiasm for investing in AT&T, an enthusiasm cooled considerably by flaws in telephone service.

For the majority of Americans, AT&T is *the* telephone company. There are in reality nearly 2,000 others, of which General Telephone and Electronic, operating 10·4 million telephones, largely in Southern California, is the largest; together the independents, as they are called, provide about 15 percent of local telephone service in the United States. The Bell System provides all the rest, and all of the national interstate telephone links. Bell's province is greater still, for it supplies telephones to and coordinates the telephone system for the Department of Defense, and it holds the responsibility, among other things, for seeing that there are telephone circuits, abundant and untapped, wherever in the country the President of the United States chooses to go.

The American domestic telephone business accounts for the lion's share of the assets and revenues of the entire industry supplying the American public with telecommunications. In 1969, for example, the seventy-eight telephone carriers subject to the FCC, because their operations crossed state lines, had revenues of $16·8 billion, of which slightly more than $16 billion was received by Bell companies. In contrast, the revenues from all international telephone traffic through cables amounted only to $249 million in 1969, and the revenues of the domestic and international telegraph traffic together were only $571 million.

AT&T itself is a holding company. The actual telephone services, the installation of wires and the collection of money from subscribers, are in the hands of twenty-four operating companies. AT&T holds all of the shares in sixteen of the companies, the majority of the shares in the rest. The parent company also owns the Long Lines Department, which has the responsibility for the long-distance network, both its physical plant and its management, and which looks after AT&T's interests in international cables and satellites.

AT&T also owns outright the Western Electric Company, a manufacturer of telephone equipment which is itself the tenth largest company in the United States. Apart from contracts performed for the federal government, Western Electric does not sell its telephones, cables, exchange equipment to any but Bell companies. Again this is no small business – Western Electric sold $4 billion worth of goods to its Bell customers in 1969.

The Bell system, therefore, has not been plagued with the problems of the British Post Office in wresting equipment from outside suppliers. Western Electric over the years has given Bell the telephones, transmission equipment and exchanges it needed on time and at steady prices.

Whether Western Electric should be pried free of AT&T and allowed to compete on its own as an independent company, selling its products in competition with other telephone equipment manufacturers at home and abroad, is a subject of perennial fascination to the Justice Department. AT&T is convinced that the divestiture of Western Electric would raise the cost of its telephone service and reduce the quality. AT&T's critics maintain just the opposite view – that the lack of competition has kept Western Electric's prices higher than they need be. The independent management consultants, McKinsey & Co, told the FCC in 1971 that without taking sides on the desirability of Western Electric's relationship with AT&T, there was only one conclusion: 'that Western Electric has been a very efficiently managed company which has served its Bell telephone company customers well.' Nonetheless, Western Electric's potential for independent growth makes it AT&T's most vulnerable point.

Together AT&T and Western Electric own and support Bell Telephone Laboratories, the complex of research establishments centered in the green fields of New Jersey, from which much of the invention that has produced the revolution in communications technology has come. Bell Labs attract scientists from all over the world; the number of British accents there is startling. The scope of the research done at Bell Labs tantalizes others in the communications industry. The cable television industry, for example, has little hope of having a research establishment of Bell's depth to explore the possibilities of broadband cables. But scientists at Bell Labs also know frustration. They are conscious that they work for the telephone company, not for a university department of research into pure science. They know that the fruits of their inquiries, like the transistor, may some day be declared out of bounds for direct commercial exploitation by AT&T. By and large, however, what Bell Labs invents, Western Electric produces and the operating companies put in service to the public. AT&T is a classic example of a self-contained, vertically integrated company.

When AT&T was formed in 1900, with capital of half a billion dollars and controlling interest in most of the original local telephone companies licensed by Alexander Graham Bell, it set out to fight the great number of competitors that had sprung up after Bell's original patent had lapsed. It did so in three ways. First, it offered a service of superior quality and scope.

Second, it refused to sell competitors equipment or inter-connection. Third, it bought them up. Such aggressiveness did not protect Bell's share of the growing telephone market, .however. By 1907 only 51 percent of the telephones in service belonged to Bell.

In 1913 the Justice Department began to take steps to see that Bell did not gain a full monopoly. It prodded the Inter-state Commerce Commission (which had acquired authority in 1910 to regulate Bell's interstate service) into forcing Bell to stop buying small companies and to supply them with connections to each other and the Bell system. But the Justice Department's zeal was blunted by the fact that telephone service is what is called a natural monopoly – one best provided by no more than one company. The ban on acquisition was modified in 1921 to allow AT&T to buy companies in towns which had been left with two telephone systems, one Bell and one not. The independent companies are growing, not declining, but nonetheless many of the telephone users who today are outside the Bell system fervently wish that they were not.

Over the years AT&T has tried to move into other branches of communications, but it has been blocked, usually by the Justice Department. It bought a large interest in Western Union in 1910 but was forced to give it up several years later (yet it managed to hold onto its private-line telegraph service.) After the First World War the company ventured into radio and owned part of the new Radio Corporation of America (and introduced the commercial advertisement to American radio) but retreated from that after criticism. In the 1930s, it intensified its competition with Western Union by offering a switched teleprinter service, called TWX, and finally (not until 1969) after a long battle before the FCC in which Western Union accused AT&T of selling its telex too cheaply in order to under-sell Western Union's Telex, AT&T agreed to sell the service outright to Western Union.

The major confrontation between the AT&T and the federal government came in 1948 when the Justice Department took AT&T to court to try to force it, under the Sherman Anti-Trust Act, to give up Western Electric. AT&T fought to hold onto its captive manufacturer, allegedly even seeking President Eisenhower's intercession on its behalf – and it won, but at a price which, in the long run, may prove to have been too dear. The case was settled with a 'consent decree' in 1956 in which AT&T promised that it would engage in no activity which was not regulated by a federal agency. In order to keep Western Electric, in other words, AT&T forsook the chance to sell data-processing services to customers or to own cable television systems and to sell the information services that these can offer. In the May 1970 issue of *The Nation*, which was devoted entirely to the evolution of cable television into a broadband communications network for the United States, the author, Ralph Lee Smith, declared that AT&T may have 'lost its bid to own the physical plant of the Wired Nation'. He judged that 'the struggle has been one of the least known and most important to take place in Washington in recent times'.

II

After the consent decree of 1956, AT&T thought it was safe within its established monopoly on the interstate telephone network. It even considered that this monopoly would extend to the interconnection of computers. Yet in 1965 the FCC announced a sweeping and unprecedented inquiry into the rates charged by AT&T for its interstate services which launched a whole series of challenges and investigations which have left AT&T with a diminished monopoly and an uncertain defensive attitude toward its regulators.

The result of the rate investigation was a shock to the company, whose shares had begun to fall as soon as it was announced (and which, by the end of the 1960s, had shown little sign of regaining the height of $75 a share reached in July, 1964). The FCC in 1967 placed a ceiling of 7·5 percent – the first such restriction in the company's history – on the rate of return it might earn on its investment in interstate service. As AT&T was earning at the time around 8 percent, the FCC ordered it to reduce the revenues brought in by long-distance and foreign telephone calls. Since then AT&T has had to defend its financial policies before the FCC much more publicly than in the past. Its old defense – a record of rates constantly reduced since 1940 – has gone. In 1971 it found itself having to beg before the FCC for permission for the first rise in interstate rates since 1953 at a time when its popularity, because of flawed telephone service, was low.

Since the rate inquiry, the FCC has delivered three major blows at AT&T's established position. In 1968 it ruled that the AT&T's refusal to attach equipment not supplied by itself (except in special cases) to the public telephone network was illegal. The ban on what AT&T referred to as 'foreign attachments' (that is, not made by Western Electric) was ostensibly to protect the telephone system and its intricate electrical codes for signaling and billing from being distorted by electrical interference fed in by incompatible equipment. But the ban also served to reinforce AT&T's grip on the whole telephone system, right down to its ownership of the telephone instruments. The FCC, in its celebrated Carterfone decision, recognized that technical advances had turned such a restriction from a necessary protection into a restraint on development of new uses for the telephone network.

The case was brought by Thomas Carter from Texas, who had invented a device that would allow private two-way radio systems (such as taxis use) to be able to receive and to send telephone calls into the public telephone network. When Bell had refused to allow the Carterfone to be linked to its lines, Carter protested to the FCC, without expecting to win. But win he did, and the FCC, after long deliberation, decided that customers had to rent only a cheap protective device from Bell in the interests of protecting the network. The British Post Office, which still believes that acoustical attachments like the Carterfone are as desirable in the telephone networks as poison in the water supply, still can hardly believe that the Carterfone decision was intended to be far-reaching. But it was, and although a great many technical details about electrical standards remain to be resolved, the day is drawing near when nothing on the customer's side of the telephone line need be supplied by Bell.

The new devices that now can be bought from suppliers other than Western Electric and owned by the customer as his personal property include architect-designed private telephone systems that dial into the public network and computers with built-in telephoning equipment. AT&T, for its part, now refers politely to 'customer-supplied devices' rather than 'foreign attachments' and speaks optimistically about the increased use of the telephone network that these will bring.

Until 1969 no company but AT&T and Western Union had licenses to sell public communications service on a national scale. But in 1969 the FCC decided to give permission for a small company to set up its own microwave links in order to furnish private communications lines for business customers between St Louis and Chicago. The company was Microwave Communications, Inc., and, like the Carterfone case, it was David against Goliath, David winning again. John D. Goeken, who had a radio and television service in Joliet, Illinois, ventured to the FCC with the novel idea that special communications common carriers might be allowed to sell communications facilities tailored to the needs of each particular customer. When his company became the first ever to win a license from the FCC to run a transmission service that competed directly with the existing common carriers, it set off a flood of hundreds of other applications to the FCC from others hoping to do the same thing.

The MCI decision also revealed how discontented the computer industry was with the interconnection service provided by AT&T. Many of them argued that the telephone industry had slowed down American economic and social growth by failure to provide adequate facilities for data transmission and forcing data to travel on the voice of telephone lines. They did not like the clumsy translation of digital codes into analogue signals which the telephone network requires. They did not like having to wait fifteen seconds to be connected. They did not like to have to rent lines by the month. And they did not like the refusal of AT&T to let small users share private lines once they had rented them. (AT&T was forced to relax this ban early in 1969.)

The computer users' complaints and the flood of applications which followed the MCI decision raised a larger question for the FCC. Why should the provision of special communications services to specific customers be a government-regulated business? There seems to be little of what is called a 'natural monopoly' about it. Obviously a telephone system works best if the entire operation is under the control of one organization.

But why should data transmission and other kinds of private communications not be sold like dry cleaning – in different forms of service and prices, each of which attracts its own particular clientele?

Under pressure from its Common Carrier Bureau, the FCC began to consider that competition itself might be a useful tool of regulation. But AT&T presented a strong argument for keeping competitors out, even of special communications services. If there were to be competition in the lucrative business of carrying messages and data between big cities, who would subsidize the less profitable services to small towns and thinly settled states? The Bell system's pricing generally has followed the historic practice (which goes back to Britain's penny post in the nineteenth century) of having the same rates for all parts of the country. The practice is called 'rate averaging'; the profitable services subsidize the less profitable. The alternative to it is 'cream skimming' – operating only where the money is good, forcing areas of low traffic to pay higher rates or do without service.

The FCC resolved the controversy in 1971 by throwing the whole field of special communications services open to competition – and by allowing AT&T to skim some cream itself. The commission ruled that any company that could demonstrate that it had the money and technical ability to provide a service that would not interfere with existing communications systems could enter the market, AT&T and Western Union included. They could charge whatever they wanted for their services, without regulation by the FCC, and were free to fail if they lost money. The only restrictions on the two established carriers was that they were forbidden from engaging in cross-subsidization – that is, from using their earnings from their regulated monopoly services in order to price their specialized competitive services low.

The decision did not touch AT&T's telephone monopoly at all, which covers by far the bulk of its business. In 1970, of AT&T's total revenues of nearly $17 billion, barely $1 billion derived from the supply of private line services and data transmission to businesses. But this specialized market is where the fastest growth in communications lies. Its total revenues are expected to be an annual $10 billion by 1980. The specialized carriers decision was, in effect, a warning to AT&T that it had not been quick enough to introduce technological innovation and that its hold on its monopoly was only as good as its service. But – the Republican-dominated FCC as much as said – AT&T can, if it is clever enough, scare much of the potential competition from ever daring to enter the race.

The struggle between AT&T and the new special carriers will be fascinating to watch in the 1970s. Of the main challengers, one should be MCI, whose plans have grown to encompass a national system of private voice telephone circuits for business customers. The other is expected to be the Data Transmission Company (Datran). Datran has plans to build a network for computer users in thirty-five major cities that would, like the telephone network, be switched – that is, any subscriber could dial another. It hopes to attract the computer industry by guaranteeing no more than one error for every million bits transmitted, no more than one busy signal in one hundred calls and a complete computer-to-computer connection in three seconds or less. The Datran network will not rely, as MCI will, on the Bell system for local distribution but will build its own, giving door-to-door digital service.

It would be unwise to think that AT&T has anything but an enormous advantage over its new competitors. It has a million miles of local digital transmission circuits already and expects, by connecting these to its new national digital facilities, to have its own all-digital intercity network operating by 1974. Western Union also has a head start, with its microwave digital system already in operation, one designed to serve customers more interested in transmitting data in bulk than in speed – hotels, airlines and credit firms, for example.

What AT&T must not do, if it is not to lose more of its monopoly, is to promise more and better data transmission than it can deliver. It could fall into that trap if the growth in data traffic is greater than it has estimated – and the company's prediction that data will represent 5 to 10 percent of all communications traffic by 1980 is so much lower than the Stanford Research Institute's estimate of 10 to 50 percent that AT&T has been suspected of producing a deliberately low estimate in order to diminish the apparent need for new specialized carriers. If AT&T is wrong, it will have more congestion on its lines in a few years and then it will really be in trouble, for underestimating growth was largely responsible for what went wrong in New York City.

III

In February 1969 the *Wall Street Journal* carried a story revealing that all over the country something was drastically wrong with the telephones. Americans were getting the kind of frustration that people in other countries had long endured: long waits for dial tones, busy signals before they finished dialing or dead silence when they expected the other telephone to ring. The worst of the trouble spots was New York's financial district. Customers telephoning the New York Stock Exchange could not get through to place their orders. By mid-summer, the failings of the New York Telephone, one of the Bell system's largest operating companies, were a joke. The joke became national, and even caught the attention of the international press, when the advertising agency of Benton and Bowles placed a full-page advertisement in *The New York Times* to give a list of 'all the people you can't reach at Plaza 8–6200'. Few people stopped to reflect that AT&T was one of the few telephone authorities in the world that could be hurt by humiliation.

AT&T recognized that its entire national reputation was at stake. It rushed engineers and repairmen in from all over the country, putting them up in hotels, to install new equipment. Western Electric went on a three-shift working day. New York Telephone got a new president from the top ranks of the parent company. The annual amount of capital invested in new equipment for the New York area alone went from $400 million in 1967 to $1·1 billion in 1971. Yet restoring the old smooth service turned out to be no simple matter. The trouble was too deep and the crash program itself was disruptive; the imported workmen caused discontent among the local unions, and there were strikes which held up the installation of new equipment.

Three misjudgments seem to have been the cause of the trouble, not only in New York but elsewhere in the Bell system. The most serious was the underestimation of the growth in demand for new telephones. In the Bell system's operations there is a temptation to make low estimates, for the lower the expected growth, the less the amount of new exchange equipment that will be needed, and the higher, therefore, the operating company's profit and the happier AT&T's shareholders. Another was not to ask the state public utility commissions, which act as mini FCCs within state borders, for permission to raise local telephone rates. During the 1960s the private companies that sell electric power under similar terms of regulation as those imposed on the telephone industry had asked for, and won, rate rises. But the Bell system chose to boast during the decade that it had offered better service to more telephones without putting up its prices. The third error was to work with a minimum of spare capacity. When the demand for new telephones surged unexpectedly, the Bell companies were caught short.

The New York company was the hardest hit because it had actually cut back capital expenditures in 1966 and 1967 under pressure to keep profits up and because growth, in the financial district, was far higher than had been anticipated. In 1968 the telephone company had planned on 980,000 daily outgoing calls from Wall Street; instead there were an average of 1.5 million. The congestion was made even worse by the decision of the Stock Exchange in 1969 to shorten its working day by closing in mid-afternoon. This compressed the enormous volume of telephone calls into a shorter stretch of hours.

The pattern of work and life in New York City also changed. More new office buildings were built than had been expected, and their tenants wanted direct inward dialing – each office telephone to be reached straight from the public telephone network without going through an internal switchboard. Yet if there is a larger flow of calls than has been expected the traffic backs up at the public telephone exchange, not at the switchboard. Once upon a time frustrated telephoners would curse the switchboard operator. But in New York they cursed the telephone company.

What was unexpected was that public welfare directors, in one district after another, began to decide that telephones were a necessity of life. They included telephone subsidies in the welfare payments – and a very substantial share of people who actually live in New York are on public welfare rolls. Thousands of new subscribers opened up new patterns of telephone traffic; there was a 20 percent growth of telephones in the Bedford-Stuyvesant area of Brooklyn, which developed a heavy volume of traffic with the Spanish-speaking district of East Harlem.

The exodus of New Yorkers to the suburbs also altered the telephone traffic. The busiest hours of the day moved from the morning to the evening, and there were many more calls than there had been between the suburbs and the center city. AT&T is now belatedly adding sociologists and environmentalists to its staff, and New York Telephone has become public-spirited to the extent of wondering how to recycle the millions of telephone directories that are discarded every year so that they will not pollute the landscape.

If there is a lesson for telephone authorities in other countries in the plight of the New York Telephone Company, it must include the problem of finding enough people to run the telephone system. The British Post Office, for example, has lately claimed that it is expanding its telecommunications service without any increase in staff, because of automation. But the Bell system has found that the benefits of automation wear off. Ultimately, an increase in new telephones means an increase in people, and they must be more highly trained than in the past for their function is to deal with people, not plugs and sockets. There is no possibility in sight of using automation to answer directory inquiries and emergency calls, to make person-to-person calls, or to explain how to perform the long-distance direct dialing that the machinery now allows.

But cities like New York do not have large untapped pools of labor. Of those who are available, many are new to urban living and have never made a long-distance telephone call. They may not know the names of the city's streets and districts, they may not know English, and they stay for comparatively short periods of employment. Bell companies, especially that of New York, feel that they have done well in training unskilled labor to the job. Others do not.

IV

AT&T is in a vulnerable position. It needs to raise more than $4 billion a year from external sources if it is to meet its five-year capital investment program and to introduce millimeter waveguides, picture telephones, digital transmission and possibly domestic communications satellites by the 1980s. It also must have rises in telephone rates now that its operating costs are rising faster than revenues. Yet both new investment and rate rises are dependent on the public's good will, and that is in short supply. Such rate rises as it has won have been grudging, both from the FCC and the various state regulatory agencies, and rarely in the amounts requested. That a vicious circle may be in progress – unpopularity leading to insufficient investment which restricts expansion and therefore encourages further deterioration of telephone service – has not escaped the notice of either company or its critics, who have begun to realize their power.

The New York State Public Service Commission in 1971 refused to allow picture telephone service to be initiated because the ordinary service still was below standard. A non-profit organization, Grassroots Action Inc., began a publicity campaign to persuade consumers to withold part of their monthly telephone bills for the same reason. The organization objected to the lack of representatives of the public interest, or indeed of any other group than AT&T, on New York Telephone's board; it also complained that the subsidiary had paid the parent company 20 percent more in dividends than it had earned in a year when it was asking to raise telephone charges to produce a $391 million increase in revenues. This kind of criticism, if mounted on a national scale, could lead to AT&T's downfall, and the company is now hypersensitive.

Late in 1970, while the AT&T was waiting to hear whether the FCC would allow it the first increase in interstate rates since 1953, a new branch of the federal government attacked it. The Equal Employment Opportunity Commission (along with the National Association for the Advancement of Colored People and the National Organization for Women) declared that the company should not have its rate rise because it discriminated against the poor, the female and the black in its hiring policies. In defense of AT&T, the chairman of the board, Haakon Romnes, declared that the company as a whole had increased its employment of non-whites by 265 percent since 1963, and that more than 12 percent of all the staff were from minority groups. But, he said, this percentage could not be reflected straightaway in management.

'We are an up-from-the-ranks company,' he declared, expressing in one breath the great strength and intrinsic weakness of the Bell system. Its management is stable, loyal, inbred. There are few women, Jews, blacks or homosexuals high up in AT&T. There are also few who have worked long for any other company – thirty-three years is the average length of service among top management. But at least they have been confident that, conformist or not, they have managed their great company well.

Their right even to that satisfaction was challenged by FCC Commissioner Nicholas Johnson in October 1970. He accused it not only of failing to serve the public but also of serving its shareholders badly with its poor management. The attack on AT&T was one of this eccentric FCC commissioner's virtuoso performances. In it, he displayed his perplexing talent for showing off, making dreadful puns, and hitting slightly off the target, yet at the same time advancing the public interest by saying what few people in comparable high office have dared to say so bluntly or clearly before.

'You all recall the telephone company,' Johnson said in his speech to a small group of customers of the Digitronics Corporation in Illinois. 'You have to recall the telephone company. You lose your dime the first try.'

In his speech, 'For Whom Does Bell Toil?' Johnson threw at AT&T all the major criticisms of it that had been floating around the FCC for years. He ridiculed AT&T for adopting financial policies that not only produced high prices and bad service for the public, but lower profits for its investors. He said that it had diluted the value of its shares by issuing too much new stock, rather than raising capital through debt, on which the interest is tax-deductible. He claimed that it had resisted the kind of accelerated depreciation of its expenses that the law had allowed, preferring a more conservative kind of bookkeeping that cost the company money. He accused it of unimaginative pricing and of pretending for years that it was impossible to use a public telephone without putting in a dime first. Johnson revived the charges of repressiveness of outsiders' equipment and reviewed the plight of the New York telephone service. Then he said: 'There is no one who I have ever been able to discover within AT&T – management, sales, or scientific research – who has a sense of the social political-economic role of the telephone in modern-day industrialized society . . . they are seemingly incapable of thinking about the ways in which people might use that instrument in their lives . . . What would be the social impact of universal availability of a low-price WATS service (trunk calls charged on a flat monthly basis)? They don't know.'

It is a charge that could apply to almost every telephone authority in the world.

Johnson's attack was belated because AT&T had acknowledged most of the criticism already. It had begun instaling dial-tone-first telephones in which callers can speak with the operator even if they don't have any money. It had changed its bookkeeping to produce an accelerated cash flow and, most conspicuous of all, it had begun to increase the ratio of debt to equity capital dramatically – from 36 percent to 48 percent in ten years.

To survive, Ma Bell must remain attractive to investors, obedient and cooperative before the FCC, quick with the new technology in order to keep rivals at bay but not so aggressively competitive as to anger the Justice Department, all the while providing virtually flawless telephone service. It is not an impossible task for the biggest private company in the world, and the telephone business seems certain to be healthy for some time to come. But what counts is not bigness but agility and courage. AT&T needs to see the forced abandonment of its monopoly on equipment and of its traditional pricing for what it really is – a chance to break with the past and to create new markets for communications. AT&T would also do well to see Western Electric for what it is – an albatross around its neck. If AT&T really wants to compete (and if it does, no other company can overtake it) it should let Western Electric become independent and try then to persuade the Justice Department and the FCC to let it become active in some of the fields from which the consent decree bars it. For eventually, perhaps within the decade, the question critical to AT&T's future is going to come up. The FCC will have to decide who will extend broadband communications by means of coaxial cables into cities and into homes and offices. Telephone lines will not suffice; they have insufficient capacity. Will AT&T be allowed to wire the Wired City?

AT&T's best hope for believing that the answer might be yes is the American cable television's industry's dread of regulation, its reluctance to become a common carrier, forced to parade its books and profits before the FCC. But if the answer is no and cable television or some other combination of companies is given the right to own the new communications wire that will carry the electronic traffic of the future, then AT&T may wonder whether its second century will see it in second place.

Part Five

Conclusion

Chapter 14
Contours of the Future

If the past is any guide, the future is unpredictable. Most forecasts about change in communications will turn out to have been too conservative and few will have been wildly optimistic. Even more uncertain than the future state of the technology itself is the effect that easier, cheaper communications will have on the organization and quality of life. Optimism is not universal. A bleak vision is offered by the British science writer, Nigel Calder, in *Technopolis*:

> Free countries cannot guarantee that they will always be free, and the existence of such potent public technologies as bugging and the electronic file may actually reduce their chances of so remaining. ... Given a fully operational network the dictator would have a very easy life.

Calder stresses the possibility that some day human beings might have electrodes implanted in their skulls at birth. Then their brains could be stimulated and controlled by remote signals, like toy boats on a pond. He can also imagine that humans might line up willingly for the devices if the result were sensually stimulating, just as they now smoke too much and drive too fast and indulge in other forms of pleasureable self-destruction.

In *The Year 2000*, Herman Kahn and Anthony Weiner of the Hudson Institute raise the possibility that computers might some day monitor an appreciable percentage of all telephone conversations, and more:

> ... Indeed future computers and programs should be able to carry out much more complex operations – possibly responding to nonverbal information, such as an unusually angry or threatening tone in a voice. Such computers may also be able to apply a great deal of inferential logic on their own – they may become a sort of transistorized Sherlock Holmes making hypotheses and investigating leads in a more or less autonomous or self-motivated manner, all

the while improving their techniques as they accumulate information about patterns of criminal behavior – or any other kind of behavior that authorities decide ought to be observed.

These are chilling prospects, but it is difficult to imagine them in practical operation. How would controllers keep themselves segregated from the controlled? How could they protect their children from the furtive implantation of electrodes? What would be the point? If the computer is to be programed to look for suspicious words, what words should they be – revolution, strike, male chauvinist? If every telephone, household, office, car, park bench and pine tree is to be bugged and all the conversations filtered through a computer, then legions of people are going to have the dreariest job in the world: reading through the lists of what the computer thought it heard. Perhaps by the end of the century computers will be able to understand human speech, but the technical progress in this direction has been discouraging in recent years. Computers have not been able to be made to serve as language-translating machines and have in fact given very poor performances in distinguishing one simple word from another, let alone the difference in meaning between 'the read book' and 'the red book,' 'flee' from 'flea' and 'in great' from 'ingrate'.

In fact it is even difficult to see how a fully operational electronic network would give a dictator an easy life, for it would probably include facilities for mobile and two-way communications. A dictator relies on one-way communication. Big Brother wants to watch everybody; he does not want them watching him. If television sets had two-way transmission and were connected in a switched network, he would not have an easy life at all.

Time will tell whether the new communications technology can be an efficient instrument of repression. But to believe that large groups or even whole populations can be monitored and kept in place by electronic devices is to place great faith in machines, not to mention in the power of governments to restrict the use of these machines to official hands. It could be done, but it would not be easy.

Undoubtedly the enormous capacity of electronic files presents a new temptation to the official surveillance of private citizens. The congressional hearings on computers and the invasion of privacy, conducted by Senator Sam Ervin of North Carolina in 1971, revealed that the American military were keeping aimless dossiers of information on civilians who engaged in antiwar or pro-black political activity. There is also the unpleasant prospect that data banks, even used properly, will mean that more crime will be detected and punished, especially the kind which can now escape notice – speeding, failure to pay traffic fines and tax evasion. In future, the public will feel more vulnerable to unexpected arrest as police, equipped with mobile teleprinters connected to computer networks, can stop a motorist to confront him with evidence of an offense committed at another time or in another place.

The alarm about the spread of data banks will have been productive if new laws are passed to give people the right of access to information recorded about themselves. Yet exaggerated fears can be harmful, for two reasons. First, electronic files offer much better protection of privacy than usually exists today; in large corporations and in professional offices, many of the files are accessible to any temporary secretary or disgruntled employee and a Xerox machine is usually handy. Second, the current anti-computer sentiment leads to a belief that information-storage itself is an evil, obscuring the fact that the threats to freedom are political, not technological. Obviously a totalitarian government will use data banks and electronic eavesdroppers to keep itself in power, but it will not have been made totalitarian by these devices. Dictators do not need electronics. Fabricating evidence is an art, not a science. A quick look around the world shows more tyranny where communications are poor.

An Up-to-Date World

There is a great deal to be said in praise of data banks. Instead of one great national information box, there are far more likely to be a great number of data banks, like universities and libraries. Their existence will mean that information will be able to be exchanged at high speeds among offices of government, hospitals, laboratories, newspapers, factories and shops. Until now the ability to make decisions based on information that is both voluminous and up to the minute has been virtually restricted to national defense and space programs. But plans affecting the organization of a city's welfare program – to take just one example – are often based on statistics that are months to years out of date. It is the businessman and the scholar, the newspaper editor and the doctor, who are going to have a much easier time because of electronic networks. A study by Datran forecast that the seven major areas of the American economy most likely to undertake a dramatic increase in data transmission by 1980 were insurance, banking, securities exchange, manufacturing, retailing, information-processing and health care. (The total of their yearly transactions is expected to rise from 14 billion in 1970 to 250 billion in 1980.)

Some of the more benign data banks are already taking shape. The *New York Times* has begun to prepare a data-retrieval service through which both printed information and photographs will eventually be able to be called out of its vast files. Business information banks are also being started up, to tell subscribers all they want to know about virtually any commercial subject – telephone poles or the organization of ITT or the predicted market for washing machines in Ireland. Medical information banks are expected to grow as medical records will come to be stored electronically; they will be invaluable, to patients as well as doctors. Who can remember, when he has just cut his foot, when he last had a booster shot against tetanus?

In the future small firms, publishing houses and craftsmen will be able to have overseas branches and outlets and to keep in touch with them at will during the working day in the way that only the giant corporations enjoy now. The pace of all commercial transactions will be speeded up. With computers compiling inventories and organizing transport schedules, the delivery of goods should become more efficient. The pace of communication in scientific research is enormously slow, for example; scientists learn of each other's results only through the exchange of letters and the reading of published articles. If they could transmit their data on the day that they reached their conclusions each one individually could accomplish more in his lifetime. Similarly, the quality of historical research should improve when information-retrieval services are extended to include public record offices and the libraries around the world.

It is possible that the worldwide sharing of information at

enormous speeds will actually raise the collective intellectual potential of the human race, just as the printing press and the computer have done. A fanciful idea perhaps, but less unreal than the fantasy of a human race mind-deadened by electronics.

If intelligence is exchanged at such a pace, will there not be a reduction in traffic on the roads and on air travel? The British Post Office, which has developed a system called Confravision for intercity business conferences, believes that company executives may some day choose to spend an hour in a Confravision studio rather than to devote an entire day to traveling in order to speak for an hour with a group of men in another city. Some transport engineers have also speculated that improved telecommunications must be taken into account in designing road systems of the future. They are probably wrong. There is no way of telling yet. There is no evidence for the future, only speculation. While some of the speculation has been based on mathematical calculation and wide research, the conclusions reached have been problematic at best and the researchers disagree among themselves. Perhaps it is not too presumptuous, therefore, to make some forecasts of the future based on simple intuition.

Improved telecommunications will probably not make a discernible difference to road traffic. The increase in population should more than fill the places left empty by those who will find themselves able to work at home or at a decentralized office. It is more likely that devices such as the picture telephone will actually encourage travel as they will increase the numbers of people in vast corporations who feel personally acquainted. Once they recognize each other's faces, they will feel the need to travel to Los Angeles or Birmingham or Tokyo to discuss business in person. In other words, while there may be fewer motor and rail journeys to work, there could be a rise in long-distance travel. Moreover, not only do people need personal contact with their colleagues, but they need to move about because of the random information that a physical journey brings. It is possible that human nature itself will change and people will some day be less inhibited before a camera. And perhaps not. Picture telephones and closed-circuit television demand the speakers' full attention and best behavior: they discourage idle nose-picking and looking at one's watch. They also discourage argument and interruption and the general stimulating abrasiveness of impromptu conversation.

Shopping by telephones or television will reduce some road traffic but not much. Certainly, the consumer will not have to travel out to shop, and in the future, as more women take jobs outside the home, they will lose the temptation to go out and buy something (shopping is the normal woman's shoplifting). But the goods will have to reach the consumer by road. There does not yet seem to be a communications device that will deliver six tins of peaches. Moreover, the electronic screen could encourage people to travel farther to make a purchase. If a computer could search around and locate a particular boat or car or piece of sculpture, one might then want to drive out and have a look at it. Finally, television itself increases the desire to travel by making remote places appear accessible.

It seems a safe guess also that cities will not disappear. Decentralization is of limited usefulness. Even now, as large corporations build themselves headquarters in the suburbs and the countryside, the staff who are transferred there tend to feel in exile. (One might trace the decline of the political importance of atomic energy in the United States with the Atomic Energy Commission's move in 1958 out to Germantown, Maryland, (thirty miles from Washington). Activities such as government, finance and scholarship need to be carried on in communities, and such communities will continue to draw others to them.

Home Life of Tomorrow

To read some of the tomorrow's-world predictions, one might think that the families of the future were never going to leave the house. The usual scenario goes something like this: Father, the engineer (he is always an engineer), is working at his computer. Mother is ordering the groceries by three-dimensional color picture telephone. The eldest child, a scholar, is curled up with a book delivered by long-distance Xerox from the Vatican Library. Another child is in the kitchen, doing his homework on the computer. In the living room, the youngest performs on the piano for his grandmother in Australia, who promptly signifies her delight by transferring a small sum from her bank account to his. The cat's lackluster coat has just been diagnosed as worms by a world-famous veterinarian 500 miles away, and all the members of the family live and work in an electronic, multichanneled nest as isolated from the world outside as if they were nineteenth-century homesteaders.

It is not going to happen that way. If the new communications technology means anything, it is the freedom to wander about the face of the globe. It is not going to closet people in their homes. It will not shore up the nuclear family. It may instead reduce some of the claustrophobia of family relationships by allowing the various members to remain in touch with each other without the fuss of writing letters or making ritual attendances at Sunday lunch. Portable telephones, for example, will give children more freedom to travel about their cities, for they can be connected to home, like astronauts, by an umbilical cord of chatter.

Improved communications should make cities pleasanter and safer. Perhaps the surveillance of parks and bus stops may seem like a nightmare to some, but probably not to the very young and the old who are afraid to venture into places where a source of help is not visible. If cars are equipped with telephones, it will be safer to walk about at night. The main reason now why Britain's streets are safer than American streets after dark is because in Britain there are a great many people out on foot. But American streets are not empty; they are full of cars. If each of those cars had a means of calling for assistance if the driver saw trouble, then the pedestrian would be infinitely less vulnerable.

Public transport will become less capricious. It will be easier to get a bus or a taxi. The flow of traffic will be regulated by computers and the drivers of buses will have contact by radio with their stations so that great queues of empty buses do not form, like chains of elephants, leaving passengers to wait for a half hour or more until the next queue comes along. Perhaps by the end of the century some of the more radical proposals now being offered for public transport will actually have been made to work. Then a pocket radio or telephone will summon an empty self-drive vehicle to any spot within a certain radius of a large city. The driver can then instruct it by pushing buttons where he wants to go, either within the city or into the long-distance transport network that connects cities. And when he has finished with the car, he can dispatch it automatically to a collection point. Billing, it goes without saying, will be done electronically so that there will be no need to do without the service for lack of pieces of metal of the right shape.

It is almost inconceivable that in twenty or thirty years' time the delivery of letters by hand will still be offered as a national social service. There still will be messengers, but they will be much better paid. There will always be messages worth the expense of delivery by hand, but the price will be set by the market place. What will be available at a subsidized and standard national rate will be electronic communication. Sentimentalists in any case should not moan about the disappearance of the personal letter. A study by the management consultants, Arthur D. Little, Inc., showed in 1967 that only 13 percent of the post in the United States consisted of personal correspondence between private citizens.

There also seems no question but that newspaper printing will be decentralized – to the advantage of the reader. A paper printed in several regions or even in a number of small neighborhoods within a city can have much more local news, as well as national and international news, without succumbing to the provinciality of the usual suburban daily newspaper. Regional printing, even multinational printing, is inevitable once satellites plus broadband cable networks really get going. For current methods of distribution cannot go on much longer, and it is a testament to inertia that they have survived this long. A product whose value depends on its physical delivery to hundreds of thousands of people within several hours is manufactured in a city, often in the middle, sometimes on the edge, and then bundled into small vans which make their way through traffic jams to railway stations, airports and news-stands from which it must be collected and distributed by hand.

If and when newspaper printing takes the next leap forward and presents itself through the television set, rather than through the letter box or on a news-stand, the reader will be able to compose his own paper. By some sort of signal, the reader will be able to indicate to the newspaper's computer which portions of the news he wants in greater detail. And from which newspaper in which city he wishes it to come. What can be delivered electronically can also be ordered electronically. From London, sooner or later, one should be able to have the *Washington Post* or *Le Monde* printed out – perhaps not every morning but on those days when one is particularly interested to know what a particular paper is saying. Remote printing by satellite, in fact, is one of the most cheerful prospects of the new technology, for it offers the world's great newspapers the chance to reach international audiences – not only those who are able to pass special news-stands in sophisticated cities – but anyone who has a television set.

Opinions differ on the use that the reader will make of these facilities. Alvin Toffler in *Future Shock* questions whether man is prepared to cope with the increased choice of material and cultural wares available to him.

For there comes a time when choice, rather than freeing the individual, becomes so complex, difficult and costly, that it turns into its opposite. There comes a time, in short, when choice turns into overchoice and freedom into un-freedom.

Ben H. Bagdikian, in *The Information Machines*, acknowledges the same worry – that the consumer in control of his own newspaper-television delivery system might take television without the news, or a newspaper's comic and sports pages only. But he decides:

If the consumer has a free choice and if he makes an 'unenlightened' decision, that, too, is a cost of doing democratic business. But the data on audiences for public-affairs information show that the demand for serious news is widespread.

If what is now known as a newspaper is to survive at all, however, it cannot be as a blank roll of paper to be filled by the customer's whim. A newspaper's function is to offer a full yet selected presentation of the news. The reader must get more than he knows he wants and it must be on some form of paper. The urge to turn back, to re-read, to cut out and to browse is unlikely to atrophy in anyone now literate.

The new technology, therefore, will have to make its way against entrenched habits as well as the established communications organizations. A good while will pass before people give up the reassurance of print and come to accept an electronically verified facsimile signature to be as reliable as one written in ink which drops through the letter box. Ironically, the new techniques which arrive soonest may be those which are now most unfamiliar – such as the delivery of printed material by satellite transmission to buildings with antennae on the roof. Services which are totally new and can be offered by new companies with the minimum of disturbance to existing communications can begin to recruit customers as soon as the hardware is in place.

Chapter 15
Consuming Communications

In spite of the impediments, the new communications technology will inevitably take hold. The rate of expansion of existing systems is so great as to ensure that they will be entirely renovated in twenty or thirty years' time. The rotary dials, the Strowger exchanges, the VHF television sets and the old letter-sorting machines will disappear. What is less inevitable is that official attitudes toward communications will have shaken off the past. The boundaries of commercial and political responsibility will be redrawn, after a good deal of hard debate. But will these debates be held in the public view and will anyone speak for the private citizen? Who will argue successfully for the social uses of the new technology?

Past experience is not reassuring. The organizations dedicated to representing the consumer have not been able to make their views prevail. Too many of the voices raised on the public's behalf in the field of communications do not appreciate the social value of the technology that exists. The outcry has been about data banks and all-figure telephone numbers, for example, not about the inequitable distribution of telephones and the need for their compulsory installation in new residential buildings. The civilizing influence of television has also been underestimated. How much international feeling would have been aroused about Vietnam, Biafra or Canadian baby seals if they had not been seen on television? People and places which do not appear on television news cannot expect international public opinion to support them. There are some well-minded reformers – in Britain's liberal Acton Society, for example – who believe that the great mass of the population must be protected from too much television and that televising the routine debates of a body like Parliament would weaken respect for authority. Such elitism is anachronistic in the face of the declining cost and increasing supply of communications channels.

The world needs more television – seeing over distance – and satellites, coaxial cables and waveguides have provided the means by which it can be obtained.

The new technology needs to be fought for. People have a right to use their telephones and television sets for a wider variety of personal expression and enlightenment. The greatest danger about the future in communications is that it will resemble the present: too few people will have too little access to what means of communications are available. There will be too much walking, too much paper, too few telephones where they are most needed, and the ubiquitous television set useful only as a national entertainment box.

So what is to be done? First, consumers' associations and political action groups must put communications on their lists. They must demand more and cheaper telephones, local television and broadband electronic distribution networks just as they demand safe cars and pure sausages. Second, governments must do their part by elevating communications to the status of a recognized social need, like housing or education. There does not need to be a burst of ministries and departments of communications all over the world. But communications must be taken at least as seriously as transport. It would not be a bad idea if communications and transport were combined in the same department. They are two forms of carriage which often substitute for each other and which should be planned together.

In any case, the responsibility for national communications policy must be centralized. The major decisions to be made in the next decade or two ought not to emerge from a tug-of-war among half a dozen government departments and agencies jealous of each other. Which ministry in Britain, for example, should decide if the country should invest in a national satellite system? Which part of the United States government should recommend the development of broadband communications networks as a national goal? In the United States, the formation of the President's Office of Telecommunications Policy was a step in the right direction, but the office cannot, no matter how much its director protests, be considered apolitical. Neither is the FCC in a good position to make long-range policy. Not only is it weak in relation to Congress, but its semi-judicial function of settling the day-to-day disputes of the telephone and broadcasting industries forces it to consider issues shortsightedly. Neither the OTP nor the FCC can finance the kind of technical and economic research that is needed before major decisions can be taken on the design of the communications networks of the future. In Britain, the Ministry of Posts is both too politically oriented at the top and too inadequately staffed to make broad decisions of policy. The Post Office is too preoccupied with the business of running a labor-intensive nationalized industry to be able to formulate plans that affect education, social welfare, foreign affairs and air navigation.

International communications policy needs to be made centrally as well, and the ITU will have to be the organization which does it. There have been suggestions that an entirely new organization be set up, but these are unrealistic. No new body could gain the support of a comparable global range of countries. The alternative to a stronger, more intellectually vigorous ITU is global communications policy made by the United States. That is what has been happening, and not only in matters of satellites. The kind of sixth transatlantic telephone cable that the FCC approved was much more sophisticated and capacious than the European telecommunications authorities wanted to build. Their own plans were, in effect, vetoed by the FCC when it turned down AT&T's application to build an 825-circuit TAT-6.

It is possible that Intelsat may provide a source of coordinated international planning in communications. Perhaps if it acquires an imaginative Director General before the end of the decade, Intelsat could become a bolder organization. It might resolve disputes about places in orbit among its own sizable membership, and it might even carry on its own program of loans and technical assistance to developing countries, providing advice more expert than is now offered by teams from UNESCO and the ITU. Were some form of consultation worked out between Intelsat and Intersputnik, some of the advantages of a new international policy-making organization might be obtained without the political bother of setting one up.

If it is unrealistic to hope for major changes in the planning of communications, it may also be rash to suggest that citizens' committees and consumer groups can have much influence. Organizations like Intelsat and the British Post Office are virtually immune to public opinion. There are signs in the

United States, however, that AT&T may find itself subjected to the kind of social pressure that has been brought against General Motors, and be forced to take representatives from the public at large among its directors.

The International Organization of Consumers' Union has shown the kind of thing that needs to be done – chiefly demanding that the services which are technically possible should become available in actuality. At the invitation of the European Conference of Posts and Telecommunications, IOCU put forth in November 1970 ten proposals for future services which it believed should be provided by the European telephone authorities. Among them were simple requests for the conveniences made possible by semi-electronic exchanges: message-taking, automatic transfer of calls to another number. Others were for services already being considered by the ITU's telephone committee: different tones to distinguish between busy telephones and busy exchanges and the introduction of time signals when three minutes have lapsed on customer-dialed international calls. The IOCU also asked for a facility that telephone subscribers should have had years ago and would have had if telephone authorities had been competitive commercial enterprises – a button to switch the telephone off.

What needs to be sought even more, however, is a thorough renovation of telephone pricing. There should be a cheap flat rate for international telephone calls anywhere in the world. The idea is hardly new. As long ago as 1961 an official of Hughes Aircraft declared that satellites would permit a telephone call to be made for ten cents to any spot on the globe. Since then there has been a steady decline in the proportion of the cost of a long-distance telephone call that concerns its transmission. The bulk of its cost reflects the expense of the terminal equipment, local distribution lines and the system's supporting staff. The economic distinction between a local and a long-distance call is in fact fading, but the flat-rate global call is still not in sight. Richard Hough, president of AT&T's Long Lines Department, does not believe that it will come into practice even by the end of the century.

Even within national boundaries, the rates charged for telephone services need to become both simpler and more flexible. There is little doubt that the present finicky price structure based on distance inhibits the use of the telephone; volume of calls falls off as distance increases. On the other hand, residential telephone subscribers should be able to enter into the kind of particular private contractual arrangements for bulk services that business communications customers enjoy. Most important of all, telephone authorities need to make formal and comprehensive plans for offering telephone service at a discount to those who cannot afford to pay the full rate. In the past, telecommunications men have tended to shrug off the suggestion with a rhetorical 'Who will pay for it?' The question is a legitimate one and one that now needs to be answered as well as asked. There is no single easy answer, but it does seem possible that telephone corporations, which enjoy steady profits and expanding numbers of customers, and public housing departments, which accept the responsibility for providing a decent standard of living for those in their charge, might share the burden in the first instance. Ultimately it will fall on the taxpayer, just as the cost of education, transportation and law enforcement does.

A revolution in pricing policies will not come about if the matter is left to the telephone authorities, with their concern for rate averaging and of making the new subsidize the old. (Just imagine what transatlantic air fares would be if the aircraft were owned by the companies that run ocean liners.) The pressure will have to come from outside, and the problem of subsidy will have to be solved before the spread of high-capacity home-delivery systems. A communications outlet will no longer be a luxury but a basic facility like a letter box, and no new system can go into operation on a large scale unless the outlets are fairly distributed throughout the population.

The new communications technology offers a great deal to wish and to work for. International satellite broadcasting, for example, will be useful and enjoyable only if professional broadcasting organizations can keep the world's ministries of information out of it – but they themselves must be compelled by politicians and public-spirited groups to become more tolerant of new entrants to their existing national television systems. As for the programs shown to international audiences, it would be good if they were not all specially prepared and culturally homogenized. One advantage of dialing a program through an international satellite would be to be able to tune in and see what other countries were watching. It might also be possible to have, dubbed or with subtitles, a weekly presentation of the best national television programs – uncensored for foreign consumption. Conceivably there might some day even be an international common-carrier television channel so that program-makers, like authors, could offer their work to audiences outside their own countries, free of the patronage of their national broadcast organizations.

The advantages of broadband communications networks need to be advertised like soap if they are to be in operation before the postal services collapse. They may not accomplish any of the social reformation expected of them, but they should be able to use the television screen to accomplish what public libraries and adult education classes have never quite achieved – to put knowledge on tap.

The new communications technology is complex and the political, economic and legal obstacles in its way more so. But the prizes to be won for overcoming them are clear – a greater exchange of information, news, and opinion among greater numbers of people in more parts of the globe than has ever been possible, and a more humane, efficient and agreeable organiza-tion of urban life. It is now as easy to communicate across long distance as across a room. The freedom to do so should be demanded with equal passion.

Glossary

aerial – an antenna usually made with wires for collecting or transmitting radio waves.

analogue transmission – the sending of signals in the form of an electrical current which physically simulates the signal.

antenna – a device for receiving or transmitting radio or radar waves.

band – a range of radio frequencies allocated to a specific use.

bandwidth – the width of the band of frequencies occupied by a particular communications channel.

bit – the smallest measurable unit of information in a communications channel.

broadband – the term used to describe a communications channel that occupies a wide band of frequencies. Broadband channels are used for sending a large amount of information in a short time.

broadcast – the sending out of waves of radio communication to be received by the public at large.

cable television – a means of transmitting television through a wire or cable rather than through the air.

channel – a band of frequencies within which a radio or television station operates.

circuit – an electrical or electronic path; a term commonly used to describe the bandwidth taken up by a telephone conversation (roughly 4,000 cycles a second). Thus a television circuit can be described as requiring the equivalent of 600 to 1,200 telephone circuits.

cycle – one complete to-and-fro motion of an electrical current or an electromagnetic wave.

digital transmission – the sending of signals in the form of units of information, usually the code used by computers.

electromagnetic radiation – a phenomenon including radio waves, radar waves, infra-red radiation, light, ultra-violet light, and also X-rays.

electromagnetic spectrum – the range of frequencies at which electromagnetic radiation can be propagated.

exchange – the switching center in which teleprinters or telephones can be connected to any other within the system.

frequency – the number of times a second an alternating current makes a complete cycle. (See Herz.)

frequency allocation – the assignment of frequencies for use by the various radio services and classes of stations recognized by the ITU.

gigaHerz – unit of frequency equal to one billion cycles a second. (See Herz.)

Hertz – a unit of frequency equal to one cycle a second. It takes its name from Heinrich Herz (1857–94), a German physicist and early experimenter with radio waves, and is rapidly replacing the term 'cycles per second' as a way of describing the frequency of radio waves.

high frequency (HF) – frequencies within the range of 3,000 to 30,000 kilocycles per second (not high by today's standards).

integrated circuit – a chip of semi-conductor material which combines a number of miniature transistors to make one electrical circuit.

laser – acronym for Light Amplification by Stimulated Emission of Radiation. A laser produces a powerful, highly directional, monochromatic, coherent beam of light which may someday make light waves usable for communications.

microwaves – electromagnetic radiation with wave lengths ranging from very short radio waves almost to the infra-red region (from thirty centimeters to one millimeter in length).

millimeter waves – those above the microwaves on the electromagnetic spectrum and so short that to be useful for communications they must usually be sent through pipes called waveguides.

optical communications – possible communications method of the future in which highly concentrated beams of light are made to carry message codes.

pay TV – a television service in which the viewer pays to see special programs or channels.

private line service – a service in which two or more designated points enjoy the exclusive use of communications circuits for specified periods of time.

pulse code modulation (PCM) – a way of sending signals by intermittent pulses.

radar – an acronym for Radio Detection and Ranging; a term used to describe any systems using microwaves to detect and identify moving objects.

radio – the use of electromagnetic radio to communicate electrical signals without wires.

radio spectrum – the part of the electromagnetic spectrum used for radio communication.

radio telegraphy – the sending of coded messages over distance without wires.

radio telephony – the use of radio waves for carrying telephone conversations.

relay (broadcasting) – to re-transmit a signal received at a given point. Cable television began as a method of relaying television signals.

(electrical) – a device by which the electrical current flowing in one circuit can open or close a second circuit and thus control the switching on and off of a current in the second circuit.

satellite (communications) – an artificial earth satellite used for relaying radio and television signals around the curved surface of the earth.

semi-conductor – an electrical conducting material whose resistance, unlike that of metals, decreases with rising temperature and the presence of impurities – the basis of the transistor.

Strowger – the step-by-step telephone switch invented by an American undertaker, Almon Strowger, in 1889, which is still the basis of most of the world's telephone exchanges.

switching – the central process of telephone and telex systems: the acceptance of calls and sending them along a route to their designated destination.

synchronous orbit (or stationary orbit) – the orbit of an artificial earth satellite which takes twenty-four hours to circle the earth, traveling parallel to the equator, and which appears to hover over a fixed spot. The altitude corresponding to such an orbit is about 22,300 miles. It is the most useful orbit for communications satellites.

telecommunications – the transmission, emission or reception or signs, signals, writing, images and sounds or intelligence of any nature by wire, radio, visual or other electromagnetic systems.

telex – an automatic teletypewriter exchange service. Various national systems are linked by the international telex system through which typed messages can be sent to any other machine in the system by dialing the appropriate number.

transistor – a small device made of semi-conductor material used to amplify electrical current in a similar manner to that of vacuum tubes or valves. Its advantages are lightness, cheapness and durability.

ultra high frequency (UHF) – the band of frequencies extending from 300 to 3,000 million cycles a second, likely to provide opportunities for further expansion of television broadcasting.

valve (or vacuum tube) – a device capable of amplification of electrical current.

very high frequency (VHF) – the band of frequencies extending from 30 to 300 million cycles a second. The band in which most American and British television has been broadcast.

waveguide – a hollow metal conductor through which microwaves may be propagated.

Bibliography

Books

Ayer, A. J. and others, *Studies in Communication* (London: Secker and Warburg Ltd., 1955).

Bagdikian, Benjamin H., *The Information Machines & Their Impact on Men and Media* (New York: Harper & Row, 1971).

Barnouw, Erik, *A History of Broadcasting in the United States*, Vol. II, *The Golden Web* (New York: Oxford University Press, 1968).

Briggs, Asa, *The History of Broadcasting in the United Kingdom*, Vol. I, *The Birth of Broadcasting*, 1961; Vol. II, *The Golden Age of Wireless*, 1965; Vol. III, *The War of Words*, 1970 (London: Oxford University Press).

Brown, Ronald, *Telecommunications: The Booming Technology* (London: Aldus Books Ltd., 1969).

Calder, Nigel, *Technopolis* (London: Macgibbon and Kee, 1969).

Carnegie Commission on Educational Television, *Public Television: A Program for Action* (New York: Bantam Books, 1967).

Caves, Richard E. and Associates, *Britain's Economic Prospects* (Washington, D.C.: Brookings Institution, 1968; London: Allen & Unwin Ltd., 1968).

Chayes, Abram, Ehrlich, Thomas, and Lowenfeld, Andreas, *The International Legal Process* (Boston: Atlantic – Little, Brown & Company, 1969).

Clarke, Arthur C., *The Promise of Space* (London: Hodder & Stoughton Ltd., 1968).

Friendly, Fred, *Due to Circumstances Beyond Our Control . . .* (New York: Random House, Vintage Books, 1967).

Goulden, Joseph C., *Monopoly* (New York: G. P. Putnam & Sons, 1968).

Halloran, James, editor, *The Effects of Television* (London: Panther Modern Society, 1970).

Johnson, Nicholas, *How to Talk Back to Your Television Set* (Boston: Atlantic – Little, Brown, 1970).

Kahn, Herbert, and Weiner, Anthony, *The Year 2000* (London: Collier-Macmillan Ltd., 1967; New York: The Macmillan Company, 1967).

Kappel, Frederick R., *Business Purpose and Performance* (New York: Duell, Sloan & Pearce, 1964).

Kock, Winston E., *Lasers and Holography* (New York: Anchor Books, Doubleday and Company Inc., 1969).

McGinnis, Joe, *The Selling of the President 1968* (London: André Deutsch, 1970; New York: Trident Press, 1969).

Michaelis, Anthony, *From Semaphore to Satellite* (Geneva: International Telecommunications Union, 1965).

McLuhan, Marshall, *Understanding Media: The Extensions of Man* (London: Routledge and Kegan Paul Ltd., 1964; New York: McGraw-Hill Book Company, 1964).

Page, Arthur W., *The Bell Telephone System* (New York: Harper Brothers, 1941).

Pierce, John R., *Symbols, Signals and Noise* (London: Hutchinson, 1963; New York: Harper & Row, 1961).

Robertson, J. H., *The Story of the Telephone* (London: Sir Isaac Pitman, 1942).

Schiller, Herbert I., *Mass Communication and American Empire* (New York: Augustus J. Kelley, 1969).

Sopkin, Charles, *Seven Glorious Days, Seven Fun-Filled Nights* (New York: Simon and Schuster, Inc., 1968).

Taton, René, *Science in the Twentieth Century* (London: Thames and Hudson, 1966).

Toffler, Alvin, *Future Shock* (London: The Bodley Head, 1970; New York: Random House, 1970).

Tunstall, Jeremy, *Media Sociology* (London: Constable & Co., Ltd. 1970).

Wiener, Norbert, *Cybernetics* (Cambridge, Massachusetts: Massachusetts Institute of Technology Press, 1948).

Articles, Papers, Pamphlets, Reports

American Civil Liberties Union, 'Response to the FCC's Inquiry Regarding the Cable Television Industry' (New York, 1968).

American Newspaper Publishers Association, 'Response to FCC's Inquiry into Cable Television' (New York, 1969).

American Telephone and Telegraph Company, 'Response to FCC's Inquiry into Policy to be Followed in Future Licensing of Facilities for Overseas Communications' (New York, 1970).

Aviation Week and Space Technology, 'U.S. Contractors Get Most Intelsat Funds' (December 21, 1970).

Barnett, Harold J., and Greenberg, E., 'A Proposal for Wired City Television' (Santa Monica, California: Rand Corporation, 1967).

Barnett, Harold J., 'Resistance to the Wired City' (St. Louis: Washington University research monograph).

Blonstein, J. L. (Plessey Radar Ltd), 'The Role of Small Earth Stations in Civil Communication Satellite Systems,' *Telecommunication Journal*, Vol. 37 (Geneva: June 1970).

British Broadcasting Corporation, 'BBC School Broadcasts: Facts and Figures' (London: School Broadcasting Council for the United Kingdom, 1969); 'In the Public Interest' (London: BBC publication No. 10442, 1971); 'Broadcasting in the Seventies,' compiled by Gerald Mansell (London: BBC publication No. 8562, 1969).

Brown, Ronald and others, 'Telecommunications: The Expanding Spectrum,' *New Scientist* (London, 1970).

Bourn, D., and Howard, N., 'The Future of Telecommunications' (London: Fabian Research Series 289, 1970).

Burke, Charles G., 'Directory of the 500 Largest U.S. Industrial Corporations,' *Fortune* (New York, 1971).

Business Week, 'Cable TV Leaps into the Big Time' (New York, November 22, 1969).

Caine, Sir Sidney, 'Paying for Television' (London: Institute for Economic Affairs, 1968).

Carnegie Endowment for International Peace and the Twentieth Century Fund, 'Communicating by Satellite' (New York: Report of an International Conference, by Gordon L. Weil, 1969).

——, 'Planning for a Planet,' Report of an International Conference (New York, 1971).

Centre for Educational Television Overseas, Annual Report 1968–1969 (London, 1969).

Chayes, Abram, 'Unilateralism in United States Satellite Communications' (McGill University, Montreal: Institute of Air and Space Law Conference, 1970).

Communication News, 'Who's Who in Data Transmission' (Wheaton, Illinois: December 1970).

Corditz, Dan, 'The Coming Shake-up in Telecommunications,' *Fortune* (April 1970).

Dawidziuk, B. M., and Preston, H. F. (Standard Telephones and Cables Ltd.), 'Comparative Evaluations of Modern Transmission Media for Global Communications' (Los Angeles: American Institute of Aeronautics and Astronautics conference, 1970).

Demaree, Allan T., 'The Age of Anxiety at AT&T,' *Fortune* (May 1970).

Dordick, Herbert, and Lyle, Jack, 'Communication Crisis Points in Urban Development' (Kyoto, Japan: International Conference on Future Research, 1970).

Duncan, C. C. (AT&T), 'Plowing Cables Under the Sea' (Institution of Electrical and Electronic Engineers conference, Philadelphia, 1968).

Electronics Industries Association, Industrial Electronics Division, 'The Future of Broadband Communications,' response to the FCC's inquiry into cable television (Washington, D.C., 1969).

Feldman, N. E., 'Cable Television: Opportunities and Problems in Local Program Origination' (Santa Monica, California: Rand Corporation, 1970).

Feldman, N. E., 'A Scenario for the Future of Cable Television Distribution' (New York: IEEE conference, 1970).

Ford Foundation, response to FCC inquiry on Domestic Communications satellites (New York, December 1966).

Gabriel, R. P., 'The Wired City – A Single Network' (London: Rediffusion Ltd., 1970); 'Cable Television: Submission to the Canadian Radio and Television Commission' (London: Rediffusion Ltd., 1971).

Gargini, E. J. (Rediffusion Ltd.), 'Dial-a-Programme Communication Television' (London: Royal Television Society, 1970).

Goldhamer, Herbert (editor), 'The Social Effects of Communication Technology' (Santa Monica: Rand Corporation, 1970).

Gross, William B. (General Electric Company), 'Distribution of Electronic Mail over the Broadband Party Line Communication Network' (New York: IEEE, 1970).

Gross, Gerald C., 'The New ITU – A Plan for the Reorganisation of the Union,' *Telecommunication Journal*, Vol. No. 2 (Geneva, October 1963).

Hough, Richard A., 'Testimony before FCC on AT&T's Capital needs for Future Interstate Facilities,' *Telecommunications Reports*, Vol. 36, No. 47 (November 23, 1970).

Hult, John H. (Rand Corporation), 'Broadcasting Opportunities with Satellites and CATV and Their Control in the Public Interest' (Cocoa Beach, Florida: Seventh Space Congress, 1970).

Institution of Electrical Engineers, 'Man-Computer Interaction,' Conference Publication No. 68 (London, 1970).

IEE, 'Earth Station Technology,' Conference Publication No. 72 (London, 1970).

International Broadcast Institute, Newsletter (Rome: Winter 1970).

Jacobson, Harold K., 'International Institutions for Telecommunications: the ITU's Role' (McGill University, Montreal: Institute of Air and Space Law Conference, May 1970).

Johnsen, Katherine, 'France Backs UN-Intelsat Control,' *Aviation Week and Space Technology* (August 28, 1967); 'Intelsat Vote Expected for New Satellite,' *Aviation Week and Space Technology* (February 13, 1967); 'Intelsat's Third Conference Seeks Lasting

Agreement,' *Aviation Week and Space Technology* (April 27, 1967). 'Compromises Permit Intelsat Agreement,' *Aviation Week and Space Technology* (May 31, 1971).

Johnson, Leland L., 'The Future of Cable Television: Some Problems of Federal Regulation' (Santa Monica, California: Rand Corporation, 1970); 'Cable Television and the Question of Protecting Local Broadcasting' (Rand Corporation, 1970).

Johnson, Nicholas, 'Dissenting Opinion on Intelsat IV Contract' (Federal Communications Commission, May 1967); 'Why I Am a Conservative, or For Whom Does Bell Toil?' (Chicago, Illinois: Digitronics Users Association Conference, 1970).

Jones, R. E., 'The Changing Face of Telecommunications,' *New Technology* (London, March 1969).

Killick, John (UK Foreign and Commonwealth Office), 'Progress of Intelsat Negotiations,' Tenth Paris Space Symposium (Paris, 1970).

Legg Industry Review, 'CATV: A "Cool" Medium Turned Hot' (Baltimore, Maryland: Legg & Co., 1969).

Leive, David M. (Communications Satellite Corporation), 'Regulating the Use of the Radio Spectrum,' *Telecommunication Journal*, Vol. No..37 (Geneva, June, 1970)

Little, Arthur D. Inc., 'Implications of Regulatory Developments in U.S. Telecommunications' (Cambridge, Massachusetts, 1969).

Marks, Norman, 'TV Dregs Planned for Cable,' *Chicago Daily News* (May 4, 1970).

Mickelson, Sig, 'Communications by Satellite,' *Foreign Affairs* (New York, October 1968).

National Academy of Engineering, 'Telecommunications for Enhanced Metropolitan Function and Form' (Washington, D.C., 1969).

National Journal, 'New Communications Office Struggles for Acceptance,' Vol. 3, No. 7 (Washington, D.C., Center for Political Research, February 13, 1971).

National Project for the Improvement of Televised Instruction, 'Toward a Significant Difference' (Washington, D.C.: National Association of Educational Broadcasters, 1969).

New York City Mayor's Task Force on CATV and Telecommunications, Report of (New York, 1968).

O'Lone, Richard G., 'U.S. Dominance Seen Hindering Intelsat,' *Aviation Week and Space Technology* (August 28, 1967).

Pay TV Ltd., 'Pay Television in the United Kingdom,' unpublished (London, 1967).

Pope, D. G. (British Post Office), 'Possible Earth Station Techniques for a Survival Craft Distress Service by Satellite' (London: IEE conference, October 1970).

Posner, Richard A., 'Cable Television: The Problem of Local Monopoly' (Rand Corporation, 1970).

Post Office Telecommunications Journal, 'We Mean Business,' Vol. 22, No. 4 (London, 1970–1971).

RCA Ltd., 'A Canadian Satellite to Serve Canada's Domestic Requirements' (Montreal, 1968).

Relay Services Association of Great Britain, 'Submission to the Committee on Broadcasting 1960' (London: 1960); 'Submission to the Broadcasting Committee 1949' (London: 1949).

Reid, Alex, 'New Directions in Telecommunications Research,' prepared for the Sloan Commission on Cable Communications (London: University College, Communications Studies Group, 1971).

Schramm, Wilbur, 'Communication Satellites for Education, Science and Culture' (Paris, UNESCO, 1968).

Shields and Company, Comsat: Report for Institutional Investors (New York, 1969).

Smith, E. Stratford, 'The Emergence of CATV: A Look at the Evolution of a Revolution,' *Proceedings of the IEEE,* Vol. 58, No. 7 (July 1970).

Smith, Ralph Lee, 'The Wired Nation,' *The Nation* (New York, May 18, 1970).

Telecommunications Reports, 'FCC Announces Policy of Free Entry by Specialized Common Carriers,' Vol. 37, No. 22 (Washington, D.C., June 1, 1971).

Thorp, Bruce E., 'Office of Telecommunications Policy Speaks for President,' *National Journal* (Washington, D.C., February 13, 1971).

Twentieth Century Fund Task Force on International Satellite Communications, First Report: 'International Satellite Communications,' by Paul Laskin (New York, 1969); Second Report: 'The Future of Satellite Communications,' by Gordon L. Weil (New York, 1970).

Wall Street Journal, 'Dial-a-Snafu' (New York, February 3, 1969).

Which?, 'How Bad Is Our Telephone Service?' (London, July 1966).

Which?, 'Telephone Service' (London, September 1969).

Whyte, J. S., 'Thirty Years On,' *The Post Office Electrical Engineers Journal,* Vol. 62, Part 3 (London, October 1969).

Official Publications

UNITED STATES

Executive Office of the President

Office of Emergency Preparedness, Office of Telecommunications

Management, *The Radio Frequency Spectrum, United States Use and Management*, July 1969.

————, *Intragovernmental Committee on International Communications*, April 1966.

Office of the President, *Memorandum on Domestic Communications Satellites*, January 1970.

Office of the President, President Nixon's message transmitting to Congress the reorganization plan establishing the Office of Telecommunications Policy, February 9, 1970. USGPO, 1970.

Federal Communications Commission

'In the Matter of the Use of the Carterfone device,' June 27, 1968. Docket Nos. 16942 and 17073.

'In the Matter of Domestic Communication Satellite Facilities by Non-governmental Entities,' March 24, 1970. Docket No. 16495.

'In the Matter of Geographic Reallocation of UHF-TV Channels 14 through 20 to the Land Mobile Radio Service,' May 21, 1970. Docket No. 18261.

'In the Matter of Regulatory and Policy Problems Presented by Interdependence of Computer and Communication Services and Facilities,' April 3, 1970.

Notice of Rule-making and Proposed Rule-making Relative to CATV, June 23, 1970.

Inquiry into Policy to Be Followed in Future Licensing of Facilities for Overseas Communications. June 10, 1970. Docket No. 18875.

House of Representatives

Committee on Education and Labor, 'To Improve Learning,' report to the President and Congress by the Committee on Instructional Technology, U.S. Government Printing Office, 1970.

Committee on Foreign Affairs, subcommittee on national security policy and scientific developments, 'Satellite Broadcasting and Implications for Foreign Policy,' hearings May 1969. USGPO, 1969.

Committee on Foreign Affairs, subcommittee on national security policy and scientific developments, 'Foreign Policy Implications of Satellite Communications,' hearings, April 1970. USGPO, 1970.

Committee on Foreign Affairs, subcommittee on national security policy and scientific developments, report of the Special Study Mission to Latin America on I. Military Assistance Training and II. Developmental Television. USGPO, 1970.

Committee on Interstate and Foreign Commerce, subcommittee

on communications and power, hearings on 'Subscription Television' December 1969. USGPO, 1970.

Committee on Science and Astronautics, subcommittee on space science and applications, 'Assessment of Space Communications Technology,' hearings, December 1969. USGPO, 1970.

Senate

Committee on Aeronautical and Space Sciences, hearings on Communications Satellite Legislation, February and March 1962. USGPO, 1962.

Committee on Commerce, hearings on Communications Satellite Legislation, April 1962. USGPO, 1962.

Committee on Commerce, communications subcommittee, hearings on continued financing for the Corporation for Public Broadcasting, April 1970. USGPO, 1970.

Committee on Commerce, communications subcommittee, hearings on FCC's proposed rule-making for CATV, June 1671. USGPO, 1971.

Committee on Foreign Relations, hearings on Communications Satellite Legislation, August 1962. USGPO, 1962.

State Department

Text of multilateral agreement establishing interim arrangements for a global commercial communications satellite system, with special agreement and supplemental agreement on arbitration. Treaties and Other International Acts Series 5616. As reprinted, June 1968.

Report of the Interim Communications Satellite Committee on Definitive Arrangements for an international global communications satellite system. ICSC document 36–58. December 1968.

Documents of plenipotentiary conferences and inter-sessional working groups concerned with definitive arrangements for the International Telecommunications Satellite Consortium, 1969, 1970, 1971.

Justice Department

Comments on the FCC's inquiry into cable television, April 7, July 11 and September 5, 1969.

Comments on the Federal Communications Commission's Proposed Public Dividend Plan for Cable Television, Docket No. 18397-A, December 7, 1970.

U.S. President's Task Force on Communications Policy

Final Report (the Rostow Report), December 14, 1968. USGPO, 1969.

Staff Papers. USGPO, 1969.

U.S. Laws, Statutes, etc.

Communications Satellite Act of 1962, Public Law 87–624. August 31, 1962.

Communications Act of 1934, Public Law 416. June 19, 1934. 73rd Congress.

UNITED KINGDOM

Committee on Broadcasting, 1960, Report of, HMSO, London, 1962. Cmnd. 1753.

Committee on Broadcasting, 1949, Report of, HMSO, London, 1950. Cmnd. 8116.

House of Commons

Estimates Committee, Third report from, 'The British Broadcasting Corporation,' HMSO, 1970. Cmnd. 4259.

Select Committee on Nationalized Industries, First report from, 'The Post Office,' HMSO, 1967.

Estimates Committee, Subcommittee D, Minutes of evidence on hearings on the British Broadcasting Corporation, HMSO, 1969. 93-i-xii.

Official Report of Parliamentary Debates (Hansard)
Vols. 772
     773
     783
Post Office Bill, HMSO, 1969.

Parliament, Acts of,

Post Office Act, 1969.

Television Act, 1964.

Post Office

Memorandum on the Report of the Broadcasting Committee 1949, HMSO, 1952. Cmnd. 8550.

Memorandum on the Report of the Committee on Broadcasting 1960, HMSO, 1962. Cmnd. 1770.

Further Memorandum (including recommendations for Pay-TV Experiment) on the Report of the Committee on Broadcasting 1960. HMSO, 1962. Cmnd. 1893.

Copy of the Licence and Agreement between Her Majesty's Postmaster-General and the British Broadcasting Corporation. HMSO, 1952. Cmnd. 8579.

Copy of a new Charter of Incorporation granted to the British Broadcasting Corporation. HMSO, 1952. Cmnd. 8579.

Copy of the Licence and Agreement between Her Majesty's

Postmaster General and the British Broadcasting Corporation.
HMSO, 1952. Cmnd. 8579.
HMSO, 1961. Cmnd. 1537.
HMSO, 1963. Cmnd. 2236.
HMSO, 1969. Cmnd. 4095.
Copy of the Royal Charter for the continuance of the British
Broadcasting Corporation. HMSO, 1962. Cmnd. 1724.
Supplemental Royal Charter for the BBC, HMSO, 1964. Cmnd.
4095.
Supplemental Royal Charter for the BBC, HMSO, 1969. Cmnd.
4194.
Post Office Prospects, 1968–69. HMSO, 1969. Cmnd. 3539.
Post Office Prospects, 1969–70. HMSO, 1969. Cmnd. 3959.
Post Office, Report and Accounts for the year ended March 31,
1969, HMSO, 1969.

Posts and Telecommunications, Ministry of,
An Alternative Service of Radio Broadcasting, HMSO, 1971.
Cmnd. 4636.
Post Office Report and Accounts for the six months ended Sept. 30,
1969. HMSO, July 1970.
Post Office Report and Accounts, for the six months ended
March 31, 1970. HMSO, November 1970.

Technology, Ministry of (now Ministry of Trade and Industry)
'Idex: a Mobile Satellite Communication Station,' by Signals
Research & Development Establishment, Christchurch, Hamp-
shire, 1967.

BRAZIL

Comissão Nacional de Atividades Espaciais (CNAE), 'Brazilian
Educational Radio and TV Experiment on ATS-F – Experiment
Proposal,' (São Jose dos Campos, SP, 1970).

JAPAN

Japanese Science and Technology Agency, 'Space in Japan',
(Tokyo, 1970).

CANADA

Drury, C. M., 'White Paper on a Domestic Satellite Communication System for Canada', (Ottawa, 1968.)

UNITED NATIONS
Development Programme (UNDP), *Pre-Investment News*, February, 1971.

General Assembly

'Review of the Administrative and Management Procedures concerning the Programme and Budget of the International Telecommunication Union,' by the Advisory Committee on Administrative and Budgetary Questions, UN Document A7765. New York, 1970.

International Telecommunication Union

Telecommunication Journal
    Special issue: Telecommunications and Education, Geneva, June, 1970.
    Special issue: World Administrative Radio Conference, Geneva, May, 1971.
'Planning for a World Telecommunication Network,' ITU Press Release, October, 1968.
World Plan, 1967.

Unesco

World Radio and Television, Paris, 1964.
Communications in the Space Age, Paris, 1968.
'South America: Preparatory Study of the Use of Satellite Communication for Education and National Development,' (by E. Ploman, W. B. Pierce and J. B. Torfs), Paris, 1970.
Statistical Yearbook, Paris, 1969.
Broadcasting from Space, Paris, 1971.

Annual Publications

The following have been helpful in preparing this book: (from Washington), Annual Report on Activities and Accomplishments under the Communications Satellite Act of 1962 from the President to the Congress. Report to the President and The Congress of the Communications Satellite Corporation, Annual Report of the Federal Communications Commission, Common Carrier Statistics of the Federal Communications Commission, Broadcasting Yearbook published by Broadcasting magazine; (from New York) annual report of the American Telephone and Telegraph Company, annual report of the New York Telephone Company; (from London) Annual Report and Accounts of the British Broadcasting Corporation, of the Independent Television Authority and of the British Post Office; the BBC Handbook, the ITA Guide and the Post Office Guide; (from Geneva) Radio Regulations published by the International Telecommunication Union.

Index

All-India Radio, 138
American Broadcasting Company, 99–100, 169
American Civil Liberties Union, 145, 163–4, 176
American Telephone and Telegraph Company, 18, 44, 47, 60, 94, 230; and international telephone calls, 21, 22, 233; and telephone equipment, 31, 218, 219, 221, 233–4, 237–8, *and see* Western Electric; and telephone cables, 33, 74, 75, 98, 99, 163, 173–4; and waveguides, 35; and satellites, 68–9, 83–5, 102–103, 108, 114, 231, 232; and television, 99–100; and telephone communications organization, 202, 235–6, 238–40, 244–5, 263, 264; and *The World's Telephones*, 203; and picture telephones, 207–208; and computers, 212, 232, 238–40; and Bell Telephone System, Chapter 13 *passim, and see* Bell Telephone Laboratories, Bell Telephone System; and finance, 232, 233, 236–7, 239, 244, 245–6; and data transmission, 238–41; and New York Telephone Company, 241ff.
Americans for Democratic Action, 145, 164
amplifiers, 30, 33; *and see* transistors
Annan, Lord Noel, 190
Annan Committee, 190–1
Aviation Week and Space Technology, 101–102

Bagdikian, Ben H., 259
Bell, Alexander Graham, 230, 234
Bell Telephone Laboratories, 9, 26, 28, 30, 31, 34, 68, 218
Bell Telephone system, 218, 224, 227, Chapter 13 *passim*; and cable TV, 174; finances of, 232–3, 236–7, 239,

242, 244, 245–6; company organization, 233ff, 244–6; and telephone equipment, 233–4, *and see* Western Electric; and New York Telephone Company, 241ff; *see also* American Telephone and Telegraph Company
Beveridge Committee, 185, 189
Bevins, Reginald, 214–15
Bhaba, Homi, 122
Bourn, Derek, 227
Brattain, Walter, 30–1
Braun, Wernher von, 67
Briggs, Asa, 184
British Aircraft Corporation, 97, 139–140
British Broadcasting Corporation, 9, 60, 180–1, 187, 193, 194; and commercial broadcasting, 20; and broadcasting organization and policy in Britain, 53ff, 180–1, 194; finances of, 55–6, 193; and satellites, 112; and education, 129, 134, 139, 140; and *Sesame Street*, 135–6; and relay radio and TV, 183, 184, 185; and UHF broadcasting, 187–8; future of, 189–191, 194, 196
British Institution of Radio Engineers, 188–9
British Relay Wireless Ltd., 183, 186
British Telephone Users Association, 226
broadband communications, 32–3, 36, 37, 38–9, 65, 197, 232, 262, 266; and picture telephones, 35, 38, 208; and letter carrying, 37, 197; and cable TV, 147, 159–60, 162–4, 181, 236
broadcasting control and organization, in Britain, 20, 22–3, 43, 50, 52–7, 193–7; in United States, 20, 23, 43, 44ff, 156, 175, 178; via satellite, 20, 70–1, 116ff, 76; international, 42–3, 57ff; *see also,* British Broadcasting

Reeves, A. W., 29, 36; *and see* pulse code
modulation
Reith, Lord, 184, 185
Relay Services Association of Great
Britain, 9, 183–4, 193, 194
relay television, *see* cable television
Reliance Telephone Company Ltd., 9
Romnes, Haakon, 245
Rostow, Eugene, 103
Rusk, Dean, 84

Sarabhai, Dr Vikram, 122
Satellite Instructional Television Experiment (SITE), in India, 122–5
satellites, communications, 11, 15, 18,
19, 23, 24, 26, 31, 44, 57, 62, 65
passim, 205, 258, 259, 260; space, 26,
30; and United States, 41, 45, 46, 47,
48, 68, 69ff, 83–5, 99–100, 113, 114,
126, 161, 230, 244; and Britain, 50,
86–7, 191; and international television, 56, 65, 112, 116ff, 121ff, 161,
262, 265–6; and international organization and control, 62, 65, 86–106,
263, *and see* Intelsat; and education,
65, 82, 121–5, Chapter 7 *passim*, 152,
230, *and see* satellites, and India;
Telstar, 65, 68, 83, 86, 103; and telephones, 66, 69, 70, 71, 73, 112, 115,
125, 126, 128, 161, 226, 231, 232, 264;
Russian, 67, 78, 84, 90–1, 126–7,
263, *and see* Intersputnik; random
orbiting, 68–9; synchronous orbit,
68–9, 74, 78, 80–1, 114, 115–16, 123,
125, 126; Early Bird, 70, 71, 73, 78,
79, 91, 92, 93, 94; economics of, 70,
71, 73, 74–5, 76–8, 88, 93ff, 99–100,
125, 140; military applications, 78–
80, 139; distribution, 116–17; and
India, 121–5, 127, 129, 130, 137, 138–
139, 140–1, *and see* SITE; Canadian,
125–6; and Latin America, 127, 129,
130–1, 138–9, 140–1; European, 127,
139, *and see* ELDO, ESRO; and Iran,
128, 140; and cable television, 146,
161, 164
Schildhause, Sol, 147–8
Schramm, Dr Wilbur, 137–8
Sesame Street, 134–6
76 Group, 190, 196
Shannon, Dr Claude, 28–9, 30, 31
Shockley, William, 30–1
Siemens A. G., 222

Skinner, B. F., 135
Sloan Commission on Cable Communi-
cations, 9, 164
Smith, Ralph Lee, 236
Snow, Lord, 229
sputnik, *see* satellites, Russian, Inter-
sputnik
Standard Telephones and Cables
Limited, 9, 29, 74, 219, 223
Stanford Research Institute, 152, 240
Stashevsky, Guennadi, 90–1
State Department (US), 9, 48, 85, 87,
94–5, 105, 108, 111, 113
Steffens, Lincoln, 122
Sterling Manhattan Cable Television
Company, 153
Stonehouse, John, 51, 180, 190, 217
Strowger, Almon B., 210; and Strowger
switching, *see* telephones
Subscriber Trunk Dialling (STD), *see*
telephones

tape recorders, 67, 131, 136–7
teachers, 23, 130, 137, 138; teaching
machines, 131, 137; *and see* television
and education, cable television and
education, educational technology
technology of communications, development of, 11–12, 15ff, 43, 47, 54, 139ff,
251ff, 261ff; and cable television,
147, 189–91; social implications of,
251ff, 261ff
Technopolis, 251
telegraph, 21, 24, 41, 44, 46, 202; and
Morse code, 28, 41; international,
41–2, 57, 58, 59, 62; and satellites,
126
telephones, 11, 16, 18, 19, 20, 21, 23,
24, 31, 38, 40, Chapters 11, 12 and
13 *passim*; push-button, 16, 206–7,
224–5; mobile, 19, 22, 38, 155, 197,
201, 202, 217, 257; equipment,
manufacture and technology, 19,
203–204, 209, 211, 217, 218, 222–4,
228; cables, 21, 24, 26, 74–5, 86, 91,
98, 99, 205, coaxial, 32–5, transatlantic, 50, 69, 73, 74, 99; rates, 21,
22, 45, 210, 214, 217–18, 225–6, 229,
232, 239, 242, 264–5; picture, 24, 35,
38, 146, 163, 167, 192, 201, 206, 207–
209, 224, 244, 255–6; and microwaves, 26, 125; and pulse code modulation, 29, 221–2, 228; and wave-